D0230437

Tourism in Major Cities

Issues in tourism series

Edited by Brian Goodall, *University of Reading* and Gregory Ashworth, *University of Groningen*, The Netherlands.

The Advisory Board includes K.H. Din, *University of Kedangsaan*, Malaysia; C.R. Goeldner, *University of Colorado*, USA; J. Jafari, *University of Wisconsin*, USA; and D.G. Pearce, *University of Canterbury*, New Zealand.

The growing significance of tourism as an economic activity is reflected in the increased recognition it has been given at national and local levels. There has been a rapid development of specialist educational and training facilities for academics and professionals, including widespread research activity, and the discipline could now be said to have 'come of age'. The books in this series provide rigorous, focused discussions of key topics in current international debates on tourism. They tackle the social, economic and environmental consequences of the rapid developments, taking account of what has happened so far and looking ahead to future prospects. The series caters for all those wanting to understand what is happening at the forefront of the field and how it will filter through to general tourism practice.

Other titles in the series

Change in Tourism
Peoples, Places, Processes
Edited by Douglas Pearce and Richard Butler

Tourism and Heritage Attractions
Richard Prentice

Tourism and the Environment
A sustainable relationship?
Colin Hunter and Howard Green

Tourism in Major Cities

Edited by Christopher M. Law

INTERNATIONAL THOMSON BUSINESS PRESS
I (T) P An International Thomson Publishing Company

London • Bonn • Boston • Johannesburg • Madrid • Melbourne • Mexico City • New York • Paris
Singapore • Tokyo • Toronto • Albany, NY • Belmont, CA • Cincinnati, OH • Detroit, MI

Tourism in Major Cities

Copyright © 1996 Selection and editorial material Christopher M. Law
Individual chapters to individual authors

First published 1996 by International Thomson Business Press

I ⓣ P   A division of International Thomson Publishing Inc.
   The ITP logo is a trademark under licence

Whilst the Publisher has taken all reasonable care in the preparation of this book the Publisher makes no representation, express or implied, with regard to the accuracy of the information contained in this book and cannot accept any legal responsibility or liability for any errors or omissions from the book or the consequences thereof.

Products and services that are referred to in this book may be either trademarks and/or registered trademarks of their respective owners. The Publisher/s and Author/s make no claim to these trademarks.

British Library Cataloguing-in-Publication Data
A catalogue record for this book is available from the British Library

First edition 1996

Typeset in Times 10/12pt by Saxon Graphics Ltd, Derby
Printed in the UK by St Edmundsbury Press, Bury St Edmunds, Suffolk

ISBN 0-415-08986-7

International Thomson Business Press
Berkshire House
168–173 High Holborn
London WC1V 7AA
UK

International Thomson Business Press
20 Park Plaza
14th Floor
Boston MA 02116
USA

http://www.thomson.com/itbp.html

Contents

Figures

Tables

Contributors

Kazutoshi Abe is Professor of Geography at the Aichi University of Education, Japan. His Ph.D. was in urban geography and he has published a book on the urban system of Japan.

Uel Blank. Currently Economic Development Consultant to the travel/tourism industry. Emeritus Professor of Economics, University of Minnesota. Author of book: *The Community Tourism Industry Imperative*. Associate Director, Institute for Community Development, Michigan State University.

Paul Bull is Lecturer in Geography at Birkbeck College, University of London. He teaches the regional economic development of Western Europe. His research interests have recently shifted to the geography of the hotel and catering industry, consumer services and tourism.

Andrew Church is Lecturer in Geography at Birkbeck College, University of London. He lectures on urban and economic geography with a focus on Western Europe. His research interests include the economic geography of hospitality and tourism, local economic policy and the application of geographical information systems to urban and regional policy.

Klaus Grabler acquired his masters degree from the Vienna University of Economics and Business Administration (Wirtschaftsuniversität Wien). He has been Assistant Professor at the Institute of Tourism and Leisure Studies of the WU Wien since 1994. His main research interests include models of tourist behaviour, tourist decision processes, urban tourism and multivariate methods.

Christopher Law is Reader in Geography and Chairman of Department at the University of Salford, Manchester. He is interested in urban and regional development, problems and policies. His book *Urban Tourism: Attracting Visitors to Large Cities* was published by Mansell in 1993.

Josef A. Mazanec acquired his Ph.D. and venia docendi from the Vienna University of Economics and Business Administration (Wirtschaftsuniversität Wien). He has been full professor and director of the Institute for Tourism and Leisure Studies of the WU Wien since 1981. His main research interests include models of consumer/tourist behaviour, strategic planning, tourism and hospitality marketing, multivariate methods, and decision support systems.

Gerda Priestley is Senior Lecturer in Geography at the Autonomous University of Barcelona. Her main fields of interest are the geography of tourism and cartography. Recent research has focused on the spatial aspects of tourism development on the Catalan coast, and golf tourism in Catalonia and in the Canary Islands.

Peter Schnell is in the Institut für Geographie, Westfalische Wilhelms-Universitat Munster, Germany.

John Tuppen is currently Head of Tourism in the School of Policy Studies at the University of Humberside. He has written extensively on the French economy and spent nine years working in France, first at the University of Lyon III and subsequently at the Group Ecole Supérieure de Commerce de Lyon (The Lyon Graduate School of Business).

Karl Wöber acquired his Ph.D. from the Vienna University of Economics and Business Administration (Wirtschaftsuniversität Wien). He has been Assistant Professor at the Institute of Tourism and Leisure Studies of the WU Wien since 1990. His main research interests include information and decision support systems, strategic planning, and multivariate methods.

1 Introduction

Christopher M. Law

The large city as an important tourism destination came of age during the 1980s. By then television travel programmes and the travel sections of newspapers were regularly featuring city breaks while game shows were offering them as prizes. At the same time governments came to recognize that tourism could have a role in urban economic development. Slowly funding for tourism increased and tourism related projects began to appear in economic strategies.

In spite of these trends the scale, importance and significance of tourism in cities is often not recognized. Many academic books and papers are still written as if tourism only happens in coastal and ski resorts, and the role of tourism in urban economies is often ignored. This is probably because tourism in cities is not understood. As will be discussed below, tourism in cities is a complex phenomenon. It cannot be grasped as easily as, say, tourism in a seaside resort. There is a discussion as to what should be included. There is still often a debate as to whether it should be encouraged in cities. Others debate whether its impact is wholly desirable. Before these issues can be fully debated we need to know more about tourism in major cities. We need to explore how it has grown, its character and the diverse nature of its impacts. There is clearly scope for several books on this topic each approaching it from a different perspective. The purpose of this book is to draw on experience in different parts of the world. To what extent are there common processes operating across the world? To what extent are there differences between the industry in different countries reflecting political, cultural and social factors? To what extent does the varying resource-base of cities determine the character of the industry? How does the leadership of the public and private sectors and the institutional structure of a city effect the development of the industry? How do problems caused by the industry vary across the world?

The focus of this book is deliberately on the large or major city. Tourism now impacts on most urban settlements whatever their size, but its importance can obviously vary. In smaller settelements it ranges in importance from very little to very great, examples of the latter being resorts and historic towns. Resorts have been brought into existence by the tourist function while towns with a strong historic character have found their economy taken over by tourism. The large city, almost by definition, cannot be dominated by tourism. It has become the size it is because of the growth of several functions, and it is multifunctional. The tourism function will be in competition with other activities for a share of resources, whether they be public expenditure, private investment, labour or space. Tourist functions and tourists may either be concentrated or scattered, and if the latter is the case, then tourism may hardly be noticed. All large cities are likely to have a significant tourism industry. Because of their size, functions and facilities will have been developed to serve residents and these will be of such a scale as to make them attractive to visitors. These will include museums, theatres, sports teams and facilities, and business activities which bring in visitors. These facilities will be a base on which to build a tourism industry. Of course some large cities will have extra advantages, world famous buildings, museums and events. It is possible then to classify major cities into types depending on the scale and nature of their tourism industry. One example of a typology is given below (see also chapters by Blank and Schnell in this book):

1 *Capital cities.* Examples London and Paris. They have major administrative and/or business roles which will attract visitors. In addition they usually have national museums of world standing and historic monuments and buildings. Consequently they are important for both business and leisure tourism and attract visitors from a large geographical area.

2 *Industrial cities.* Examples Baltimore and Manchester. While these cities are the product of industrial development, they usually also have significant commercial roles. Their size in terms of population has meant that many facilities, attractive to tourists have also developed. However, their industrial character and image is a barrier for the evolution of their tourism industry, and business tourism remains most significant for hotel-staying visitors. Geographically their leisure visitors are drawn mainly from the region and state in which they are found.

3 *High-amenity cities.* Examples Munich and San Francisco. These cities have a wide range of amenities from natural scenery, attractions and entertainments whilst at the same time they may have important business functions. They attract both business and leisure visitors, often from a wide area.

4 *Major attractive cities.* Examples Florence and Miami. This category includes cities which whilst multi-functional also are perceived to be tourist cities either of a resort or historic nature. These cities are mainly concerned with the leisure tourists who are often drawn from a distance.

Any typology such as the above is bound to be crude and oversimplistic. All attempts to classify cities on the basis of their functions have failed as there are no clear boundary lines for the significance of a function, only a continuum. Further, as will be discussed below, the scale and nature of tourism is evolving, and cities may change their position in any system of classification.

This book does not attempt to define a major or large city in terms of size whether this be population or employment. The functional characteristics of cities do not suddenly change when a threshold level is passed whether this be 250,000, 500,000 or 1 million. The significance of absolute size may vary from one country to another depending on the level of economic development and geographical characteristics. Each author of the following chapters was given a free hand to include whatever size cities they thought appropriate. Below we examine the nature of urban tourism, how and why it is being developed, some of the problems, and how cities can be ranked on the basis of the industry.

THE NATURE OF TOURISM IN MAJOR CITIES

As mentioned above, one of the reasons why tourism in major cities has been underestimated is that it has been misunderstood. This misunderstanding concerns the tourist, what they do and the components of the industry. Cities are multi-motivated travel destinations, unlike many resorts.

At least in the mind of the general public, a tourist is a person who goes away from home for several days, typically one or two weeks, and visits a place for pleasure activities. Many would baulk at the idea of 'business tourism', but this type of visitor is very important for cities. The business visitor may come in the usual course of his or her work, say to visit a factory or office, but the term also covers the conference or exhibition delegate. People visit cities for many purposes: for business, for entertainment and leisure activities, to visit friends and relatives, and to undertake personal business. Often they visit a city for more than one reason. They may primarily come for business reasons, but wish at the same time to visit an art gallery. Or they may come to attend a football match but at the same time wish to see a friend or relative. Overseas visitors may use the city as a gateway to visit surrounding regions. Many visitors to Britain stay in London and have day trips to places such as Stratford-upon-Avon, Oxford and Bath.

The official definition of a tourist is a person who is away from home for more than 24 hours (i.e., is away overnight). Many visitors to cities do stay overnight, but a large number are day trippers. With improved travel they may come from a distance. From Manchester there are day air trips to places as distant as Rome and Vienna. Many business trips can now be made within a day which previously would have required an overnight stay. Most visitors to cities either come for a day or stay only two or three nights. This contrasts with the long stays made at resorts.

Given the importance of day trippers it is important to be able to define the necessary distance travelled before a person is counted as a visitor. A tourist can be considered to be a person travelling outside his/her normal area of movement, but quoted distances would vary from person to person, region to region, and country to country. Usually for cities a visitor is considered to be someone coming from outside the metropolitan area, which could be variously defined from 15–150 kilometres. Unfortunately, either cities use different definitions or the statistics refer to different types of area, so that it is often difficult to compile comparable figures. There are also reasons why different studies may define a visitor in different ways.

Many cities are now attempting to use tourism as a means of regenerating inner city areas (see p. 12). In some cases, owing to decline and poor environment these areas have become deserted or largely avoided even by people living only a short distance away. If tourism projects are able to persuade urbanites to revisit these areas should they not be counted as visitors? In many American cities suburbanites had ceased to visit downtown and inner city areas. Subsequently revitalization projects with a strong tourism dimension have persuaded them to return, but too narrow a definition would exclude them being defined as tourists.

These thoughts raise another issue for the nature of urban tourism – that of defining a tourism project or attraction. With a seaside or ski resort the nature of the attraction is obvious and clear. But for cities tourists are using facilities which are also patronized by the local population. These include museums, art galleries, theme parks, historic buildings, sports stadia, theatres and concert halls. They may even use the same shops and restaurants. At what point are these facilities considered part of the tourism resource-base? In order to assess the role of tourism in cities it is vital to have statistics on the origin of visitors to these facilities. In a city where tourism is significant the majority of visitors are likely to come from a distance, whereas for a minor tourism centre only a small proportion will do so.

This discussion illustrates how many projects in cities are multi-purposed. A new concert hall may be designed to provide better amenities for the local population, to be able to host high-quality concerts which will attract visitors from a distance, to show the executives of firms that might consider moving to the city that it can offer a high-quality lifestyle and perhaps to be a prestige symbol for the city. Given these various motives it is often difficult to assess the success of a scheme, and to which heading the costs and benefits should be attributed.

This diversity of consumers in cities is another reason why it is difficult to assess the significance of tourism. Visitors are usually not distinguishable from locals. The owners of the facilities which they visit are often not able to say what proportion of their trade comes from tourists. The pound or dollar spent by the tourist goes into the same till as that of the local. Without wide ranging and expensive surveys it is often difficult to calculate the impact of visitors in terms of jobs created. As a consequence there is much ignorance about the impact of tourism in cities, which allows scope for debate on this topic.

However, it is clear that tourism in major cities involves shorter stays, a high proportion of day trippers, visitors coming for a wide range of reasons, and that it is less seasonal than that of tourism in many other types of destination.

THE RISE OF URBAN TOURISM

Why should more people be visiting major cities? What are the processes creating the rise of this activity in cities and how do they vary spatially? There are no simple answers to these questions. It is a result of the conjunction of a number of trends in society. We have seen above that visitors to cities include visits to friends and relatives, short break leisure visitors, visitors using the city as a gateway, conference and exhibition visitors and business travellers. These very broadly can be divided into the leisure (or pleasure) and business markets, which can be considered in turn.

During the twentieth century the combination of a growth in leisure time and increased affluence has resulted in the growth of leisure industries. Leisure time can be defined as free time or time which can be used at the discretion of the individual. Overall the amount of time worked for pay has fallen, whether this is measured in terms of hours per week, days per year (after holiday deductions) or years of working life. At the same time the amount of domestic and other essential non-paid work has tended to fall with smaller families and more domestic appliances. Of course these general trends vary greatly between individuals. Some middle-class workers think that they are working harder than ever, while the unemployed and retired appear to have vast amounts of leisure time. These trends can be considered in relation to rising incomes. Once again discretionary income, that is income available after basic living costs have been paid, has been rising rapidly for many in society. Some households where there are two earners have significant amounts of both discretionary time and income available, while at the other extreme some households are having to work long hours just to make ends meet. The combination of free time and discretionary income enables the consumer to spend money on a range of activities which may be broadly considered as leisure activities. These could include in-home entertainment, out-of-home entertainment, day trips, short breaks, holidays, eating and drinking and visiting friends and relatives. As a consequence of this type of expenditure, employment in pubs, clubs, restaurants, hotels, theatres and museums has been increasing rapidly in recent years. Along with producer services (see p. 8) it has been one of the two main growth sectors of the economy in the late twentieth century. The patterns of leisure activities have almost certainly varied over time, reflecting several factors. When work dominates, leisure time may be predominantly used for relaxation and refreshment. As free time and discretionary income increases, leisure time is used more actively for amusement and entertainment. With higher levels of education being attained by increasing proportions of the population, cultural activities are likely to become more important.

The growth of these leisure activities and expenditures is the context for the expansion of tourism but the two are not simply casually related. Leisure activities may take place in the home area or outside. Tourism may be regarded as the consumption of leisure activities outside the home area. Why should people want to travel? This can happen for very many reasons. Friends and relatives may live elsewhere and to see them one has to travel. With increasing movement for employment and retirement migration this is a major reason for travelling to visit friends and relatives. Many people also travel because the activities they are interested in are taking place elsewhere. These might be sporting, cultural or entertainment events. At the same time education and the media have made people more aware of their common world heritage and created a desire to travel to see famous buildings, landscapes and works of art. These desires might be created by our culture, but they become very real motives for travel (Urry 1990). Another reason for travel is the concept of a break or holiday. Having a holiday means, for many people, getting away from the normal, usual things and going somewhere else. People use their holidays to visit the seaside, rural areas, mountain areas, and to experience their cultural heritage. For many the 'good life' is going away on holiday, visiting an exotic place, and this has become possible for an increasing number. The choices individuals make when travelling will obviously vary greatly depending on a wide range of factors such as inclination (taste), age, income, health and education. Young people and young adults with children may prefer active holidays including the seaside, walking, climbing, skiing, etc., while older people may prefer visiting cultural attractions, shopping, etc. One reason for the growth of cultural tourism is that the population is ageing and that many remain healthy and affluent well into old age and continue to desire to travel.

The choice of destination made will obviously depend on the opportunities. Easier, cheaper and faster transport has greatly widened the choice of destinations available. The private sector, aware of growing demand and the opportunities for profit, has invested in attractions, hotels and catering as well as providing companies to arrange and organize trips. The public sector has also provided a great deal of infrastructure and attractions, often as a deliberate policy to encourage tourism.

With so much choice available, how do individuals decide what to do and where to go, and how do we explain the resulting pattern of outcomes? How do large cities compete with other types of destination and why should cities be growing in importance? Because cities are multi-purpose destinations there is no one answer to these questions. They attract many vistors to friends and relatives because they have a large population. They draw visitors to their attractions and events because these are often much better developed in them than in other types of destination area. These amenities are being further developed at the moment as a deliberate policy on the part of cities to expand their tourist industry. Museums, concert halls, theatres, arenas, stadiums are being built or improved and potential tourism quarters being redeveloped and renovated. Cities also have other advantages to attract tourists. With airports and scheduled services they are easily accessible. They often have a large stock of hotels built to serve the business traveller which are underused at the weekend. Accordingly, cheap weekend breaks can be offered. Cities also appeal to the different tourist markets. A more educated population is attracted to the cultural heritage of cities. A more elderly population is also likely to appreciate cultural heritage and prefer it to active outdoor holidays. At the other end of the age spectrum young people are attracted to the excitement found in the city, the entertainment, the night life and sporting events. The large city attracts visitors because of the wide choice of attractions which enables the tourist to make their own selection. In this sense it is the ultimate post-Fordist, post-modern tourist destination.

Winchester does not really have a wide choice of attractions to enable tourists to make their own selection.

The large city is also the destination for the business traveller. Cities have always been important as business or commercial centres. They still remain important as the location of producer or business services, a fact which will bring many visitors. At the same time and for these reasons, many companies have their headquarters in major cities. With the emergence of the global corporation the activities of companies have become widely scattered. There is a need for executives to meet for planning and training sessions, which they frequently do in cities because of the facilities and accessibility which they have. These business tourists have been the basis of city tourism for many decades. They have created the demand for hotel accommodation and more recently the growth of scheduled services from local airports, both resources being important for leisure tourism as discussed above.

Another type of business tourism partly included above is the conference and exhibition market. Corporate conferences, just described, are very numerous but usually have only up to about a hundred participants. They usually take place in hotels. On a larger scale the association conference may have up to several thousand delegates. They require a large hall and, increasingly, a purpose-built facility. Attendance at conferences has been growing in recent years, only occasionally halted by a recession. This growth reflects the increasing number of associations, which may be social, political and religious as well as linked with the professions, and their national and international span, necessitating the need to bring people together. In theory it might be thought that there would be less need for conferences as new forms of telecommunications, including the teleconference, might obviate the necessity for meeting. But conferences have an important social and spontaneous component which requires a face-to-face meeting. The growing complexity and interconnectedness of different regions and countries will almost certainly ensure that conference numbers continue to expand. Conferences can be held in many types of location and not just cities. But large cities have the resources in a way other destinations do not. They usually have good communications, including airports, hotels, conference centres and the ancilliary facilities which delegates want. Conferences and exhibitions are often associated with each other. Small exhibitions are laid on with conferences, and conferences are laid on with exhibitions. The convention centre, pioneered in the United States, provides for both of these activities in a flexible way. The number of exhibitions, both trade and public, has been growing in the post-war period. Trade exhibitions provide a good way of bringing sellers and buyers together, being convenient and saving time. They are likely to continue to grow in number, becoming more specialized. Since nearly all specialized exhibition centres and convention centres are found in cities, the growth of this activity will favour these places which have good facilities, and which have carved out a niche in the increasingly competitive marketplace.

TOURISM AND URBAN GROWTH

Perhaps one reason why urban tourism has been so little recognized is that its evolution does not fit easily into urban growth models. Early ideas about urban systems focused on Christaller's Central Place Theory. In this model cities provide services for their surrounding area and are classified into a hierarchy with higher order cities serving a larger area and lower order ones a small local area. Growth in the system takes place in conformity with this hierarchy. In so far as tourism attractions can be classified and ranked we might expect the higher order cities to have good facilities such as museums, theatres and sports, drawing people in from a large area, whilst the lower order centres would have few attractions and of only local appeal. There is some validity in this idea. Higher order centres will generally be larger in population and so have the threshold to support significant attractions. Interestingly, Christaller (1964) in his paper on tourism completely ignored the appeal of cities. However, the quality of attractions cannot simply be correlated with size and rank in the urban hierarchy. Historical factors have left some cities with better endowments than others, whether these be of museums, buildings or physical environment. The physical characteristics of the site may also be an attraction, and this will vary from one place to another. Finally leadership in cities, which can influence tourism development, will vary and not simply be correlated with rank. Central place hierarchies were generally conceived in terms of national areas. With the emergence of free trade areas and global interconnectedness, it now may be time to think of a world system of cities and related hierarchy. However, once again tourism may not fit neatly into the scheme (see pp. 15–16).

Another popular idea about urban growth relates to concepts of a pre-industrial, industrial and post-industrial city. The pre-industrial or mercantilist city was based on trade, monopolies and military power. From the late eighteenth century the industrial city emerged, growing on the basis of manufacturing activity within a capitalist system. Within the industrial period there were several phases, the latest of which is sometimes referred to as Fordist, involving mass production and consumption. Many commentators believe that since the early 1970s a new economic system has been emerging, variously described as post-Fordist, neo-Fordist or flexible accumulation. With respect to cities, Harvey (1989) perceives the principal characteristics to be entrepreneurial cities, public–

private partnerships and increased inter-urban competition. The latter takes the form of competition within the spatial division of labour for mobile investment, competition with respect to the spatial division of consumption, competition for the location of command functions (finance, business, information and government) and competition for the receipt of government funds. Harvey makes it clear under the second heading that the major cities are competing for the tourist's income and that success or failure in this sphere could be crucial to the future of a city. This competition has resulted in a spate of innovations from convention centres, sports stadia, theme parks to downtown paradises. For Harvey the post-industrial city is characterized by increasing class polarization, which city leaders seek to conceal through the use of community spectacle. This same spectacle will also make them more attractive to tourists.

Another idea about the modern post-Fordist city involves the concept of industrial districts (Scott 1988). Emerging from Fordism, industries may become smaller, seeking external rather than internal economies of scale. Linked with just-in-time systems there may be a reconcentration of industries into areas held together by linkages akin to those which developed at the end of the nineteenth century and early twentieth century, but possibly on a larger geographical scale. In some respects the tourism districts appearing on the edge of city centres fit into this pattern. The product which the city offers is a multi-faceted experience. Tourists may be drawn by the main attractions but they often patronize shops, restaurants and other facilities. Thus there is a group of producers who combine together in a small geographical area to offer the visitor a product. The more producers there are, the higher the quality of their offerings, and the stronger the linkages the better the product will be.

TOURISM AND URBAN ECONOMIC DEVELOPMENT

Since the early 1980s the case for using tourism to promote economic development in cities has been widely discussed (Law 1993). Deindustrialization has created problems for most large cities. Jobs have disappeared, unemployment has increased and derelict sites have emerged, often in the inner city. It is apparent that the perceived economic stability of the early post-war years has come to an end. Global competition combined with continual technological change means that cities as well as regions and countries must constantly be renewing their economies or face decline and death. Consequently the leaders of cities are looking for growing sectors which can be developed to create jobs and raise incomes in the locality. There is no desire to specialize in any activity, but rather to diversify the economy. It is in this context that tourism has been adopted and promoted in a large and varied range of cities. It is not perceived as a panacea to all problems, but it is certainly an industry which it is thought will be able to breathe new life into old cities. Rightly or wrongly, it is perceived to have long-term growth potential based on growing affluence, increased leisure time and easier travel, and to be capable of development in urban locations.

As mentioned above, most cities already have, even if unrecognized, a tourist industry and also a range of tourism resources. These include museums and art galleries, theatres, concert halls, sports stadia and teams, arenas and large halls. They often have good transport accessibility, including air transport, and a range of hotels, restaurants and a night life. These can be developed, improved and extended to attract tourists. Even if lacking high ranking attractions, events can be created to woo the visitor.

The invisibility of tourism in cities partly arises from the fact that many facilities are used both by residents and visitors. Improving these facilities therefore provides benefits for residents as well as assisting the promotion of tourism. Visitors who pay to use these facilities contribute to the viability of an amenity and thus safeguard its long-term use for residents.

The kinds of facilities which are being developed as part of a tourism strategy tend to be of the type that appeal to mobile business executives. These include theatres, concert halls and museums. They are important therefore as part of a wider strategy to attract inward investment to the city, whether this be manufacturing or business services. It has become obvious in the late twentieth century that business location decisions are not made simply on the basis of narrow economic advantage, but take into account the lifestyle opportunities of executives. This is apparent from the literature put out by economic development agencies. Tourism development therefore is congruent and supportive of these wider economic development strategies.

Another link with these strategies arises from the advertising of the city, which is an essential part of tourism promotion. Advertising the city to potential tourists raises the profile of the city, keeps it in the public eye, and so links itself with the other type of promotion to firms who are potential movers. Of course tourism advertising is highly selective, concentrating on those aspects of the city which can appeal to outsiders. Through this form of advertising a new image for the city can be created. As later chapters will show, the image of a city is very important in the attraction of the leisure tourist, although much less so for the business tourist. This advertising often involves slogans. Thus Birmingham has recently promoted itself as 'Europe's Meeting Place'. Such a slogan combines an attempt to attract conferences and exhibitions as well as general business activities.

Another value of tourism is its perceived association with physical regeneration. Many new projects, such as convention centres and arenas, are centrepieces of the regeneration of derelict areas on the downtown area. Some of the most spectacular redevelopments, involving waterfronts, have contained major leisure and tourism themes. In the case of places like the Inner Harbour, Baltimore, they have become attractions in themselves. Once again such projects have helped to transform the image of the city.

A final advantage of tourism development linked to the above point is that it is generally located in the city centre and/or adjacent inner city. It is these areas which have generally suffered the most from deindustrialization, defined here broadly to include transport and distribution. The city centre has often, particularly in North America, suffered competition from new suburban nodes. In spite of these obvious problems in the city centre and inner city, tourism strategies have tended to focus on this area. This is not simply so that tourism can be used to regenerate these areas, but because so many of the existing tourism resources are found here. They form the basis for improvement and extension. The city centre is still amongst the most nodal and accessible points in the city. For these reasons development is focused here.

The promotion of tourism in cities requires vision, leadership, partnership and funding as well as the will to pursue a policy over many years. It requires a vision which can combine both economic and physical (landscape) perspectives to create a range of products of great appeal. These products should be of high quality and unique. Generally it is the public sector which is best placed to give this leadership. It has control over physical planning and often has access to funding for key schemes. Most tourism strategies involve anchors such as museums and convention centres which are likely to be publicly funded. Once the key pieces of infrastructure are in place the private sector is likely to follow with investment in smaller attractions, hotels, entertainment and catering. Partnerships between the two sectors are most common in promotion and it is by such organizations that the private sector can sometimes make its input into tourism planning (Bramwell and Rawding 1994).

THE COSTS AND DISADVANTAGES OF TOURISM IN CITIES

The image of the tourist industry is one of casual and seasonal employment with poor pay. This is only partly true for the entire industry, and much less valid for the industry in cities. Many of the activities mentioned above such as business travel, conferences and exhibitions and cultural and sporting events take place throughout the year and if there is any seasonality it is not only much less marked but may be inverse to the usual trends (see Schnell on Germany, Chapter 4 in this book). As the work is often not seasonal, jobs can be more permanent. While there is a proportion of poorly paid jobs, they are jobs for the unemployed, who often live in the inner city near to the tourist attractions and are not noticeably poorer paid than such people would get in other industries.

A second criticism is that the development of the tourism industry diverts attention and resources away from social needs in the city. In its promotional literature a city will try to create an appealing image and ignore/obscure the problems which exist. This alone may cause complacency about the problems. The amenities and environments which attract tourists are usually those which appeal to middle-class values. The values and lifestyles of the working class and those organizations which fight for them are therefore likely to be ignored and possibly downplayed in the life of the city. This divergence was highlighted in the debates which took place when Glasgow was European City of Culture (Boyle and Hughes 1991). The new tourism projects are likely to appeal to middle-class tastes, museums and concert halls, and the finance needed for their construction may directly or indirectly divert funds from social spending. This is alleged to have been the case in Birmingham where the huge resources needed to build the convention centre are said to have been diverted from the repairs to educational buildings (Loftman and Nevin 1992). In the short term the question that is often asked is: a tourism industry for whom? Funds appear to be used for the affluent middle classes and for people who do not live in the city. Nearly always the city leadership will defend the policies on the basis that visitors will bring income to the city and that their expenditure will create jobs. This is obviously true to a certain extent, but the true costs and benefits are rarely calculated. The true costs should not only include the investment in new facilities but also a wide range of other costs including funds for promotion, the cost of the time officials spend in planning the industry, the costs of wear and tear, the cost of policing and the costs of congestion. Equally of course the benefits of tourism should be evaluated fairly broadly to include a change of image, extra investment brought to the city and the impacts of enhanced physical environments. Unfortunately the costs are often short term while the benefits are likely to be long term. By the time an evaluation has been made, it may be too late to correct any mistakes.

The development of tourism not only shows investment decisions, but there is also a geographical component. Tourism resources and infrastructure are often concentrated, usually in the city centre, so these areas receive priority in investment over other areas where social need may be great (Madsen 1992). Many cities, in order to create the right image for tourists, have also invested in scenic entrances or corridors, again at the expense of other routes.

One of the problems of evaluating the costs and benefits of tourism is that it is not clear what projects to count. Investment in a museum caters for the needs of both residents and tourists. Should this be counted as a tourism project, half tourism or not a tourism project? Whereas in the past investment in a museum would have been perceived to be catering for the needs of residents, this would rarely be the sole reason given today.

Investment in tourism projects is inherently risky. In theory the investment should be recouped over a number of years, but in many cases the tourism future is very uncertain. To be successful the project must attract visitors, and in this a city is in competition with other cities for the same trade. This can be illustrated by reference to the construction of convention centres by cities in the United States. Nearly every city now has one, but there is insufficient trade to go round. In order to attract business, a subsidy has to be given to conventions. Accordingly most convention centres are run at a loss, since even popular destinations are frequently compelled to reduce their charges. A particular tourism resource or even a whole city may be successful in attracting tourists for a number of years, but then suddenly find its trade draining away. This could be because a rival or rivals have come along with a better, newer or more novel product, because fashions change or because of an international event, war or currency change, which reduces demand. In such cases the expected return does not materialize, and the community is left footing the bill.

The costs of tourism in cities are often experienced at the local level. In cities where tourism is very successful or is very localized, particular areas may suffer from congestion, rising property prices, changes in the character of the area, including shops, which may result in conflicts between residents and tourists, and a sense of alienation on the part of the former. In London and San Francisco the expansion of hotels has either resulted in a reduction of apartments to rent, or an increase in their price. In either case residents – often the poorer ones – may be driven out of the area. For many cities this is not a problem; rather, a lack of demand in the fringe of the city centre has resulted in a zone of decay. Newer activities are welcome because they regenerate these areas.

It is not possible to generalize about the benefits and costs of tourism in major cities. Each city is unique, and the situation should be examined for every case. All cities will attempt to maximize the benefits and reduce the costs. The strategy they adopt and the way they go about it will depend on the characteristics of the place and how it relates to other cities, a topic to which we now turn.

CITY TOURISM CENTRES: HIERARCHY AND GROWTH MODEL

The scale and relative importance of tourism varies from one city to another. Various measures can be used to quantify the industry including: number of day visitors, number of visitors staying in serviced accommodation and the number of overnights, other visitors including those to friends and relatives, expenditure, and employment. The industry can also be divided between leisure and business. Such statistics, if available on a comparable basis, which unfortunately they are not, could be used to rank cities by the scale of their industry. However, there is another dimension which concerns the draw of cities; from what distance and in what proportions do their visitors come? This dimension would separate those cities which draw significant numbers from around the world from those which mainly gain visitors from their own locality. While cities having a world pull might be expected to have large absolute numbers the rankings on the two dimensions might not exactly agree. Using the second dimension the following hierarchy can be constructed:

Rank	*Origin of visitors*	
1	World	Significant share from world
2	Continental	Mainly from same continent
3	National	Mainly from nation in which city found
4	Regional	Mainly from macro-region of country
5	Local	Mainly from local region

Such a scaling could only be used within large countries. For small countries the criteria would have to be adapted. The world tourist city is one that will be familiar to many travellers. It includes cities such as London, Paris, Washington and St Petersburg. The main features of such cities is that they contain attractions of world-class rank in the hierarchy of attractions (see Butler 1991). In many cases these cities have been capitals and their attractions have resulted from this status. Art galleries and famous buildings are particularly important in attracting tourists. Examples include the Louvre in Paris, the Uffizi in Florence, the Hermitage in St Petersburg, the Prado in Madrid, and the National Gallery in Washington. Famous buildings include royal palaces, cathedrals, castles and icons such as the Eiffel Tower. Sometimes, but necessarily so, these cities are also world financial centres. These cities appear frequently on the TV news and in films, thus becoming familiar around the world and creating a desire amongst travellers to visit them. Their cosmopolitan nature will be most visible at the leading attractions where guidebooks will be sold in several languages and in Europe where coaches from many countries will be queuing to pick up parties.

At the other end of the spectrum the 'local' tourist city will draw the majority of its vistors from a day visit range. Its attractions will only be known by those in the region and will have little appeal to people elsewhere in the country. The city will not appear frequently in the national and international media, and thus its visibility will be low.

This ranking might also be used as a stage of growth model. An aspiring tourist city would be attempting to move up ranks by developing higher order attractions and seeking wider coverage in the media. It would be seeking to develop elements of uniqueness which would give it world-class status including distinctive landscape trade marks.

As with all hierarchies there is the question as to whether there are, and can only be, a limited number of places at the top level. Potential tourists can only absorb so much information about cities and have only a limited time to visit them. This suggests only a limited number of 'world' tourist cities. While the industry may be growing and most cities benefiting, the rankings may stay much the same. Currently there is intense competition between cities. This has partly arisen because air transport has made long distance travel so much easier, so that visiting cities around the world is becoming possible for the ordinary tourist. This inter-city competition has also happened because cities are vigorously promoting the industry in a way that did not happen twenty years ago. As has been discussed above, many industrial cities in Western Europe and North America are attempting to expand the industry but they usually lack the world-class attractions and a good image (see Chapter 7). At the same time other geopolitical and transport changes are bringing new cities into the marketplace. The ending of the Cold War has opened up much more of Eastern Europe and the former Soviet Union to 'Western' tourists. Cities such as Budapest, Prague, Moscow and St Petersburg have much to offer and once their infrastructure has been improved will be able to compete strongly with other European cities. Easier travel is also bringing East Asian and possibly Australian cities into the global marketplace. Hong Kong, Beijing, Bangkok and Singapore can offer distinctive cultural elements not found in Europe. In so far as there is a kudos associated with foreign travel, those for whom this is an element will be looking for something more exotic than is found in Europe. These trends suggest the emergence of a global hierarchy of tourist cities superseding the continental ones that now exist. An example of such a hierarchy in Europe will now be discussed.

TOURISM IN EUROPEAN CITIES

Ideally European cities could be ranked according to the importance of tourism using data from comprehensive studies including income, visitors, days and nights and employment. Since, owing to cost, very few such studies have been undertaken, any attempt to rank cities must rely on specific indicators for which there is information and consequently the results will only be partial. An example of such a study is that by Rubalcaba-Bermejo and Cuadrado-Roura (1995) which uses data on fairs and exhibitions. Another indication of the importance of cities as tourist centres is the number of nights spent by visitors. Many countries in Europe collect data from hotels which is collated to provide aggregate statistics for cities. Unfortunately the definitions adopted do not always agree. Small hotels are often not included, but the cut-off point varies from one country to another and may vary over time. Further city boundaries may not coincide with the built-up area and there could be an underestimation. On the other hand, where the figures are provided for provinces there could be an overestimation. All these caveats make the comparison and interpretation of published statistics difficult. In any case hotel figures exclude visits to friends and relatives, and self-catering. Tables 1.1 and 1.2 provide data for the major tourist cities. London, Paris and Rome are the most important centres. Most of the cities in Table 1.1 are capital cities but there are also historic cities such as Venice and Florence as well as major business and industrial cities such as Frankfurt and Birmingham. The importance of Barcelona partly reflects the year 1992 when it hosted the Olympic Games. Table 1.2 shows the figures for foreign nights. Some second cities, such as Milan, fall in rank in this table suggesting that they are less successful in attracting both foreign leisure and business visitors.

The importance of these cities for the pleasure tourist is reflected in the number of times they appear in travel brochures. Van den Berg *et al.*'s (1994) figures are shown in Table 1.3. The main feature to note is that business and industrial cities are absent from this list, and that fourteen cities have widespread appeal in Europe.

IS THERE AN URBAN TOURISM? IS THERE AN URBAN TOURIST?

There is no doubt that tourism is a significant activity in many towns and cities and that its importance is likely to grow in the future. Because of this it is useful to understand the phenomenon, to be able to describe it, to interpret it and to suggest the forms it may take. Towns and cities have become tourist destinations. This fact must be taken on board by planners and politicians as well as academics. But are the concepts of urban tourism and the urban tourist meaningful ones? The term 'urban tourism' has become widely used in the literature (see Ashworth 1989; Haywood

1992; Law 1993; van den Berg *et al.* 1994; Page 1995) but it has not been subject to analysis, and there is the possibility that it is a chaotic concept.

Table 1.1 Hotel nights in European cities, 1992

Rank	City	Millions	Rank	City	Millions
1	Paris	31.0	16	Amsterdam	4.0
2	London	29.4[a]	17	Venice	4.0
3	Rome	12.4	18	Birmingham	4.0[a]
4	Madrid	7.7	19	Brussels	3.2
5	Vienna	6.9	20	Lisbon	3.2
6	Munich	6.5	21	Frankfurt	3.2
7	West Berlin	5.7	22	Manchester	3.0[a]
8	Milan	5.6	23	Copenhagen	2.9
9	Dublin	5.0	24	Istanbul	2.9
10	Edinburgh	4.7[a]	25	Lyon	2.8
11	Budapest	4.5	26	Stockholm	2.6
12	Prague	4.3	27	Glasgow	2.6[a]
13	Barcelona	4.3[b]	28	Cologne	2.4
14	Florence	4.2	29	Zurich	2.0
15	Hamburg	4.1	30	Geneva	1.9

Sources: Marktbericht (1994) *Tour MIS Stadteberich 1994*, Osterreich Werbung, Vienna; KPMG (1993) *European Tourism Cities*, Amsterdam (and other sources)
Notes: [a] Estimate; [b] Barcelona figure is for 1993

Table 1.2 Foreign hotel nights in European cities, 1992

Rank	City	Millions	Rank	City	Millions
1	London	22.9[a]	16	Lisbon	2.1
2	Paris	21.9	17	Copenhagen	2.1
3	Vienna	7.5	18	Istanbul	2.0
4	Amsterdam	3.8	19	Geneva	1.7
5	Budapest	3.7	20	Frankfurt	1.7
6	Madrid	3.4	21	Zurich	1.7
7	Prague	3.2	22	West Berlin	1.5
8	Venice	3.1	23	Salzburg	1.4
9	Edinburgh	3.1	24	Glasgow	1.4[a]
10	Brussels	3.1	25	Manchester	1.2
11	Florence	2.7	26	Birmingham	1.2
12	Dublin	2.7	27	Stockholm	1.1
13	Munich	2.7	28	Hamburg	1.0
14	Barcelona	2.6[b]	29	Cologne	0.9
15	Milan	2.4	30	Lyon	0.8

Sources: As for Table 1.1
Notes: [a] Estimate; [b] Barcelona figure is for 1993

Table 1.3 City short-break destinations in Europe, 1993

Featured in the travel brochures of at least six foreign countries	
Amsterdam	Madrid
Budapest	Moscow
Dublin	Paris
Florence	Rome
Istanbul	St Petersburg
Lisbon	Venice
London	Vienna
Other popular cities	
Athens	Munich
Barcelona	Oslo
Berlin	Prague
Brussels	Seville
Copenhagen	Stockholm
Edinburgh	

Sources: J. van der Borg (1994) 'Demand for city-tourism in Europe: tour operators catalogues', *Tourism Management* 15, 66–9, and L. van den Berg *et al.* (1994). Based on travel brochures in Belgium, Denmark, France, Germany, Great Britain, Italy and The Netherlands

The argument that urban tourism is a chaotic concept might hold if the term is used to describe a wide range of phenomena. Some have suggested that tourism itself falls into this situation (Hughes 1991). Certainly the term is used to cover a wide range of situations. Page (1995) uses the term and includes case studies as diverse as Canterbury, Dover, Lourdes, the London Docklands, and Wellington (NZ). Others might include resorts as well as major industrial centres. 'Urban tourist' is also a term which can include diverse types: for example, a day visitor, business traveller, an attender of cultural and sports events, a visitor to museums, an observer of historic buildings and a visitor to friends and relatives. Can all of these be part of the same phenomenon, or are they a series of phenomena which just happen to take place in an urban area?

These terms might be meaningful if it can be shown that the sum is greater than the parts, or at least so on a significant number of occasions. Thus, when visitors are asked about why they went to London and Paris, many do not reply that it was because they wanted to visit the Tower of London or the Louvre, but rather that they just wanted to go there. The image of these cities conjures up many things, from excitement and romance to the fact that there are so many things to do. Of course some people do go to these cities for a single purpose, say a business visit, to see a friend or relative, or to go to an event, but equally large numbers go for multiple purposes. There is a range of activities in these cities which not only provides excitement but a feeling that there will always be plenty of things to do. The enjoyment of these activities and the sheer range is such that frequently visitors will say that they would like to come back again, because amongst other things they did not have time to do all that they wanted to do.

Quite obviously it is possible to speak of an urban tourism and an urban tourist when discussing tourism in cities like London and Paris. It is not quite so obvious that these terms are useful when describing what happens in small cities and towns like Canterbury, Lourdes or Eastbourne. These places have a narrow range of attractions, although of course, as with Canterbury Cathedral, they may be of a very high quality. Accordingly the visitor is likely to only want to stay in such places for a few hours. There will only be limited linkages to other activities, one of which is often shopping and another catering. To this reviewer, then, it is useful to use the terms 'urban tourism' and 'the urban tourist', but only when describing the phenomenon found in large cities, where the sum is greater than the parts. Once again it is not possible to define a size when this happens. As cities get larger in size they develop activities which bring in the visitor for these multiple-purpose stays. However, cities vary in their characteristics. An industrial city might not have the appeal of another city of the same size, which perhaps for historical reasons has more attractions. Where cities have very large numbers of visitors they develop a range of attractions. Thus Blackpool and Brighton originally developed as seaside resorts but the large number of visitors has meant that many other attractions have been introduced. Large numbers of visitors go to these places with no thought of bathing. The sea has merely become a themed background for entertainment, conferences and shopping. However, as mentioned earlier, major cities do have a range of attractions for the tourist because they have large populations and facilities developed for the residents. In conclusion the term 'urban tourism' is a useful concept when describing visitor behaviour to large cities where 'large' is understood in terms of the range of facilities/attractions and of the numbers using them.

CONCLUSION

The purpose of this chapter has been to discuss the scope and characteristics of tourism in major cities and thus provide the background for the chapters which follow. While the material will be useful to practitioners it has not attempted to be a guide as to how to do tourism. For this perspective the next chapter by Grabler, Mazanec and Wöber will be more useful. It adopts a strategic marketing approach and, using the best statistics available, analyses the markets of the major city tourism destinations in Europe. The remaining chapters are national case studies. The first three of these on France, Germany and Spain illustrate how an understanding of tourism in cities can often best be interpreted from the perspective of the national picture. Chapters 6 and 7 discuss the British situation, typically – for this country – dividing it between London and other cities. Moving outside Europe, Chapters 8 and 9 examine the situation in the United States and Japan. In these large and highly urbanized countries it is more possible to characterize tourism in the major cities. All the case studies illustrate the quickening pace of tourism promotion and development in large cities. They confirm the reason for producing this book that tourism in cities has become, and will remain, an important topic for the management and planning of large urban areas.

REFERENCES

Ashworth, G.J. (1989) 'Urban tourism: an imbalance in attention', in C.P. Cooper (ed.) *Progress in Tourism, Recreation and Hospitality Management*, 1, 33–54.

Boyle, M. and Hughes, G. (1991) 'The politics of representation of the real discourses from the left on Glasgow's role in European City of Culture', *Area* 23, 217–28.

Bramwell, B. and Rawding, L. (1994) 'Tourism marketing organisations in industrial cities', *Tourism Management* 15, 425–34.

Butler, R.W. (1991) 'West Edmonton Mall as a tourist attraction', *Canadian Geographer* 35, 287–95.

Christaller, W. (1964) 'Some considerations of tourism location in Europe: the peripheral regions – underdeveloped countries – recreation in areas, *Papers Regional Science Association* 12, 95–105.

Harvey, D. (1989) *The Urban Experience*, Oxford: Basil Blackwell.

Haywood, K.M. (1992) 'Identifying and responding to challenges posed by urban tourism', *Tourism Recreation Research* 17(2), 9–23.

Hughes, G. (1991) 'Conceiving of tourism', *Area* 23, 203–7.

KPMG (1993) *Overview: Comparative Analysis 34 European Cities*, Amsterdam.

Law, C.M. (1993) *Urban Tourism: Attracting Visitors to Large Cities*, London: Mansell.

Loftman, P. and Nevin, B. (1992) 'Urban regeneration and social equity; a case study of Birmingham 1986–92, Research Paper No. 8, University of Central England in Birmingham, Faculty of the Built Environment.

Madsen, H. (1992) 'Place-marketing in Liverpool: a review', *International Journal of Urban and Regional Research* 16, 633–40.

Marktbericht (1994) *Tour MIS Stadteberich 1994*, Osterreich Werbung, Vienna.

Page, S. (1995) *Urban Tourism*, London: Routledge.

Rubalcaba-Bermejo, L. and Cuadrado-Roura, J.R. (1995) 'Urban hierarchies and territorial competition in Europe: exploring the role of fairs and exhibitions', *Urban Studies* 32, 379–400.

Scott, A.J. (1988) *New Industrial Spaces*, London: Pion.

Urry, J. (1990) *The Tourist Gaze: Leisure and Travel in Contemporary Society*, London: Sage.

Van den Berg, L. van der Borg, J. and van der Meer, J. (1994) *Urban Tourism,* Rotterdam: Erasmus University.

Van der Borg, J. (1994) 'Demand for city-tourism in Europe: tour operators catalogues', *Tourism Management*, 15, 66–9.

2 Strategic marketing for urban tourism

Analysing competition among European tourist cities

Klaus Grabler, Josef Mazanec, Karl Wöber

MANAGERIAL ISSUES OF STRATEGIC MARKET PLANNING

Marketing a city to tourism generating countries, in terms of strategic reasoning, is not fundamentally different from marketing branded products to consumer target groups. Consider the management of the municipal tourist board or of a comparable organization in charge of promoting tourism. The managers have to take long-range decisions on which urban tourism products should be offered to which segments of the international tourist demand. Thus, a planning exercise equivalent to product positioning and market segmentation must be completed (McDonald 1989; Calantone and Mazanec 1991). These strategic decisions cannot be reversed in the short run. They inspire subsequent action planning and need continuity and lasting effort to gain results. An issue such as image advertising for a city, for example, is designed along the guidelines of a positioning strategy and accompanied by co-ordinated product planning of tour operators and other private and public service providers. The regular evaluation of various market segments contributes to making market operation selective and to maintaining a reasonable ratio of promotional input to segment response.

On the simplest level of strategic thinking in urban tourism, managers acknowledge the city as a whole as their 'product' and the tourism generating countries as their potential market segments. As this perspective raises least requirements for data collection, and may be implemented with the available (but somewhat refined) international tourism statistics, it will be implemented here. The database originates from the TourMIS marketing information system of the Austrian National Tourist Office. It comprises a selection of time-series 1975–92 with bednight figures for twenty-six European cities (listed in Table 2.1) and eighteen major origin countries. The principles of strategic analysis remain unchanged if managers start to pursue a more sophisticated approach – for example, aiming at consumer lifestyle groups as its market segments (Mazanec and Zins 1994). The need for costly data, however, will increase markedly. The investment into market research may be justified more easily if the management has learned to utilize data already available to full capacity.

Prior to taking strategic decisions the management performs an in-depth review of their destination's strengths and weaknesses *vis-à-vis* its competitors. In today's managerial routine this analytical step employs some variant of the portfolio model to be outlined on pp. 38–46. The entire procedure depends on the appropriate identification of one's competitors and the size of the overall market in which they are competing with each other. This is not a trivial problem and has gained considerable attention in the marketing literature. The forthcoming treatment for urban tourist destinations in this chapter, however, is new and specifically elaborated for the severe data restrictions in this application domain.

IDENTIFYING THE COMPETING DESTINATIONS

Supply and demand driven identification criteria

Marketing researchers have developed a methodology to systematically identify competitors and the boundaries of a relevant market made up of the brands competing within a homogeneous product class (Urban and Hauser 1993). The methods may be characterized as supply-oriented, demand-oriented, or combined examinations working either on a macro or on a micro level of analysis. A strictly supply-oriented approach using macro data is based on comparing the overall structure of tourist services in a group of tourist cities and the degree to what they might be replaced by each other's destinations. The process may also incorporate micro data if managerial judgements are brought in. Furthermore, wholesale figures on the urban destinations offered by major tour operators (Van der Borg 1994) can be used to examine the market structure.

A purely demand-oriented analysis may focus on travellers' stated or revealed preferences, measured for example by unaided awareness, constant-sum scales or conjoint analysis (Woodside and Carr 1988). These analyses require similar patterns of benefits. Thus they should not only consider persons, but preferably person-in-situation approaches to collect 'real' substitutes (Ball *et al.* 1992). The findings are not fully comparable to the most popular method suggested in the marketing literature – namely, brand (destination) switching. The reason is that different consumption goals and purposes result in different competitors (Shocker *et al.* 1984). The monitoring of destination (brand) switching is one of the behavioural approaches that outperform perceptual approaches in identifying existing competitors. However, it often fails to identify potential competitors (Fraser and Bradford 1983, 1984). The perceptual similarities of tourist cities or the monitoring of destination switching behaviour requires micro data. The same holds true for analysing what has more recently become popular as consideration set hypothesis (Crompton 1992) building on Howard and Sheth's seminal work on the evoked set concept (1969).

Crompton's comprehensive article (1992) outlines the potential vacation destination sets that have been operationalized previously (Woodside and Lysonski 1989). The sets are constructed in such a way that smaller sets (e.g., choice or decision sets) are part of bigger ones (e.g., consideration or evoked sets) with a higher chance to be finally chosen (Goodall 1991). They may be conceived as mental categories that are formed by the travellers. The concept implies that a counterpart category – a reject set sometimes further subdivided – also exists (Woodside and Lysonski 1989). In principle, all these sets can assist in identifying competitors. In most cases the decision set that comprises 'no more than seven, often fewer' destinations (Goodall 1991) will be a reliable basis for competitor detection. In this final decision phase the inhibitor variables have a stronger impact than in former stages, where facilitators are more decisive (Um and Crompton 1990, 1992). The consequence is that destinations in the decision set appear to be similarly attractive, but may be rejected because of travel cost and distance, potential health problems, or other perceived risk factors.

Combined supply/demand-oriented analyses typically would involve macro information on the marketing efforts of competing destinations and the ensuing changes in travellers' reactions. Given sufficient data on a time-series, cross-sectional (or on a pooled longitudinal/cross-sectional) basis, cross-elasticities might be derived by some econometric estimation of market response models. The forthcoming examples pick up more straightforward and practical methodology. It is the underlying hypothesis that the relative frequencies of guest nationalities represented in a destination tell about its exposure to inter-city competition. Thus more similar structures of the guest mix are indicative of tougher competition. The reasons are both supply- and demand-related. Travellers from the same origin country are likely to be more homogeneous in their travel needs, perceptions, and attitudes than tourists from different parts of the world. What makes them accumulate in some places may denote a similar degree of preference, some split of destination loyalty towards these places, a competitive threat rendering the places interchangeable. On the other hand, a bigger match in terms of guest structures may stem from uniformity in marketing objectives and strategies pursued by the tourist destinations.

There is, however, one reservation concerning the basic assumption. Two or more cities may exhibit a similar guest mix merely because they are frequently tied together in the same travel package by tour operators. The same effect occurs if individual travel patterns symptomatically contain these cities within a round trip. Fortunately, the cities visited on a round trip (e.g., by Americans touring through Europe), and also the guest nations preferring this type of travel, are well known. Taking these caveats into account a look into the guest mixes seems to be rewarding for the sake of clarifying competitive relations, sometimes with unexpected results.

A European case study

International and domestic travel

Making an assumption about who are the strong competitors is a crucial step. Of course, it is not obvious that two cities of comparable market power are tied up in a competing situation. It is also not evident that two cities which are situated close to each other are 'natural' competitors. Neither marketing strength nor geographical vicinity necessarily determines competition. Ritchie (1994) is right in observing that marketing scientists have paid much attention to consumer response to marketing actions while giving little regard to competitors' response on the tourism supply side.

To prepare the ground for the following case study, assume that all European cities base their marketing effort on a geographical segmentation approach. Actually, this is not a severe restriction as this assumption corresponds to strategy guidelines followed by many tourist organizations. They choose to allocate their budgets according to the attractiveness of the major countries of origin. With this consideration in mind, the comparison of guest mix structures is indeed a working model for discovering subgroups of European cities competing in the same markets.

It has always been an intricate question for marketing managers and researchers whether domestic travel should be included or eliminated in building the 'relevant' market volumes. Apparently there is no recipe or strategy prescription on how to treat the compatriots as potential travellers. National tourist offices tend to exclude domestic travel in such a situation. Their major concern is foreign exchange earnings, though, like the Austrian NTO, they might be obliged by their statutes to promote domestic tourism as well. For a city tourist board the position is different in its effort to attract outside purchasing power into the municipality. The minds of some tourism managers seem to operate on two levels of competition – pulling-in foreign visitors and holding back locals inclined to go abroad. The shrinking importance of national boundaries in Europe and the growing predominance of the concept of regions may change views in future.

Without twisting the meaning of competition two separate analyses exclusive and inclusive of domestic travel will be presented. The strictly international version has the merit of detecting competitive links between cities deliberately targeting at the foreign visitor (see pp. 28–30 and 30–3). The all-inclusive version does not truncate the guest mix and reflects the total picture. Interior competion of various cities within a country becomes visible, but may – to some extent – disturb the similarities on the international scale.

Origin, quality, and processing of data

As mentioned earlier the data originate from the TourMIS system of the Austrian National Tourist Office (NTO). The NTO annually collects the material via its representatives abroad. In most cases statistics from official sources are transmitted and (after sometimes painful translations) checked for plausibility. The whole process lasts about one and a half years (by June 1994 the data for 1992 were available).

Vandermay (1984) thought that his study about urban tourism was limited because of the absence of fully compatible statistics and the shortage of data. One decade later the situation has not improved essentially. There is still a lack in accordance of what is being collected by municipal statistical offices. The data used in this study suffers from lack of a uniform definition of urban tourism (for example, Barcelona recently changed from zone figures to urban figures). One has to check the forms of accommodation included (non-commercial too or only hotels) and the breakdown of generating countries. Political transition (like in Berlin), changing methods or databases (London's figures, for example, are sample based), or the unclear percentage of visits to friends and relatives affects the reliability of trip, arrival or bednight figures.

Besides all these practical problems there is the more technical problem of missing data. About 1–2 per cent of the material used in this study was not available in time. As missing data may cause distortions in the results of mapping algorithms employing eigen analysis (Buldain 1988), all missing values were either interpolated through average indices for the city and the generating country or, for the most recent period, forecasted. The twenty-six cities used in this study are listed in Table 2.1.

Table 2.1 European cities used in marketing study

Name	Code	Name	Code
Amsterdam	AMS	Madrid	MAD
Barcelona	BCN	Milan	MIL
Basel	BSL	Munich	MUC
Berlin	BER	Oslo	OSL
Brussels	BRU	Paris	PAR
Budapest	BUD	Prague	PRG
Cologne	CGN	Rome	ROM
Frankfurt	FRA	Salzburg	SBG
Geneva	GVA	Stockholm	STO
Hamburg	HAM	Venice	VCE
Helsinki	HEL	Vienna	VIE
Lisbon	LIS	Zagreb	ZAG
London	LON	Zurich	ZRM

European cities in the guest mix space

The analysis of competitors – one of the primary tasks for tourism marketers – is becoming increasingly complex (Heath and Wall 1992). In particular, this holds true for international tourism. Geographical vicinity is often the only variable that managers take into account. One of the reasons for this is that a service-intensive industry like tourism has traditionally been more customer-oriented and thus spends less thought on competition. In a mature market with slow growth rates, however, this philosophy is likely to be replaced by greater emphasis on competitor dimensions (Day and Nedungadi 1994). Prior to evaluating cities in terms of their attractions, potentials and marketing strategies it is imperative to identify competitors in a systematic manner.

Mill (1990) defines those destinations that seek to attract the same tourists as competing. In the following examples the same tourists are represented in terms of their origin. Cities with similar guest mixes are regarded as competitors. As a first step in analysing competitors one of the most widely used methods in marketing science is employed: principal components factor analysis (Hackett and Foxall 1994). This data reduction technique compresses the large number of variables in the city profiles (percentages of generating countries in the guest mix) into a much smaller set of dimensions for spatial visualization. The purpose of this approach is twofold: (1) to extract the generating countries which differentiate between groups of cities and (2) to identify the competitive relationships derived from the guest mixes. 'Competitive maps' can also be constructed by using other information such as cross elasticities (Cooper and Nakanishi 1988) and by other methods such as multidimensional scaling (see the following sections).

The factor procedure of the Statistical Package for the Social Sciences (SPSS) reduced the eighteen profile variables (country percentages) into five major dimensions. Selecting the 'right' number of dimensions is always an intricate decision. The five factors explain 64.3 per cent of the total variance and were retained for further analysis because of the shape of the scree plot and the development of the eigenvalues. The solution is far from being perfect but is a compromise between ease of interpretation and methodological requirements. The Spanish and the Canadian markets are excluded from the interpretation (not from the analysis) because of their weak communalities (about 0.3).

The interpretation of the five factors is the most relevant information gained from this analysis. The meaning of the factors results from the factor loadings after varimax rotation. The first factor accounting for 20.6 per cent variance is characterized by overseas (Japanese and US) tourists and the German market with reverse signs. This means that on the western half in Figure 2.1 the cities are largely dependent on the German travellers and on the eastern half on the overseas markets. Factor 2 (15.3 per cent) is strongly related to tourist flows from the Nordic countries, especially Norway and Denmark. The third factor (10.9 per cent) appears to be rather vague as the highest loadings are a moderate 0.65 for Australia and France. Factor 4 (9.6 per cent) and Factor 5 (8 per cent), which are not shown in the plot, represent the travel demand from the UK or, less intensely, from The Netherlands, and from Switzerland or, less intensely still, from Austria.

After calculating the factor scores for each city a competitive map can be drawn (Figure 2.1). For the sake of a convenient geometric representation only the leading three factors are shown. The north-European capitals together with Hamburg and Berlin build one cluster. This cluster is also characterized by a dominance of north-European guests. Even though domestic tourism was excluded the strong regional competition between these cities is maintained. In the left hemisphere of the map a cluster is formed of cities with a dominance of Germans in their guest mix. Barcelona, Prague and the cluster around Vienna with Basel, Salzburg, Budapest, Zagreb, Lisbon are weak in the overseas markets and compete heavily for the German tourist. The remaining cities can hardly be separated into different groups and only seem to vary in their dependence on the Japanese and US markets (and, to some extent, also on the domestic travellers).

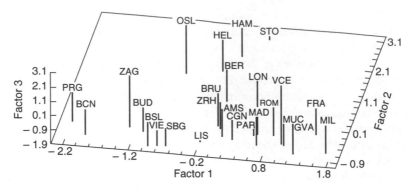

Figure 2.1 PRINCOMP guest mix space for twenty-six European cities, 1992

The visual interpretation of the competitive map is not sufficiently precise for identifying competitors. Thus a cluster analysis with the factor scores was run using Ward's method. Since the aim was to help in interpreting the map only the first three factors were used. The Viennese as well as the northern clusters are reproduced clearly. The dendrogram shows that these clusters hardly compete with other cities. The visual impression of Lisbon and Zagreb as competitors of Vienna cannot be affirmed. A reason is that the cluster method used here does not allow for a city to pop up in more than one cluster (of a non-disjunctive clustering method introduced on pp. 33–35). The bulk of the other cities form different clusters that quickly combine to bigger ones. Therefore, cluster analysis does not help much here to identify stepwise competition between these other cities.

Two distinct clusters result from the factor analytic approach competing in the German and north-European markets respectively. The results in general neither correspond to a geographical map nor to a map with 'product categories' like modern vs traditional cities. Final conclusions about the competitive situation should not yet be drawn. The three factors in the map do not even explain half of the observed variance. Further analyses using distance or similarity measures instead of correlations must be examined.

An MDS reconstruction of the guest mix space for 1992

The multidimensional scaling (MDS) method constructs a map based on guest mix profiles and displays the cities geometrically. Cities with a similar guest mix are configured close to each other and vice versa. One of the advantages of the MDS procedure is its ability to extract and to visualize an inherent underlying competitive structure. Thus it renders the data more manageable and strategically meaningful. The analysis demonstrates how multidimensional scaling establishes a pattern of the twenty-six European cities competing for the international visitor.

Many successful applications of MDS techniques in tourism research have been published. Recent examples deal with the evaluation and classification of tourist roles (Pearce 1982, with his attempt to extend an earlier article on tourist roles by Cohen 1974; or Yiannakis and Gibson 1992). MDS techniques have been applied for classifying leisure activity types (Ritchie 1975; Becker 1976; Hirschmann 1985; Russell and Hultsman 1987), for investigating the relationship between public and private recreational systems (Lovingood and Mitchell 1978), for exploring the psychological benefits a recreational park can produce (Uluch and Addoms 1981), and for demonstrating how tourists perceive and classify the setting visited (Iso-Ahola 1980; Mayo and Jarvis 1981; Stringer and Pearce 1984). Finally, MDS procedures provide a standard technique to measure and compare consumer tourist attractions (Fodness and Milner 1992; Zins 1994), tourist services (Mayo and Jarvis 1981; Grabler 1993), or recreational destinations (Goodrich 1977; Haahti 1984; Gartner 1989). A comprehensive overview of MDS methodology employed in tourism research is given by Fenton and Pearce (1988).

This analysis is closely related to a research effort undertaken by Haahti (1986). Haahti's focus is on the tourists' perceptions of alternative destinations within some predetermined dimensions of holiday choice. By defining Finland's position in comparison with competing countries along the most significant choice dimensions Haahti bridges the gap between contemporary study of consumer behaviour and the current practices of marketing decision-making for a tourist receiving country.

Multidimensional scaling uses proximities as input data. A proximity value indicates how similar or how dissimilar two objects are, or are perceived to be. For n objects to be scaled there are $n(n-1)/2$ pairs. Each pair of cities must be characterized by a (dis)similarity value. To analyse the competitive relationships between two cities, tourism volume data (measured by nights in all accommodations) have to be 'preprocessed' to remove the effect of the city size. Therefore, the raw data are transformed into guest mix shares and arranged in tabular form. The rows of this table correspond to the cities, the columns represent the guest mix shares of the eighteen most important generating countries. Each row stands for a city profile in terms of guest mix. Although domestic tourism may be an important issue for several of these cities it is removed from this analysis. All cities compete without any 'home advantage' making them less dependent on international visitors.

The usual way to derive proximities from a set of profile data is to compute correlations, contingency or distance measures (Euclidian, City Block, or more general Minkowski distances). Squared Euclidian distances are chosen here for computing the dissimilarity coefficients of 325 city pairs (twenty-six European cities in 1992).

The typical MDS analysis (SPSS ALSCAL; Norusis 1992) outputs a two- or higher-dimensional 'map' with a configuration of points. In advance it is not known how many dimensions will be adequate. The number depends on how well the distances in the map reflect the observed proximities from which the space is derived. Goodness of fit is measured by Kruskal's stress formula 1 (see Kruskal and Wish 1976: 29). For the two-dimensional solution it is 0.257, indicating a fit far from being perfect. Stress is supplemented by squared correlations. The RSQ value indicates the proportion of the variance of the observed proximities accounted for by their corresponding differences. For three dimensions stress drops to an acceptable 0.16 and the R^2 (RSQ) value rises from 0.77 to 0.87.

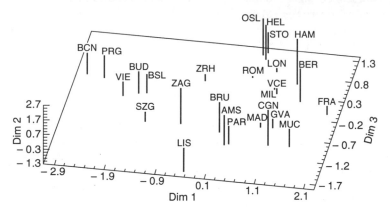

Figure 2.2 MDS guest mix space for twenty-six European cities, 1992

The most common way of interpreting the geometrical representation (Figure 2.2) is to examine the dimensions in the space and the co-ordinates of the stimuli. If the city points projected on to an axis at opposite extremes differ from each other in some discernible and systematic manner an interpretative hint may have been found. Optimal rotation and labelling of the axes can be handled more objectively with multiple regression analysis. This is particularly useful if additional variables (properties) are associated with the competitive space positions of the cities (property fitting was invented by Chang and Carroll at Bell Laboratories in the early 1970s – see Chang and Carroll (n.d.)). To prove whether or not there is a relationship between this external information and the positions in the configuration, multiple regression takes each of the new variables as the dependent variable and the co-ordinates of the configuration as the predictors. With no additional properties at hand multiple regression for learning more about the attributes of the guest mix space may also be demonstrated by exploiting the same data input matrix used for generating the space once more.[1] So which are the countries of origin where the guest mix space dimensions contribute significantly to explaining the nations' shares? According to the explanations offered by regression coefficients and variance analysis, Germany, the USA, Denmark, Sweden and Japan are the most discriminating generators of European city tourism.

Visual inspection of the guest mix space in Figure 2.2 suggests a subdivision into three main groups of competitors. The first group, located in the western hemisphere of the spatial configuration, consists of seven cities with a strong German representation in their international guest mix profile (Vienna, Salzburg, Zurich, Basel, Budapest, Prague and Barcelona). The central to north-eastern part of the 1992 space is populated by a group of nine European cities with a substantial competitive edge in the Scandinavian countries, especially in the Danish and Swedish markets (Hamburg, Cologne, Berlin, Oslo, Helsinki, Amsterdam, Brussels, Lisbon and Zagreb). Finally, the largest subgroup with ten competing European cities is located in the lower-eastern sector of the space. These cities are particularly oriented towards overseas markets (Munich, Frankfurt, Geneva, Venice, Paris, Madrid, Stockholm, Milan, Rome and London). Note that the home markets do not play a role in forming these groupings; neither does the size and tourist significance of the cities.

Time dependent guest mix spaces: an INDSCAL analysis

The next step in MDS modelling significantly increases the extent of data exploitation. So far there has been no discussion of the fact that there is an eighteen-year history of guest mix development. The guest mix structures are expected to be stable over time. However, there may be long-term shifts apparent over one or two decades. Such trends would tend to alter the competitive relationships and the managers should be aware of these changes in the environment. To add to the overall information value in this series of analysis domestic tourism now gets included in the guest mix shares. Keep in mind that for Budapest, Prague and Zagreb the shares of the nationals are not considered as Hungarians, Czechs and Croatians are not among the eighteen largest guest nations.

The INDSCAL model (Carroll and Chang 1970; Young and Hamer 1987) is adopted here to account for the eighteen 'replications' of data matrices available for the entire period 1975–92. Individual differences scaling has been firmly established as a method for perceptual mapping in the consumer research tool kit for quite some time (Mazanec 1978: 231–5, 430–3). Originally, it was introduced to allow for individual or group-specific perceptual variations within a sample of respondents. Most elegantly, the consumers share a common perceptual space of brand positions, but with individual dimension weights. This means that the relative positions of brands and ideal products in a market – though rated on a common basis of evaluation criteria – are subject to more flexibility in the preference and brand choice consequences[2] of these criteria.

In the tourist cities example the similarity information rests in a 26×18 matrix of profile data constructed for each of eighteen successive years. The time periods are considered in just the same way as individual respondents would be modelled in a standard application – as replicated measurements containing something worth knowing about individual cases (namely, time periods). The weights of the similarity/guest mix space dimensions vary over time indicating that some origin countries are gaining salience in determining competitive 'closeness' while others are diminishing. Though no dramatic fluctuations are expected, with the norm being a rather smooth and continuous change, one year or another may turn out as an 'outlier' – not an ideal basis for drawing long-term policy conclusions.

The guest mix profiles are first translated into Euclidean distances for each pair of tourist cities in each year. The subsequent INDSCAL analysis[3] condenses the resulting matrices of proximities into a configuration of low dimensionality with the distances in this space representing the original dissimilarities as closely as possible. Given the improvement in goodness of fit (Young's stress = 0.24, Kuskal's stress = 0.19, average squared correlation = 0.85) clearly favours a three-dimensional solution (of stress values of 0.34 and 0.27, averaged RSQ = 0.74 for two dimensions).[4] Before turning to the resulting guest mix space the development of dimension weights should be monitored. INDSCAL assigns each year its individual set of dimension weights thus squeezing or stretching the space to comfort the unique city profiles and similarities in each period. As has been expected the weights are not radically different. For the eighteen years they vary within [0.62, 0.73], [0.45, 0.52] and [0.33, 0.50] for the three axes. The time plot in Figure 2.3, however, indicates that there might be an imminent change. The importance of the guest space dimension no. 1 has increased in 1992 while dimensions no. 2 (recently) and no. 3 (since 1988) have dropped. Thus 1992 is either a structural break in city guest profiles or a temporary outlier not so well suited as an exclusive database.[5]

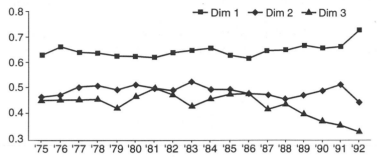

Figure 2.3 Dimension weights, 1975–92

The INDSCAL guest mix space for tourist cities in Figure 2.4 automatically accounts for the entire period 1975–92. A number of German cities gather in the south-eastern corner. Three Northern European capitals are lying south-west. Madrid and Barcelona are separating to the north, Milan and Rome are lowest down the third dimension. The bulk of Central and Western European metropoles are located in the gravity centre of the city space. A contextual interpretation of the positions of the points along axes is not strictly necessary for the purpose of competitor detection, but it is tempting. One's first impression is that geographical aspects are misleading and inconclusive. More substantial help may be gained from correlating the series of co-ordinates along each axis with the observed percentages of guest nations.[6] It reveals several facts. The best predictors of a city's position along axis no. 1 are the guest shares for Italians, Swedes, Norwegians, Finns and Spaniards; the reason is that these nationalities tend to patronize their domestic cities more than others. Spanish and Italian city tourists also influence the axes no. 2 and no. 3 positions most decisively. Germans are highly represented in their domestic cities but at the same time are holding large shares in the guest mix of various destinations outside the FRG. Most cities in the space centre are obviously depending on international travellers and, therefore, exposed to tough competition from other internationally 'open' destinations. The next section attempts to follow the competitive relationships more accurately.

Conclusions about competitive relationships between urban destinations in Europe

A clustering procedure applied to the configuration of city points in Figure 2.4 will assist in assessing the competitive relationships. Which cities aggregate to form clusters of destinations under competitive pressure? The Euclidean distances in Figure 2.4 serve as the raw material. Judging from these distances a tourist city may compete in more than just one city cluster. Hence a non-disjunctive cluster analysis would be preferred as it does not attribute a city in one, and only one, competitive group by enforcing rigorous cluster boundaries. The CLIP clustering model and program (Peay 1975; Mazanec 1976) performs this type of analysis in a hierarchical manner.

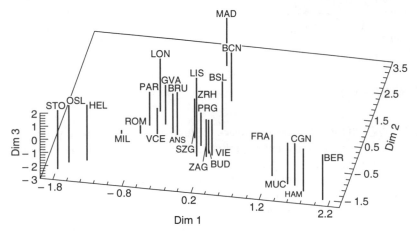

Figure 2.4 INDSCAL guest mix space for twenty-six European cities, 1975–92

Consider the stepwise groupings in Figure 2.5. Cologne and Munich, then Budapest and Vienna are most similar in terms of guest mix. Cologne closely resembles two other German cities (i.e. Munich and Hamburg), with Berlin or Frankfurt entering the cluster later. Triple-city clusters appear at distance 0.36, four- and five-city clusters at distances 0.40 and 0.50. A Euclidean distance of 0.72 in the three-dimensional guest mix space exhibits particularly plausible relationships of intense competition. (After that there is a wider gap of 0.06 distance units to reach the next level of 0.78.) Budapest, Vienna, Salzburg, Zagreb and Prague being also subject to competition from Zurich. The competitive pressure in this group has become apparent to various tourist companies. Viennese hoteliers have begun to expand into Budapest and Prague. Austrian travel agencies specializing in inbound tourism have reacted quickly in incorporating the three cities in their packages particularly offered to overseas visitors. This is an instructive example of how a competitive threat due to a similar appeal to several tourist nationalities may be transferred into a more attractive product by 'neutralizing' the rivals.

Distance × 100	C	C	L	U	S	T	E	R	S	
14	CGN, MUC									
15	CGN, MUC	BUD, VIE								
20	CGN, MUC	BUD, VIE	SZG, ZAG							
23	⋮									
26	CGN, MUC	CGN, HAM	BUD, VIE	SZG, ZAG	AMS, BRU					
27....34	⋮									
36				SZB, ZAG, PRG						
38, 39	⋮									
40	CGN, MUC, HAM	BUD, VIE, ZAG	SZG, ZAG, PRG, VIE	AMS BRU GVA	AMS, ZRH	BER, HAM	FRA, MUC	HEL, OSL	OSL, STO	
43, 47	⋮									
50	CGN, MUC, HAM	CGN, FRA, MUC	BUD, VIE, SZG, ZAG, PRG	AMS. BRU. GVA	AMS, BRU, ZRH	BER, HAM	HEL, OSL	OSL, STO	BSL, LIS	
58....71	⋮									
72	CGN, MUC, HAM, BER	CGN, FRA, MUC, HAM	BUD, VIE, SZG, ZAG, PRG	BUD, VIE, PRG, ZRH	AMS, BRU, ZRH, GVA, LIS	BRU, PRG, ZRH	HEL, OSL, STO	BSL, LIS, ZRH	BRU, GVA, PAR	MIL, ROM
78....493										

Figure 2.5 Hierarchical non-disjunctive city clusters

One remark is in order here. The fact that Budapest and Prague are 'deprived' of their national visitors is not crucial. Both capitals already featured in the 'truly' international league in Figure 2.2. Amsterdam, Brussels, Zurich, Geneva and Lisbon seem to strive for the same mixture of target segments. At the same time, each of these cities except Amsterdam is competing with one more rival such as Prague, Basel or Paris.

The Northern European capitals and the Italian metropoles (Rome and Milan, but not Venice) are largely dependent on their own nationals and stay in clusters of their own like the German cities. London and the Spanish cities (Barcelona and Madrid) are still staying aloof. With large shares of British and US visitors, and Spaniards respectively, they are quite different from all the rest in terms of guest mix.

One important weakness of the guest mix approach is that leisure and business trips cannot be distinguished in the overall bednight figures. As soon as the European Travel Monitor is mature enough to replace bednight statistics this type of separate analysis for leisure and business travellers will greatly increase its information output. The double approach with and without domestic travellers, however, pays off. One might have hypothesized for the German or the Scandinavian cities that the guest mix positions are predominantly determined by German or Nordic domestic travel. Having seen the purely international variant in Figure 2.2 this is not true. These destinations actually tend to compete among themselves. By contrast, the Italian and Spanish cities are joining the domain of tough international competition once the share of the domestic travel has been removed.

COMPARATIVE STRATEGIC ANALYSIS OF EUROPEAN CITIES UNDER COMPETITIVE PRESSURE

Adapting the growth-share matrix

One of the most widely used methods of strategic evaluation techniques in management is the growth-share matrix where a company is viewed as a portfolio of individual businesses or products and brands. It employs three assessment criteria: market growth rate, relative market share (compared to the toughest competitor), and contribution to overall sales (importance value).

According to these criteria the strategic market positions of tourist-receiving cities in Europe can be evaluated by exploiting simple bednight figures (Calantone and Mazanec 1991). The market growth rate is the percentage variation of the relevant market volume, where the relevant market volume comprises the total number of bednights sold by the major European cities to the leading generating countries in the world during one calendar year. The relative market share is defined as a ratio of two market shares. The numerator is the share of bednights sold by one particular city in the bednight total bought by a generating country from all competing urban destinations. The denominator is the share of bednights attained by the biggest competing urban destination. Thus, a relative share of 1.1 for a city in a generating country X means that this city is the market leader in X and excels the second-best competing destination by ten percentage points. The importance value is defined as the proportion of bednights sold to a particular generating country in the bednight total of guests recorded in a city destination. An importance value of, say, 10 per cent for the generating country X-Land in Y-City means that travellers from X-Land contribute 10 per cent to the bednight total produced by all guests in Y-City.

In a pictorial representation the three elevational criteria are portrayed along the vertical axis (growth rate), the horizontal axis (relative share), and through the diameter of circles (importance value) for generating countries (of the layout in Figures 2.6 to 2.9).

City tourism managers use the analysis to raise questions such as: Which cities were successful in tackling the growth markets? Are their portfolios rather one-sided or reasonably diversified? A single dominant circle would indicate an unbalanced mixture of guest nations. Which urban destination has a dominant position in one of the generating markets? Market dominance may reveal a competitive advantage by achieving economies of scale in market operation.

If growth rates are based on two succeeding years, strategic decisions may be biased by ephemeral effects. Checking for trends (e.g., estimating slope coefficients or stable variations in moving averages) should be considered as alternatives.

It is a weakness of the growth-share matrix that it relies on a limited amount of information (Wind *et al.* 1983). Tourism managers are likely to ask for additional qualitative input determining market attractiveness (disposable income per capita, spending patterns, seasonality, vacation styles and benefits sought) as well as competitive positions (exchange rates, relative prices and purchasing power, awareness level, cost of transport or travel distance, quality of tourist services). Therefore, managers in more advanced industries tend to employ multifactor portfolio models to handle a broader range of criteria determining market attractiveness and competitive position.

Static portfolios for selected European cities

A crucial prerequisite of the portfolio technique is the careful definition of the products and the markets as the units of analysis (Abell and Hammond

1979). As long as detailed data (e.g., separate data for business and leisure tourists or for other segmentation schemes) are not available the appropriate units of analysis are the generating countries. These countries will be evaluated by formally using portfolio analysis to promote a strategic approach in urban tourism marketing. A typical decision situation is the allocation of a destination's marketing budget.[7] The market definition is based on the competitive structure analysed in the previous sections. In the following study Vienna serves as an example and thus there are nine cities that build the relevant market volume – namely, Barcelona, Basel, Budapest, Lisbon, Prague, Salzburg, Vienna, Zagreb and Zurich.

The market growth rate is usually computed between two succeeding years and the market shares and importance values originate from the most recent period. In this short-term sense portfolio analysis is more of a diagnostic aid that helps to visualize data, rather than a strategic tool. Ideally, it is employed every year to observe the development of each country, but it may fail to provide a conclusive evaluation of the markets in the long run if there are erratic movements. This happens quite frequently for the market growth figures where outliers can easily distort the picture.

To smooth short-term changes a six-year period is considered in the following example. Given this reasonable span of time portfolio analysis may be called 'strategic' in the field of tourism. Market growth rate is the mean variation divided by the average market volume during the years 1987–92 for each generating country. The market share and importance value figures are also calculated after first summing up the absolute values for six years.

The portfolio chart for Vienna looks satisfactory (see Figure 2.6). Note that only eight of the most important countries are shown for ease of interpretation. Nearly all the important countries are growth markets. In five countries Vienna is market leader – including Japan, the fastest growing market. However, competition in these 'star' markets, as they would be called in classic portfolio jargon, is tough and, therefore, a portfolio like this cannot be maintained very easily. Also, countries like Spain and France would require increased marketing effort in order to reach a leading market position. Another point to mention is the degree of dependence on generating markets. In the case of Vienna the German visitors are dominant, but the imbalance is not too bad as there are other 'star' countries like USA and Italy which account for a considerable amount of the Viennese guest mix. The figure also shows that the UK is not in a favourable position. Such a position should induce the managers to think seriously about a new strategy concerning this particular country. In total, one must take into account that the market has been defined rather narrowly. Given a broader definition with all European cities the portfolio would not look that good.

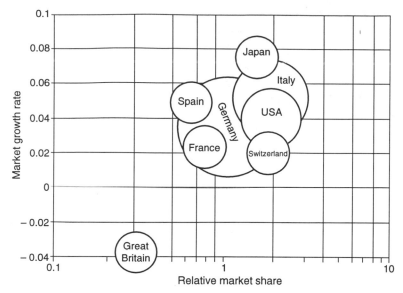

Figure 2.6 Portfolio for Vienna, 1987–92

Extending the analysis to cover the major competitors conveys a deeper understanding of the market. The competitors' portfolios inform about which markets are penetrated by others and give an idea of the marketing strategies of other cities. Budapest is one of those cities that has fully benefited from the dismantling of the Iron Curtain in the period under study and must be regarded as one of Vienna's main competitors. One can easily recognize that Budapest is in a 'waiting position' concerning the major generating countries (Figure 2.7). It has not yet become the market leader in these countries, but Vienna is in real jeopardy to lose its top position in Italy, Germany, Switzerland, or in the attractive market of US tourists. Only the Japanese have not yet discovered Budapest, but a greater time lag is likely to exist for this long-haul market.

The chart for Prague (Figure 2.8), a capital that opened its doors comparatively recently, is also indicative of these time-lags. Considerable market shares have already been gained in the short-distance countries (especially Germany) whereas in the southern European and overseas countries the market share is still half or less that of the strongest competitor. (Note that the unity line marks the right border in this figure.) With a focus on more recent data the portfolio of Prague would look more threatening to Vienna. Judging from the six-year portfolio Prague is expected to compete more strongly in the German market and to build market shares in countries like France and The Netherlands. Currently, it depends too much on the German market.

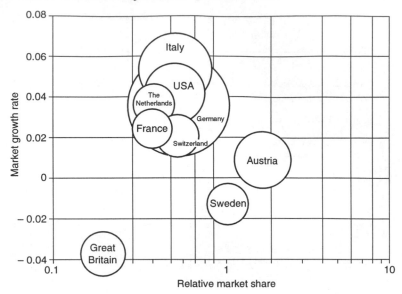

Figure 2.7 Portfolio for Budapest, 1987–92

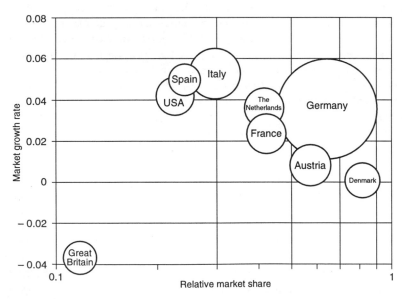

Figure 2.8 Portfolio for Prague, 1987–92

The fourth competitor here is Zurich. Its portfolio (Figure 2.9) looks quite different from the previous ones. Like Prague, Zurich is not a market leader in any country and it holds less than half the share in those markets where the others compete: Germany, Italy and France. Japan and the USA offer more chances for Zurich, whereas the UK occupies the same unpleasant position it occupies for the other competitors. (Barcelona is market leader there.) The Zurich portfolio nicely reflects the results of the previous analyses of competitive relationships. Zurich is a competitor for Vienna (mainly owing to German travellers), but the degree of competition is not comparable to Budapest or Prague as Zurich tends to serve the overseas markets. (Remember that these markets also were associated with one of the axes in the MDS and factor solutions.)

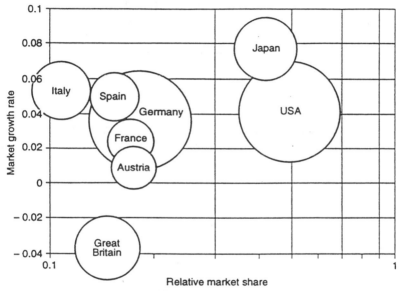

Figure 2.9 Portfolio for Zurich, 1987–92

Although a period of six years was used in this example strategic recommendations are not easily drawn. More assessment criteria and background knowledge should be invoked to generate meaningful strategic suggestions. Portfolio analysis should be regarded as a diagnostic aid and an analytical tool that can be made more 'strategically relevant' when looking over a period of several years as shown above. Of course a time-span of six years is not sufficient to recognize trends as well as short-term threats in an early stage (as became apparent in the example of Prague). Therefore, managers in urban tourism are right in using both annual and medium-to-long-term approaches. The next section will demonstrate an alternative technique exploiting time trends for portfolio analysis.

Incorporating market trends into dynamic portfolio construction

Analysing a firm's portfolio at a given point in time provides only a static perspective (Kerin *et al.* 1990). But the comparison of several portfolios using historical data shows the movement of market segments over time. It reveals trends and market dynamics. Portfolio scenarios can be developed for future time periods on the basis of projected market growth rates and tentative decisions on the market share strategy for each guest segment. Tracing these trajectories assists in detecting successful or disastrous paths taken by the various segments. The prospects for maintaining a balanced portfolio in the years to come and the guidelines for developing new markets to avoid future imbalances may be worked out.

In conjunction with a modern marketing information system the success or failure of marketing programmes can be evaluated by a deviation analysis based on the sequential presentation of portfolio diagrams (Wöber 1994). Figure 2.10 for example, shows the evolution of Vienna's growth-share matrix between 1981 and 1992 for selected generating countries. For clarity of pictorial presentation only two evaluation criteria are portrayed – market volume in million bednights along the vertical axis and relative market share along the horizontal axis.

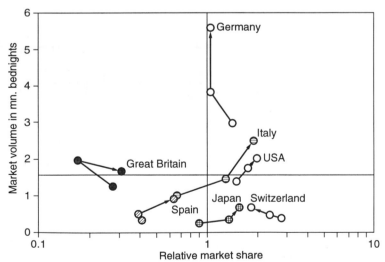

Figure 2.10 Vienna's competitive trajectory for selected generating countries, 1981–92

In the case of Vienna the most successful development emerges for the Italian, the US, the Japanese and the Spanish markets. However, similar to most of the other European cities the German market is Vienna's paramount guest segment. Although this segment nearly doubled its volume during the last eighteen years Vienna lost some of its market strongholds. A considerable decline is also apparent for the Swiss market. The comparison with Budapest's trajectory demonstrates that the Hungarian capital is Vienna's toughest competitor (Figure 2.11). During the ten years from 1981–92 in particular, Budapest improved its market position in nearly every segment. Only for the Austrian guest segment, where Budapest is defending the market leadership, did competitive losses occur recently.

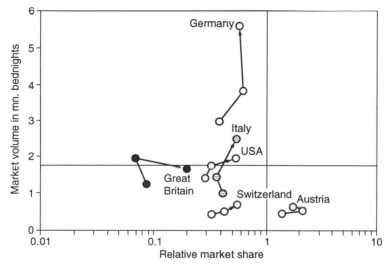

Figure 2.11 Budapest's competitive trajectory for selected generating countries, 1981–92

Each sector of the portfolio diagram represents a distinct type of success potential. However, recommended decisions and strategies for products and markets in the various parts of the matrix are only suggestive and not prescriptive. A tourist city should not base its market share strategy on its own portfolio of market segments exclusively. An attempt should be made to draw similar diagrams for all major competitors. Imbalances in the portfolios of some competitors and obvious strengths in the portfolios of others may disclose the strategies they are likely to pursue.

A more systematic approach than the simple monitoring of all competitors' plots includes an additional gain and loss analysis for the major market segments. The periodical performance and the destination preferences of the various generating countries should be watched constantly. For the Vienna Tourist Board the comparison with eight leading European receiving cities functions as a proxy for the relative profit performance. The winners and losers in each market segment are visualized by another type of plot suggested in Figure 2.12. This portfolio variant shows the competitive evolution on the Italian market between 1981 and 1992 measured by nights in all accommodations. In this diagram the vertical axis represents the segment performance in the various cities relative to 1975. It is easy to identify Vienna as market leader and Barcelona as having lost its second position to Budapest. Salzburg, Lisbon and Prague are potential competitive threats in the future.

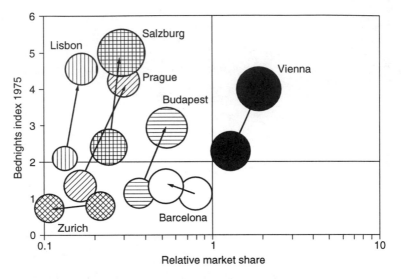

Figure 2.12 Competitive evolution on the Italian market, 1981–92

The simple visual format of portfolio diagrams offered in these examples is easy to grasp and well suited to stimulate competitive thinking. Substantial benefit lies in the process of preparing the diagrams. It enforces strategic thinking by all those involved. Discussions among managers help to recognize opportunities for future market operation and to broaden the set of strategic options.

NOTES

1 A geographical interpretation can be given by converting correlation coefficients into 'direction vectors' in the MDS diagram. A comprehensive discussion of multiple coefficients and their geometrical interpretation is available in Kruskal and Wish (1976).

2 (Hyper)spherical iso-preference curves become (hyper)elliptical which means that the space dimensions (representing product attribute bundles) are of different importance in determining brand preferences.

3 The (metric) individual differences option of ALSCAL in SPSS for OS/2 has been used.

4 This is a good fit for this bulk of data. Note that the INDSCAL model estimates only 132 parameters (3×26 co-ordinates = 78, plus 3 dimension weights $\times 18$ years = 54) out of 5,850 data restrictions (i.e., $26 \times (26 - 1)/2$ dissimilarities for each of eighteen years). The standard ALSCAL analysis (pp. 28–30) is far less determined with 52 parameters (2×26 co-ordinates from 325 restrictions imposed by the 1992 data.

5 The MDS program calculates a weirdness index for individual cases describing their degree of uniqueness in weighing dimensions; 1992 gets the only value exceeding 0.15.

6 As the INDSCAL setting processes twenty-six cities by eighteen years simultaneously only three multiple regressions need to be run with each axis as a dependent variable, and all nations' shares as predictors.

7 Another way of evaluating countries for the same purpose was demonstrated in a recent study for Australia where population size and wealth (GNP) and geographical proximity were used as assessment criteria (Faulkner 1994).

REFERENCES

Abell, D.F. and Hammond, J.S. (1979) *Strategic Market Planning, Problems and Analytical Approaches*, Englewood Cliffs, N.J.: Prentice-Hall.

Ball, D., Lamb, Ch. and Brodie, R. (1992) 'Segmentation and market structure when both consumer and situational characteristics are explanatory', *Psychology & Marketing* 9, 395–408.

Becker, B.W. (1976) 'Perceived similarities among recreational activities', *Journal of Leisure Research* 8, 112–22.

Buldain, R. (1988) 'Preparing data for mapping', in Sawtooth Software Conference on Perceptual Mapping, Conjoint Analysis, and Computer Interviewing, Sawtooth Software.

Calantone, R. and Mazanec, J.A. (1991) 'Marketing management and tourism', *Annals of Tourism Research* 18, 101–19.

Carroll, J.D. and Chang, J.J. (1970) 'Analysis of individual differences in multidimensional scaling via an N-way generalisation of "Eckart-Young" decomposition', *Psychometrika* 35, 283–319.

Chang, J.J. and Carroll J.D. (n.d.) 'How to use PROFIT, a computer program for property fitting by optimising nonlinear or linear correlation', Unpublished manuscript, Bell Laboratories.

Cohen, E. (1974) 'Who is a tourist?', *Sociological Review* 22, 527–53.

Cooper, L.G. and Nakanishi, M. (1988) *Market-Share Analysis*, Boston: Kluwer Academic Publishers.

Crompton, J. (1992) 'Structure of vacation destination choice sets', *Annals of Tourism Research* 19, 420–34.

Day, G.S. and Nedungadi, P. (1994) 'Managerial representations of competitive advantage', *Journal of Marketing* 58, 31–44.

Faulkner, H.W. (1994) 'Towards a strategic approach to tourism development: the Australian experience', pp. 231–45, in W.F. Theobald (ed.) *Global Tourism: The Next Decade*, Oxford: Butterworth-Heinemann.

Fenton, M. and Pearce, P.L. (1988) 'Multidimensional scaling and tourism research', *Annals of Tourism Research* 15, 236–54.

Fodness, D.D. and Milner, L.M. (1992) 'A perceptual mapping approach to theme park visitor segmentation', *Tourism Management* 13, 95–101.

Fraser, C. and Bradford, J.W. (1983) 'Competitive market structure analysis: principal partitioning of revealed substitutabilities', *Journal of Consumer Research* 10, 15–30.

Fraser, C. and Bradford, J.W. (1984) 'Competitive market structure analysis: a reply', *Journal of Consumer Research* 11, 842–7.

Gartner, W.C. (1989) 'Tourism image: attribute measurement of state tourism products using multidimensional scaling techniques', *Journal of Travel Research* 28, 16–20.

Goodall, B. (1991) 'Understanding holiday choice', pp. 58–77, in C.P. Cooper (ed.) *Progress in Tourism, Recreation and Hospitality Management*, London: Belhaven Press.

Goodrich, J.N. (1977) 'Differences in perceived similarity of tourism regions: a spatial analysis', *Journal of Travel Research* 16, 10–13.

Grabler, K. (1993) 'Produktpositionierung für das Wiener Plaza: Empirische Methodenvergleiche anhand der Wiener Luxushotellerie', Diploma thesis, Vienna University of Economics and Business Administration.

Haahti, A.J. (1984) 'An empirical study into tourists' cognitive choice structure', Doctoral thesis, Helsinki School of Economics.

Haahti, A.J. (1986) 'Finland's competing position as a destination', *Annals of Tourism Research* 13, 11–26.

Hackett, P.M.W. and Foxall, G.R. (1994) 'A factor analytic study of consumers' location specific values: a traditional High Street and a modern shopping mall', pp. 163–78, in G.J. Hooley and M.K. Hussey (eds) *Quantitative Methods in Marketing*, London: Academic Press.

Heath, E. and Wall, G. (1992) *Marketing Tourism Destinations: A Strategic Planning Approach*, New York: Wiley.

Henshall, B.D. and Roberts, R. (1985) 'Comparative assessment of tourist generating markets for New Zealand', *Annals of Tourism Research* 17, 14–28.

Hirschmann, E.C. (1985) 'Multidimensional analysis of content preferences for leisure time media', *Journal of Leisure Research* 17, 14–28.

Howard, J.A. and Sheth, J.N. (1969) *The Theory of Buyer Behaviour*, New York: Wiley.

Iso-Ahola, S.E. (1980) *The Social Psychology of Leisure and Recreation*, Dubuque, Ia.: William C. Brown.

Kerin, R.A., Mahajan, V. and Varadarajan, P.R. (1990) *Contemporary Perspectives on Strategic Market Planning*, Needham Heights, Mass.: Allyn & Bacon.

Kruskal, J.B. and Wish, M. (1976) 'Multidimensional scaling', in J.L. Sullivan and R.G. Niemi (eds) *Quantitative Applications in the Social Sciences*, Beverly Hills, Calif.: Sage.

Lovingood, P.E. and Mitchell, L.S. (1978) 'The structure of public and private recreational systems: Columbia, South Carolina', *Journal of Leisure Research* 10, 21–36.

McDonald, M. (1989) *Marketing Plans, How to Prepare Them: How to Use Them* (2nd edn), Oxford: Heinemann.

McNamee, P.B. (1985) *Tools and Techniques for Strategic Management*, Oxford: Pergamon Press.

Mayo, E.J. and Jarvis, L.P. (1981) *The Psychology of Leisure and Travel*, Boston: CBI Publishing.

Mazanec, J. (1976) 'BMDIC – ein demoskopischer Indikator zur Messung der Intensität der Substitutionskonkurrenz zwischen Produktmarken', *Working Paper No. 5*, Institute for Advertising and Market Research, Vienna University of Economics and Business Administration.

Mazanec, J. (1978) *Strukturmodellle des Konsumverhaltens*, Vienna: Orac.

Mazanec, J.A. (1986) 'How to evaluate a travel market, econometric modelling versus multi-attribute decision making with management estimates', *Les Cahiers du Tourisme*, Série C, No. 48, Aix-en-Provence, Centre des Hautes Études Touristiques.

Mazanec, J.A. and Zins, A. (1994) 'Tourist behaviour and the new European life style typology', pp. 199–216, in W.F. Theobald, (ed.) *Global Tourism: The Next Decade*, Oxford: Butterworth-Heinemann.

Mill, R.Ch. (1990) *Tourism: The International Business*, London: Prentice-Hall International Editions.

Norusis, M.J. (1992) *SPSS for Windows. Professional Statistics*, Release 5, Chicago: SPSS Inc.

Pearce, P.L. (1982) *The Social Psychology of Tourist Behaviour*, Oxford: Pergamon.

Peay, E.R. (1975) 'Nonmetric grouping: clusters and cliques', *Psychometrika* 40, 301–12.

Ritchie, J.R.B. (1975) 'On the derivation of leisure activity types: a perceptive mapping approach', *Journal of Leisure Research* 7, 128–64.

Ritchie, J.R.B. (1994) 'State of the art in tourism research', Opening session on the Conference on Decision-Making Processes and Preference Changes of Tourists: Intertemporal and Intercountry Perspectives, Innsbruck, Austria, November, 1993, reported in *Newsletter of the Academy for the Study of Tourism* 7, Spring.

Russell, R.V. and Hultsman, J.T. (1987) 'An empirical basis for determining the multidimensional structure of leisure, *Leisure Sciences* 10, 69–76.

Shocker, A.D., Zahorik, A.J. and Stewart, D.W. (1984) 'Competitive market structure analysis: a comment on problems', *Journal of Consumer Research* 11, 836–41.

Stringer, P.F. and Pearce, P.L. (1984) 'Toward a symbiosis of social psychology and tourism studies', *Annals of Tourism Research* 11, 5–17.

Uluch, R.S. and Addoms, D.L. (1981) 'Psychological and recreational benefits of a recreational park', *Journal of Leisure Research* 13, 43–56.

Um, S. and Crompton, J.L. (1990) 'Attitude determinants in tourism destination choice', *Annals of Tourism Research*, 17, 432–48.

Um, S. and Crompton, J.L. (1992) 'The roles of perceived inhibitors and facilitators in pleasure travel destination decisions', *Journal of Travel Research* 30, 18–25.

Urban, G. and Hauser, J.R. (1993) *Design and Marketing of New Products* (2nd edn), Englewood Cliffs, N.J.: Prentice-Hall.

Van der Borg, J. (1994) 'Demand for city tourism in Europe: tour operators' catalogues', *Tourism Management* 15, 66–9.

Vandermay, A. (1984) 'Assessing the importance of urban tourism, *Tourism Management* 5, 123–35.

Wind, Y., Mahajan, V. and Swire, D. (1983) 'An empirical comparison of standardised portfolio models', *Journal of Marketing* 47, 89–99.

Wöber, K. (1994) 'Strategic planning tools inside the marketing-information-system in use by the Austrian National Tourist Office', pp. 201–8, in W. Schertler *et al.* (eds) *Information and Communications Technologies in Tourism*, Vienna: Springer.

Woodside, A.G. and Carr, J.A. (1988) 'Consumer decision making and competitive marketing strategies: applications for tourism planning', *Journal of Travel Research* 26, 2–7.

Woodside, A.G. and Lysonski, S. (1989) 'A general model of traveller destination choice', *Journal of Travel Research* 27, 8–14.

Yiannakis, A. and Gibson, H. (1992) 'Roles tourists play', *Annals of Tourism Research* 19, 287–303.

Young, F.W. and Hamer, R.M. (1987) *Multidimensional Scaling: History, Theory, and Applications*, Hillsdale, N.J.: Lawrence Erlbaum Associates.

Zins, A.H. (1994) 'On the derivation of a common space of competing leisure attraction types', *Journal of Marketing Management* 10, 179–90.

3 Tourism in French cities

John Tuppen

INTRODUCTION

Over recent years a growing number of urban centres have sought to exploit their potential for tourism. In part this stems from a tradition of welcoming visitors due to the existence of primary attractions such as museums, monuments and historic districts within the city. However, this trend also relates to specific policies of tourist development, relying much more on complementary attractions in the form of hotels and conference centres. In these circumstances the principal aim is to strengthen and diversify the local economy, particularly where many traditional activities are experiencing decline.

The notion of towns and cities as tourist centres is still not widely accepted. Tourism continues to be more commonly associated with resorts in coastal, mountainous or rural regions where holiday-making and leisure pursuits represent the primary motives for the visit. There are obvious exceptions to this generalization – notably Paris, which has long been renowned as a tourist destination. However, in the case of other cities tourism tends to be associated with particular events (such as the film festival at Cannes) or is perceived as an offshoot of business activity rather than as an integral part of the urban economy. Even where tourism is deemed to be important, problems arise in trying to assess the scale and impact of this activity. This relates principally to the absence of precise study of tourism and in particular to the associated lack of reliable statistical data. It is rarely possible to assess with accuracy the total number of visitors to an urban centre and it is even more problematic to quantify their effect on the local economy. In general, the most reliable data relate to stays in hotels, but this of course clearly considerably underestimates the overall importance of tourism.

A further problem concerns the use of the term 'city'. France is unusual in having a highly distorted urban hierarchy, with Paris possessing an exceptionally greater size and influence than the country's second- and third-ranking cities. Outside of the capital there are only three other large urban centres in France – Lyon, Marseille and Lille, after which there is another sizeable gap in the hierarchy (Table 3.1). For this reason, and rather than restrict analysis to only four cities, many of the comments in this chapter refer generally to tourism in an urban context.

Table 3.1 The population of major French urban centres, 1990

Urban centre	Population	Urban centre	Population
Paris	9,318,821	Nice	516,740
Lyon	1,262,223	Nantes	496,078
Marseille – Aix-en-Provence	1,230,936	Toulon	437,553
Lille	959,234	Grenoble	407,733
Bordeaux	696,364	Strasbourg	388,483
Toulouse	650,336	Rouen	380,161

Source: INSEE (1994a)

In the present review there are four main sections. The first provides an overview of tourism in France and is designed to constitute a backcloth to the more detailed assessment of urban-based tourism which is considered in the second section. Then, in the third part, different forms of urban tourism, such as the conference and exhibition business, are studies in greater depth. Finally, the fourth section is devoted to the study of tourist activities in specific cities with a comparison between Paris, Lyon and Lille.

TOURISM IN FRANCE

France has a long tradition of tourist activity reflecting the richness and diversity of its natural landscapes and cultural heritage, a range of favourable climatic influences and an international reputation for its numerous culinary delights. Tourism has expanded rapidly since the 1960s and, as in many developed Western countries, this trend has been stimulated by a combination of higher living standards, longer paid holidays and far greater personal mobility. Such growth has produced various benefits, including a substantial increase in jobs and a major injection of expenditure into the economy. At the same time, however, various costs have resulted, relating notably to problems of congestion, over-use of selected sites and environmental damage (Tuppen 1991).

Tourism has come to play a major role in the French economy. It generates each year a substantial income, offers a large number of employment opportunities and represents a key 'export' industry as a result of the considerable expenditure of foreign tourists visiting France. In 1993 total spending on tourist stays and related travel exceeded 533 billion francs and amounted to 7.5 per cent of French gross domestic product (Direction du Tourisme 1994). This proportion has varied little over the last decade (Py 1992) and attests to the general resilience of the tourist sector to the negative effects of recession. A similar picture emerges concerning employment in tourism, although accurate assessment of the total number of jobs generated by tourist activities poses certain problems (Py 1992; Cazes 1993). Estimates suggest a current total of over 800,000 permanent jobs in tourism, to which up to 300,000 seasonal posts and at least 600,000 indirect and induced jobs need to be added (Py 1992; Cazes 1993). Permanent jobs have increased by slightly more than 3 per cent per annum since the early 1980s and consist essentially of employment in the café, hotel and restaurant branch (Direction du Tourisme 1994).

A further measure of the importance of tourism to the French economy is given by the 'travel' entry in the balance of payments accounts. This covers purchases of currency for the purposes of tourism and provides a measure of both foreign tourist expenditure in France and similar French spending abroad (Py 1992). Analysis of such figures (Table 3.2) shows not only the sizeable value of expenditure but also the very substantial net surplus from which the French economy benefits. In 1993 this figure amounted to over 60 billion francs, and exceeded by a considerable margin the net value of foreign exchanges in leading export fields such as agricultural, food and drink products and vehicles (Table 3.3). Furthermore, the size of this surplus has risen substantially over the last fifteen years and contrasts strongly with the situation in the 1960s when in various years a deficit of tourist expenditure was recorded (Cazes 1993). These figures attest to the importance of France for international tourism. Indeed, in 1992 foreign visitors totalled over 59 million, making France the world's leading tourist destination ahead of the United States; similarly, the volume of tourist spending (25 million dollars) was second only to the United States (Direction du Tourisme 1994).

Not only does France attract a large and increasing number of foreign visitors, but domestic tourism is also growing. Evidence of this trend is provided by the general rise in household expenditure on leisure and related sporting activities as well as the increase of spending under the heading of 'hotels, cafés, restaurants and travel' (INSEE 1994a, 1994b). In the latter case such expenditure represented 6.1 per cent of total household consumption in 1960, but by 1993 this proportion had risen to 7.1 per cent (INSEE 1994a). Such an increase may not match the growth associated with items such as health and housing, but it contrasts strongly with the declining proportional significance of spending on products such as food, drink and clothes. Logically, as tourist expenditure has increased, so too has the number of French people taking a holiday each year. Whereas only 41 per cent of the population went on holiday at least once a year in 1965 (Table 3.4), by 1993 this proportion had increased to 60.9 per cent (INSEE 1994a). The growth of holiday-making, however, has been uneven during this period; rates rose rapidly throughout the late 1960s and 1970s, but have progressed little since the early 1980s, largely as a consequence of repeated periods of recession. One indicator of the impact and respective importance of both foreign visitors to France and domestic tourism is given by the number of nights spent in registered hotel accommodation; in 1993 the total amounted to more than 145 million, of which 55 million nights were accounted for by foreign tourists (Direction du Tourisme 1994).

Table 3.2 The 'travel' entry in the French balance of payments

	Million francs	
	1990	1993
Receipts	109.9	132.5
Expenditure	67.7	72.5
Balance	42.2	60.0

Source: Direction du Tourisme (1994)

Table 3.3 Trade balance for selected goods and services, 1993

	Million francs
Agricultural and food products	56.5
Energy	− 69.3
Vehicles	27.7
Tourism	60.0

Source: Direction du Tourisme (1994)

Table 3.4 Holiday departure rates

Year	Rate (%)	Year	Rate (%)
1965	41.0	1985	57.5
1975	52.5	1990	59.1
1980	57.2	1993	60.9

Source: INSEE (1994a)

Using the same criterion of nights spent away from home, it is also possible to obtain an insight into the relative importance of different types of tourism. Surveys in France have used four broad categories of stay:

holidays (consisting of at least four consecutive days away), short breaks of less than four days, business trips and visits motivated by reasons of health (Py 1992; Cazes 1993). On this basis 66.2 per cent of 'tourist nights' spent by French people are accounted for by holidays, 19.6 per cent by short stays, 13.5 per cent by business purposes and 1.6 per cent for health; amongst foreign visitors to France the respective proportions are 69, 5.4, 25.6 and 0 per cent (Cazes 1993). As far as the growth of these visits is concerned, short breaks and trips motivated by business have expanded most rapidly over recent years (Lefol and Chaigneau 1985; Mermet 1994). Thus, between 1980 and 1990 the number of 'tourist nights' spent by French people on short breaks multiplied by an average of 3.3 per cent each year, while those inspired by business increased at an annual average rate of 4.7 per cent (Py 1992).

In response to the sizeable and rapidly growing demand for tourism, an extremely heterogeneous range of tourist firms has developed. If there is a common feature to these enterprises, it is their small average size. Py (1992) states that 97 per cent of companies in the tourist sector have less than ten employees and that 57 per cent have no employees at all. Various factors explain this situation, including the extreme diversity of tourist 'products' and locations, the relatively insignificant character of the package holiday market, the weak role played by travel agents in organizing travel and holidays and, in this latter context, legislative constraints which have restricted the development of large vertically or horizontally integrated groups (Py 1992). None the less, despite the predominance of small businesses, control of the tourist industry is becoming increasingly concentrated in the hands of a limited number of large groups, leading to the emergence of a dualistic structure.

Concentration has become inevitable with the large-scale expansion of tourism, the intense nature of competition within the industry and the increasingly international character of tourist activities. Thus, a series of large companies now play a key role in the industry (Wackermann 1992). Examples include the giant Accor hotel group (controlling chains such as Sofitel, Novotel, Mercure, Ibis and Formule 1), tour operators and holiday specialists such as Club Méditerranée and Nouvelles Frontières, and Pierre et Vacances which specializes in the sale and rent of holiday accommodation and dominates this field in France. Alliances and various other forms of association have also become an increasingly common feature of the tourist industry. A number of hotel chains such as Logis de France function in this way, more than 300 travel agencies operate under the banner of Sélectour and tour operators work closely with other firms: Club Med, for example, has formed an alliance with American Express, with each partner promoting the other's products (Py 1992). Thus, although numerous small businesses persist, major shares of the tourist market are increasingly controlled by large companies. Firms employing over a hundred people may still represent only 1.9 per cent of all tourist businesses, but they alone account for 49.2 per cent of the industry's turnover (Cazes 1993).

The public sector is also actively involved in the development and promotion of tourism. At government level the responsibility for tourism currently lies with the large combined Ministry of Equipment, Transport and Tourism, although in practice a number of other Ministries (such as Environment, Housing and Agriculture) are also concerned with tourist activities. While the government is responsible for the formulation of tourist policy and related legislation, it also intervenes directly in a series of tourist development projects through various funds such as the Fonds d'intervention pour l'aménagement du territoire (FIAT). The different levels of local government also intervene to encourage tourism, with their influence having been generally reinforced as a result of government legislation on decentralization passed in the 1980s. Communes and departments both have the possibility of investing in tourist projects (as in the case of a new conference centre), while the regions are more concerned with the wider strategic planning of tourism (Py 1992). There are also both regional and departmental tourism committees whose primary responsibilities concern the promotion and commercialization of tourist activities. Informing actual or potential tourists is also the primary task of numerous Syndicats d'Initiatives (of which there are over 3,200); in a number of large cities and major tourist centres more important centres exist in the form of Municipal Tourist Offices (Cazes 1993). The mission of these offices is not only to inform the public, but also to organize events such as festivals, to study the tourist market and even to manage certain activities such as marinas, ski-lifts or sports centres.

Local authorities are frequently directly involved in tourist development as a result of their shareholdings in so-called 'mixed economy companies' (sociétés d'économie mixte – SEM). These companies represent a form of public/private partnership. Shares are divided between both public and private investors, with the company run as a private organization. Mixed economy companies are a common feature in France, particularly in the field of urban development and regeneration. With respect to tourism their roles are varied, ranging from the management of ski-lifts to the running of exhibition or conference complexes.

TOURISM IN URBAN AREAS

Traditionally, urban centres have been perceived much more as important sources of tourists rather than major destinations for tourism. Indeed, in an urban society, the very notion of taking a holiday might be interpreted as a desire to escape the environment of the city (Michaud 1983). Certain characteristics of French holiday-making would appear to support this idea. As holiday venues, towns and cities do not play a major attractive role. Over the year as a whole they account for less than 9 per cent of tourist destinations (Cazes 1993). While the average is somewhat higher in winter than in summer, urban areas as such have far less appeal than the coast, the countryside or mountainous regions (Table 3.5). Moreover, the relative attraction of towns would appear to have decreased rather than increased over recent years. At the same time, the proportion of urban dwellers taking a holiday has steadily risen over time, not least in major cities. Thus, currently over 77 per cent of the 9.3 million Parisians go away on holiday each year (Cazes 1993).

Table 3.5 Major holiday destinations in France, 1993

Type of destination	Summer (%)	Winter (%)
Touring	4.9	7.9
Coastal areas	19.8	44.6
Mountainous regions	31.3	13.6
Rural zones	26.0	24.2
Urban areas	18.0	9.7

Source: INSEE (1994a)

This initial and partially negative view of urban centres as tourist destinations needs, however, to be qualified in various ways. First, the above trends refer only to French holiday-makers, taking no account of foreign tourists. Yet foreign visitors seem to show a far greater interest in urban destinations and, particularly in Paris (Renucci 1991). Second, these figures relate to stays of at least four days, whereas towns and cities represent a particular attraction for visits of a shorter duration. However, the average length of stay in large cities appears particularly short. Thus, Renucci (1991) quotes the examples of Paris and Lyon for which the respective figures are 2.6 and 1.6 days. In part this situation corresponds with the more general trend towards annual holidays being divided into a series of shorter stays rather than constituting only one lengthy period away from home. The substantial and continuing growth of such visits has also been encouraged by the tourist industry itself, notably as an increasing range of 'weekend breaks' is being marketed. Tourist offices have promoted such 'packages', as have tourist businesses; the Novotel chain, for example, offers weekend stays in its hotels combined with various types of activity, depending on the locality.

The importance of short stays in urban areas also reflects the frequently different character of tourist activities in these locations compared with more conventional resorts. In particular various forms of business tourism often play a dominant role. It is estimated that in towns of over 100,000 inhabitants the visits of businessmen and attendance at conferences or trade fairs and exhibitions accounts for over 70 per cent of tourist activity; indeed, in the case of Lyon (1.3 million inhabitants) this proportion rises to 78 per cent (Renucci 1991). A third important factor, which needs to be taken into account when assessing the importance of towns as tourist centres, concerns the number of day visitors. As with short breaks, such visits are not recorded in official statistics, although their number is considered to be substantial; using again the example of Lyon, it is estimated that at least half of the visitors to the city each year consists of day-trippers (Renucci 1991). The motivations for these journeys are clearly highly varied including shopping, business, visits to restaurants, theatres and cinemas or other such leisure activities, as well as attendance at conference, exhibitions or festivals. However, while the number of these visitors is undoubtedly important, their impact on the local economy is more questionable due to the shortness of the stay and the absence of expenditure on accommodation.

In reality, therefore, urban areas and particularly major cities offer numerous opportunities for tourism and attract numbers of visitors. It is no longer appropriate to assume that urban centres reject rather than attract tourists. On the contrary, their attractiveness has been progressively enhanced (Clary 1993). The expansion of urban tourism might be attributed to various influences such as increased affluence, mobility and leisure time which have underpinned the growth of tourism nationally. At the same time, however, a number of specifically urban-based factors have contributed to this trend, including investment in transport infrastructure, accommodation and specialized facilities. Furthermore, with the increased recognition of the economic benefits which may accrue to local communities through tourist activities, a growing number of local authorities has been actively seeking to promote tourism. In certain cases this forms part of a more general strategy of rendering the city more attractive to facilitate its marketing.

The historic quarters of cities and their related monuments have long represented a tourist attraction. Efforts to enhance and embellish these sites have continued throughout recent decades, encouraged as early as 1962 at a national level by the 'loi Malraux' designed to establish conservation areas of particular architectural interest in urban areas. More recently, protected 'heritage zones' (Zone de protection du patrimoine architectural et urbain), introduced in 1984, have been designed to pursue this policy (Clary 1993). At a local level numerous initiatives have accompanied or pursued further these state-led schemes. The rehabilitation of the historic core of Lyon (Vieux Lyon) and its transformation into a major tourist attraction is an obvious example; the same is true of the old centre of Rouen with the rehabilitation and pedestrianization of the quarter around the shopping artery of the 'Gros horloge'. Indeed, as in many other European cities, pedestrian streets have become common features of the majority of French city centres.

Tourism in urban areas has also been favoured by improved accessibility both to and within the city. The progressive extension of the French motorway network has enlarged the hinterlands of the country's major towns served by these routes, although even more spectacular improvements in accessibility have resulted from the continuing development of the high-speed rail network (Thompson 1994). Lyon is within two hours travelling time of Paris, Bordeaux is only three hours from the capital and central Paris can be reached within an hour from the centre of Lille. Similarly, Lyon and Lille are now only three hours apart by TGV. Business or leisure trips within the day, notably to and from Paris, already rendered possible by a dense network of air services, are now increasingly feasible. Movement within large urban areas has also been facilitated, not least by improvements to public transport. The majority of large provincial cities have seen the development of either metro or tram systems, notably serving the central areas. In Lyon, Lille, Marseille and Toulouse metro networks have been established, whereas in other large towns such as Nantes, Grenoble and Strasbourg preference has been accorded to the tram. In the latter case, the reintroduction of the tram into the city in late 1994 (trams previously disappeared in the early 1960s) was accompanied by the exclusion of cars from the historic centre and the extension of pedestrian streets within this area. These decisions should greatly entrance the already considerable tourist appeal of Strasbourg.

A further stimulus for tourism has resulted from improvements to the facilities offered by cities for tourist activities. Hotel accommodation has been substantially modernized and expanded. Such changes have been progressive and resulted largely from the development of the major hotel chains, notably the Accor group which by 1993 controlled 882 hotels in France (Theumann 1994). Much of the new investment of these groups has benefited urban locations with the result that the problem of underprovision of such facilities, which existed in the past, has largely disappeared. The relatively large size of these hotels, together with the standardized nature of their product, has also encouraged their use by tour operators. Moreover, conference and meeting rooms often form an integral part of the up-market hotels of these chains (e.g. Sofitel-Pullman,

Holiday Inn, Novotel), and thus provide a range of opportunities for business tourism. Initially new investment in such hotels was concentrated on the urban periphery where land costs were lower and accessibility easier than in the central city. This trend is still evident for the low-cost segment of the market (e.g. Formule 1, Mister Bed), but there are also signs of a new interest in inner and central sites for the location of better-quality hotels, reflecting the important concentration of tourist-related facilities in this part of the city. Novotel, for example, has invested over recent years in the centres of Paris, Lille and Grenoble as well as in the inner city of Lyon.

The public sector has also taken initiatives to encourage tourism, with many local authorities promoting the development of conference and exhibition centres. More than fifty towns now possess a conference or convention centre, although the size and quality of these facilities varies between towns. Despite the large number of centres and highly competitive nature of the market, new conference facilities continue to be provided, illustrated by recent developments in Nantes and Lille. Increasingly these purpose-built venues are designed to respond to a range of uses. Even in many smaller urban centres, where ambitions and budgets are more modest, investment in similar facilities has taken place, often in the form of multi-purpose conference or concert halls (Clary 1993).

Municipal authorities have intervened in other ways with respect to tourism. This may involve the extension of existing museums and art galleries or the creation of new facilities as in the case of Grenoble. Here, in 1994, the new Musée de Grenoble opened, housing one of the most important art collections in provincial France (*Le Monde* 1994a). The organization of festivals is another common strategy to attract tourists, as is participation in a major sporting event. In a less direct manner, the renovation or refurbishment of central shopping areas may also help bring in more external visitors to a city, although factors other than tourism also lie behind such projects: enhancing the city's image, competition from other urban centres and resistance to the challenge from large out-of-town shopping centres.

Rendering the central area more attractive has become a common and continuing theme in the majority of France's large provincial cities. To achieve this goal, a mixture of strategies has been employed, generally involving improvements to accessibility, the enlargement and modernization of retail facilities and the creation of a more appealing shopping environment. From the 1970s new, large, purpose-built covered shopping centres began to appear in cities such as Lyon, Bordeaux, Marseille and Strasbourg as part of central area redevelopment schemes (Tuppen 1988). The trend has continued with the completion in 1994 of a new central shopping complex in Lille which forms part of the large Euralille development built around the TGV station. Such changes have in general been accompanied by new public transport systems, the exclusion of vehicular traffic from parts of the central area and the addition of 'street furniture' and flower displays. In Lyon, for example, such measures have also been accompanied by the construction of a series of large underground car parks around the traditional commercial core of the Presqu'île and the refurbishment of existing pedestrian streets.

There are, therefore, many examples of investments undertaken by municipal authorities with the aim of either directly or indirectly stimulating tourist activity. This interest undoubtedly reflects the ability of the tourism industry to create jobs and to induce various multiplier effects in the local economy. However, the extent to which the promotion of tourism forms part of a coherent urban development strategy is more open to question. Certainly it appears that many cities either still lack a clear policy with respect to tourism or are ineffective in promoting this activity (Renucci 1991). This is not to say that specific projects have not been strongly defended. Many city councils have demonstrated a firm commitment to the building of conference centres. Such interest is justified by the supposedly beneficial effects of the perceived spin-offs, as well as the desire to establish a presence in what is still a growth area, despite strong competition. In certain cases, as at Lille, this logic has indeed been taken further and business tourism has been targeted as a key element within the broader tourist development strategy of the city (*Les Echos* 1994a).

Such investment and its indirect effects in the form of associated hotel accommodation have generally been greatest in the central areas of cities. Suburban zones, however, have also been the focus of tourist-related developments as in the case of the large exhibition centres created on the outskirts of Paris (Villepinte) and Lyon (Eurexpo). Once again municipal authorities have favoured such projects due to the positive multiplier effects on the local economy. Other motivations are also apparent as well as alternative forms of development. Thus, at Saint-Denis, in the northern suburbs of Paris, the local council effectively lobbied the French government to ensure it was chosen (in 1993) as the site for the capital's new football stadium for the World Cup in 1998. While the presence of the stadium itself will ensure an important inflow of visitors to Saint-Denis both for and after the World Cup, its impact is designed to be far greater. 'Le Grand Stade' is envisaged as a central feature and catalyst for the economic and urban renovation of this depressed Parisian suburb which has experienced large-scale deindustrialization and where the unemployment rate exceeded 15 per cent in 1994; the stadium and related infrastructure alone represent an investment of 5 billion francs (*Le Monde* 1994b).

Other examples might be cited where tourism has been used as a means to stimulate or regenerate the economic activity of a region. One unusual, although ultimately unconvincing scheme, was the opening in 1989 of a large theme park in the centre of the traditional steel-making regions of Lorraine. The park was located 15 kilometres to the north of Metz, adjacent to the A4 and A31 motorways and at the centre of a strongly urbanized and industrialized region. Based on the strip cartoon characters 'Les Schtroumpfs' (The Smurfs), and the result of an investment of over 720 million francs, the park was envisaged as playing a key role in the revival of the depressed economy of this area. Given its location at the 'heart of Europe', it was expected to attract over 1.8 million visitors in its first year of operation. In reality the park was visited by less than half this number; the subsequent failure to increase the number of visitors and the attendant financial problems led to its sale and restructuring.

Theme parks have been developed with greater success in a limited number of other urban locations. The most well-known example is the Disneyland Park complex located to the east of the capital. This park too has faced financial difficulties, although at the same time it is the most visited site in France. As such it has clearly become an essential element amongst the range of tourist products on offer in the region of Ile-de-France. At a local level, Disneyland has been seen as an equally important component of the economic development of the new town of Marne-la-Vallée and, more generally, of the less-privileged eastern suburbs of the capital. In western France, to the north of Poitiers, a very different and, arguably, more successful theme park known as Futuroscope was inaugurated in 1985. Since that date more than 1 billion francs have been invested by the department of Vienne in a site oriented around the theme of communications and new technologies (*Les Echos* 1993a). Visitors have the possibility of participating in the different activities and experiences proposed by the park, giving a pedagogical as well as recreational character to the visit. Moreover, the site has attracted various educational and research establishments and a series of service firms. In 1993 visitors to the park totalled 1.9 million and the mixed economy company running the park made a profit; annual turnover exceeds 300 million francs (with a similar sum estimated to be injected into the local economy), and 2,000 jobs have resulted directly from this development without counting the indirect employment benefits for the region (*Le Monde* 1994c). The proximity of such an important source of jobs and of a large potential clientele for the hotels, restaurants and shops of Poitiers might be seen as a particular advantage for the town, not least in an area previously lacking in dynamism (*Le Monde* 1989).

While there are many examples of urban authorities developing specific tourist amenities and often thus influencing a particular part of the city, in most large cities tourism depends on a series of 'products' spread throughout the urban area. In this respect Paris, not surprisingly, displays the most comprehensive range, including major conference and exhibition centres, historic sites, museums and art galleries (as well as their associated exhibitions, often of international appeal) and sports arenas, together with numerous possibilities for accommodation. Lyon and Lille provide similar opportunities, although on a much reduced scale and with far fewer prestigious sites. These same features are again present at Marseille, although the city is largely outclassed by its northern rivals as a centre for business tourism. Marseille does, however, benefit from its maritime location and related ports and beaches giving a further dimension to tourist activities. The possibility of extending and enhancing these facilities is seen as a future means of diversifying and reviving the city's ailing economy (Tirone 1991). However, as a tourist centre Marseille is currently overshadowed by its smaller neighbour, and rival, Nice.

Tourist strategies in these cities have been conceived to promote one or a number of these activities. Thus, at Lyon and Lille the further development of business tourism is a key element of policy. The same ambition is less evident at Marseille due to the absence of a modern conference centre. Instead, the city has sought to promote its attraction as a 'stop-over' point for tourists visiting the wider region. Other cities have pursued a similar strategy. Lyon and Bordeaux have both developed the theme of visits to neighbouring areas renowned for their vineyards (such as the Beaujolais or Médoc), associated with a stay in the city.

Not all urban authorities have demonstrated the same interest in exploiting tourism as a means to stimulate the local economy. Clermont-Ferrand, for example, has a long history of industrial development, linked primarily with the presence of the Michelin tyre company. With the loss of many industrial jobs and the need to diversify the town's economy, the development of the tourist sector offered one solution to this problem, not least due to the existence of certain potential advantages for tourism – the historic old town, a series of monuments and museums, a conference centre and proximity to the extinct volcanoes of the Massif Central and particularly the Puy-de-Dôme (attracting over 450,000 visitors each year). Yet local political rivalries and a reluctance to innovate with respect to tourist development have meant that this potential remains largely underexploited (Jamot 1992). In contrast, various other similar-sized towns, also faced with the need for industrial conversion, appear to have been far more receptive to the idea of developing a tourist strategy. Such is the case of Mulhouse, for example (Tuppen 1985). A further illustration of a more dynamic approach is provided by the new towns of the Paris region (Marne-la-Vallée, Cergy-Pontoise, Evry, Melun-Sénart and St-Quentin-en-Yvelines). Although an unlikely setting for tourism, guided visits to the towns are now proposed, oriented around the theme of architectural innovation in urban design. These excursions are offered in various languages and have proved particularly popular with Japanese visitors; the aim is to enlarge the initiative to include other themes (Wermes 1991).

Whatever the strategy adopted, its implementation is generally the responsibility of the Office du Tourisme. Such promotional organizations exist in all· of France's major urban centres. Although their message is directed primarily at the general public, it is also destined towards professionals working in the tourist industry. Other organizations may also be involved in promoting tourism. Specialized services may exist to manage specific activities, most notably with respect to conferences and exhibitions or hotel reservations. Often these bodies are direct offshoots of the Tourist Office. Regional and departmental tourist committees may also work with city tourist offices on promotional activity and on longer-term development strategies for tourism. Hoteliers are represented by the Chambers of Commerce and Industry, although these organizations undertake little promotional activity. Finally, many of the individual actors working in the tourist industry such as hotel and restaurant owners, transport operators and travel agencies may, either individually or collectively, be involved in the formulation and implementation of a city's tourist strategy.

In theory, therefore, tourism should be well promoted. However, in practice this is not always the case. The budgets of Tourist Offices are relatively modest and frequently the proportion spent on promotional activities is small (Renucci 1991). Similarly, deficiencies may exist in the number and quality of staff present in such offices, while in many cases detailed knowledge or studies of consumers' preferences are lacking (Clary 1993). Problems of co-ordination also arise, not only between the various and often numerous partners involved, but also in defining the range and type of tourist products to be marketed as well as an appropriate policy of communication (Boyer and Viallon 1994).

MAJOR FORMS OF URBAN TOURISM

The conference and convention business

For many cities the businessman has come to represent a major source of revenue for the tourist industry. Business trips to urban areas are generally motivated by three factors – participation in conferences and seminars, attendance at trade exhibitions and visits to individual factories and offices. With the growth of these activities, well over 50 per cent of the nights spent in hotels in large provincial cities such as Lyon is accounted for by the businessman (Tuppen 1985). Moreover, in the capital, business tourism is estimated to account for up to half the tourist income of the city (*Le Monde* 1986). New industries and services have developed to meet the needs of this market, including specialized travel agencies and caterers as well as manufacturers and assemblers of stands at conferences and exhibitions.

Amongst these activities the French conference market (including conventions, conferences and seminars) has developed significantly over the last fifteen years. In 1990 the turnover of this industry was estimated at 20 billion francs, following a decade of exceptional growth (*Libération* 1992). Since then expansion has slowed, currently averaging around 3 per cent per annum (*Les Echos* 1994b). Heightened competition and the negative impact of recession on business activity lie behind this slowdown, although it has not prevented the continuing opening of a series of new or refurbished conference centres. The strength of such development means that France now represents approximately 9 per cent of the world market for conferences and 15 per cent of the European market (Py 1992). Similarly, France is second only to the United States in the number of its international conferences, while Paris has been the leading centre in the world for international conferences since 1980 (Cazes 1993).

Conferences may be held at a variety of locations including hotels, university lecture rooms and exhibition halls, as well as in a range of more specialized facilities. With respect to this last category, a substantial increase has occurred in the number of purpose-built conference centres. Such facilities currently exist in nearly a hundred towns of various sizes, spread throughout France, although over a third of these conference centres lie in the three south-eastern regions of the country (Provence-Alpes-Côte d'Azur, Rhône-Alpes and Languedoc-Roussillon). However, while certain southern areas may be favoured in terms of the number of establishments, reflecting their advantages in terms of climate or scenery, the majority of activity is concentrated overwhelmingly in Paris. If measured with respect to international conferences, nearly 50 per cent of these events take place in the capital; Paris is followed, although with a considerably smaller total of conferences, by Strasbourg, Nice, Montpellier and Lyon (*Libération* 1992; *Les Echos* 1994b, 1994c).

This hierarchy may well be modified in future years following a wave of new investments. Conferences are seen as a lucrative business for a city, but to attract these events in a highly competitive market, modern, specialized and easily accessible facilities are essential. In addition, the provision of a new conference centre might be interpreted as symbolizing a city's ambitions to be recognized as a major focus of (international) business. Over the last decade large conference/convention centres have been opened at Nice (1985), Montpellier (1989), Deauville (1992), Tours (1993) and Lille (1994). In all cases these centres offer an auditorium with at least 1,500 seats, as well as different exhibition spaces and a series of meeting rooms (*Les Echos* 1993b); the aim is to be able to respond to a variety of demands (concert, conference, seminar) and to provide a high level of equipment and service. Such facilities imply substantial investment, as is seen in the case of Nantes or Montpellier where the conference centres cost 840 million francs and 700 million francs respectively (Table 3.6). Indeed, the supply of major conference complexes will be further enlarged with the completion of projects at Lyon and Bordeaux. New facilities are not limited, however, only to the above towns. Smaller but often equally well-equipped centres have been opened recently in a variety of locations including Reims, Grenoble, Toulouse and Mandelieu-La Napoule (near Cannes) or, on a more modest scale, at Beaune and Chalon-sur-Saône.

Table 3.6 Investment in major conference centres in France

Conference centre	Opening date	Investment (million francs)	Size of largest auditorium (no. of seats)
Nantes: L'Atlantique	1992	840	2,000
Cannes: Palais des Festivals	1982	700	2,300
Montpellier: Le Corum	1989	700	2,010
Strasbourg: Palais de la Musique et des Congrès	1975/85	700	2,000
Nice: L'Acropolis	1985	680	2,500
Tours: Le Vinci	1993	450	2,000
Lille: Grand Palais	1994	410	1,500
Paris: Palais des Congrès	1974	355	3,700
Deauville: Le Cid	1992	265	1,540
Reims: Centre des Congrès	1994	254	700

Source: Adapted from *Les Echos* (1993b)

In many cases it is the municipalities themselves that have invested directly to ensure the construction of these conference centres (Ragu 1989). Their subsequent management is then often placed under the responsibility of a mixed economy company, in which the municipality is usually still a major shareholder. However, direct intervention by the municipal authorities may also occur due to the need to subsidize the often substantial running costs of the centre, for it is relatively rare that the revenue from lettings covers these costs. The justification for all this expenditure derives from the multiple positive spin-offs that conference centres are argued to provide for the local economy. Conference delegates are seen as relatively liberal spenders, particularly as they themselves generally only bear a fraction of the costs. Average daily expenditure of a delegate is estimated by the Ministry of Tourism at around 1,300 francs in Paris and 1,000 francs in provincial cities. Such average figures clearly conceal considerable variations between localities and types of conference, with spending in general being higher for international events. If it is also assumed that the average conference lasts three days and attracts approximately two hundred participants, then it is clear that the total amount of money injected into the local economy, with its attendant multiplier effects, is substantial (*Les Echos* 1994b).

Most cities with conference centres have attempted to quantify this effect. Thus, the city of Lyon estimates that in 1990 conferences alone (excluding other forms of meeting) generated over 127 million francs of spending. Nice has one of the largest convention centres in provincial France, L'Acropolis, which was opened in 1985. Since its inauguration it has attracted a large number of events ranging from conferences and conventions to product launches and shows. Between 1985 and 1991 the centre welcomed over 430,000 people staying for 1.1 million 'conference days' and generating an estimated expenditure of 1.6 billion francs. Even smaller towns lay claim to a considerable economic benefit from conferences. Perpignan, for example, estimates that such activity injected 42 million francs into the local economy in 1991.

The major beneficiary from such spending is undoubtedly the hotel and catering sector. Nationally it is estimated that 65 per cent of expenditure is devoted to this one category of activity (*Les Echos* 1994b). Delegates may also spend money on items such as presents and souvenirs, car hire and public transport. In addition the organization of the conference itself implies various forms of expenditure – the hire of specialized equipment or decorations, the provision of hostesses or interpreters and the organization of related visits and exhibitions. Despite its advantages, reliance on the conference trade may present various problems for a city. Competition between conference centres at a national and international scale is intense, implying continuing investment in facilities which themselves rarely generate a profit. Moreover, the term 'conference' frequently covers a diverse range of activities, not all of which have the same ability to generate income for the local economy. Short, intense scientific gatherings do not offer the same potential as those meetings which build their conference programme excursions on other leisure activities.

Exhibition centres

The exhibition business displays many of the characteristics already outlined with respect to conferences. Exhibitions space and the number of events held each year both increased significantly throughout much of the 1970s and 1980s, followed by a much slower rate of progression over recent years due to the joint effects of the downturn in economic activity and heightened competition between exhibition centres (Py 1992). None the less France ranks as the second most important country in Europe after Germany for exhibitions (Mesplier 1993), and offers a wide range of facilities spread between a large number of towns. Once again, however, the market is dominated overwhelmingly by Paris.

Exhibition centres have been funded in general by public bodies and institutions (for example, local authorities or public sector banks such as the Caisse des Dépôts et Consignations) or local Chambers of Commerce and Industry. Their management has been mostly delegated to companies in which these bodies retain important shareholdings, while a series of specialized firms has developed concerned with the actual organization or particular events. As with conferences, strong competition exists between different sites to attract business and this has been one factor in the provision of new purpose-built facilities to accommodate such activity. The exhibition complex at Villepinte on the northern outskirts of Paris (first opened in 1982 and then substantially extended in 1986) and the similar, though smaller, development of Eurexpo on the eastern fringe of Lyon (opened in 1984) illustrate this trend.

The justification for such investment is once again to be sought in the substantial spin-offs that such centres are deemed to create for their local economies. Exhibitions generally take the form of large, generalized city or regional fairs (such as the Foire de Paris, or the Foire Européenne at Strasbourg) or of more specialized and frequently smaller trade fairs. In the former instance the number of visitors may be considerable; in 1993, the Paris Fair attracted 945,000 visitors *(Le Monde* 1993a), while the similar event at Lyon was visited by 455,000 people *(Le Monde* 1993b). However, many of these visitors stay only a relatively short time and spend comparatively little. In contrast trade fairs may involve longer stays and greater expenditure on hotels and restaurants. But, to a far greater extent than for conferences, one of the major benefits generated by an exhibition concerns the work of setting up, running and servicing the event. In this respect the Villepinte complex in Paris provides employment for 15,000 people, working in nearly 300 companies spread throughout the region of Ile-de-France *(Le Monde* 1992). Overall this site alone was estimated in 1992 to have injected 7 billion francs into the regional economy out of a total of 16 billion francs for the exhibition business as a whole in the region of Ile-de-France (*Le Monde* 1992).

Similar benefits, although on a reduced scale, are generated in other major city regions. However, as with conferences, these need to be balanced against certain costs. Few exhibition centres themselves make a profit and many host only a limited number of events each year, despite attempts to develop multi-purpose structures (although in part this feature reflects the time needed to assemble and dismantle exhibitions). Similarly part of the investment costs have often been borne out of public funds. In contrast, the very success of the Villepinte complex and the adjacent airport of Roissy-Charles-de-Gaulle, has generated a different type of cost related to the problems of congestion affecting the local road network.

Historic monuments, museums and galleries

The extent to which an individual museum or art gallery is capable alone of attracting tourists to a region is open to question. However, for people visiting a particular locality or for the inhabitants of this area, the existence of such facilities is likely to induce a large number of related trips. In this respect France is particularly well-equipped, with over 12,000 classified monuments and more than 1,000 museums (Cazes 1993). Moreover, these sites attract a large and growing number of visitors; for example, between 1980 and 1990 visits to the country's thirty-four national museums (under state control) increased from 9.6 to 15 million (Py 1992).

This form of cultural tourism has an obvious urban dimension, with Paris once more displaying an overwhelming domination of such activity, both in terms of the range of potential attractions and the number of visitors. Of the leading ten such sites in France, nine are located in the capital (Table 3.7). Their success in attracting visitors represents one of the factors behind the substantial development of museums and galleries over the last decade. Since the early 1980s work has been carried out at 400 different sites to provide new facilities or to extend and renovate those which existed already (*Le Monde* 1993c). Numerous municipalities have invested in this manner in the arts, their task facilitated by government grants provided by the Ministry of Culture through the Directions des Musées de France. Government spending on such construction projects has been multiplied substantially since the early 1980s, not least under the impetus of Jack Lang, the socialist Minister of Culture from 1981 to 1986 and again between 1988 and 1993; the construction and renovation budget rose from 63 million francs in 1981 to 225 million francs in 1991 (*Le Monde* 1993c). While part of the motivation for such investment is undoubtedly cultural, for many municipalities there are other considerations. Museums and art galleries, through the nature of their collections or the architecture of their buildings, frequently represent part of a wider strategy to enhance the image of the city. Not only is this policy designed to attract a greater number of visitors and tourists, but also to encourage firms, for which the quality of the cultural environment may represent an important locational determinant, to invest in the locality.

Table 3.7 Most visited national museums and historical monuments in France, 1993

Site	No. of visitors
Pompidou Centre	7,995,812
Eiffel Tower	5,537,155
Cité des Sciences et de l'Industrie	5,300,000
Louvre	4,919,702
Château de Versailles	3,668,000
Musée d'Orsay	2,579,000
Musée Centre Pompidou	988,938
Musée des Armées	874,169
Mont-Saint-Michel (Abbey)	844,133

Source: Direction du Tourisme (1994)

Museums and similar institutions have also become the focus of increasing consumer expenditure. Whereas the modest entry fees once represented the principal source of revenue, there is a growing tendency to develop related commercial activities. These take various forms ranging from the renting of space for shows or concerts to the creation of various shops, bars and restaurants (Tinard 1994). Such trends might be seen as a part of a wider movement to broaden the appeal of museums by also adding other facilities such as libraries and research centres, leading to the creation of a form of 'cultural complex' (*Le Monde* 1993c). Such a concept has represented a central feature of the development of the Louvre. Its progressive extension since the early 1980s (at a cost of 6.3 billion francs, with work due for completion in 1997) involves not only a significant extension of the exhibition space and souvenir shops, but also the opening of a large related underground complex (the Carrousel) which includes up-market retail outlets, restaurants and conference facilities (*Le Monde* 1993d). This marriage of cultural and commercial interests is justified in part by the large number of visitors (nearly 5 million in 1993), including a high proportion of foreigners (64 per cent). The result is that the Louvre itself employs around 1,500 people and produces a modest revenue (1992) of 96 million francs (*Le Monde* 1993d).

This ability to create jobs and generate a significant income lies behind many of the investment projects in provincial cities. However, in reality the situation is not always so favourable. Visitors tend to stay for a short time and in most cases spend relatively little. Moreover, while a major part of the construction costs of the museum may have been covered by the subventions of the state and various local authorities, the subsequent running costs often present a major financial problem. Such costs may be high. For the Louvre they amount annually to 600 million francs, although over 80 per cent of this figure is paid by the state (*Le Monde* 1993d). For many municipal museums this is not the case, as at Grenoble (*Le Monde* 1994a). Running costs exceed revenue by a considerable margin, with the result that local authorities are forced to provide a large and continuing subsidy. At Grenoble, for example, 18 per cent of the city's budget is devoted to cultural activities (*Le Monde* 1993e).

Finally, as with exhibition centres, the very success of certain museums may generate its own problems and costs. The Pompidou Centre in Paris provides an obvious example. It was originally designed in the expectation that it would receive an average of 5,000 visitors a day. Currently this total exceeds 25,000 with such heavy usage representing a major factor behind the current programme of refurbishment which is estimated to cost around 400 million francs (*Le Monde* 1994d).

Other activities

Urban tourism is also induced by the existence of a varied range of other attractions, although often their precise impact is difficult to assess. Certain cathedrals, churches and religious centres bring in large numbers of visitors, notably in the major cities. Each year Notre Dame de Paris and the Sacré-Coeur de Montmartre are together visited by 14 million people, while at Lyon the Notre Dame de la Garde is visited by 1.5 million people (Tinard 1994). However, many smaller towns such as Chartres or Lisieux also draw in large numbers of visitors. Indeed the most impressive example of religion encouraging tourism is provided by the small town of Lourdes and its function as the destination for numerous pilgrimages. Each year it is estimated that the town is visited by over 5.5 million people (Cazes 1993) with this one activity dominating the town's economy. Whereas visits to a famous cathedral are generally of a short duration and probably induce little direct expenditure, the situation at Lourdes is very different. Visits are much longer and represent a major source of activity for the town's hotels – over 300 hotels provide more than 13,000 rooms, totals which are considerably higher than those of a large city such as Lyon. Tourism is claimed to inject 3 billion francs each year into the local economy (*Le Monde* 1993f).

In the same way that religion may encourage tourism, so too may considerations of health. France possesses one of the largest number of spa towns and thermal baths in Europe. This activity is estimated to provide around 60,000 jobs and generate an annual turnover of approximately 5 billion francs (Cazes 1993), with the benefits accruing most to local hoteliers and restaurant owners. However, this impact concerns a series of smaller towns mainly in central and southern France, rather than the country's larger cities. Vichy, La Bourboule and Le Mont Dore, all in Auvergne, are typical examples. In part they benefit from an assured market, for much of their activity relates to treatments prescribed by doctors for which patients are reimbursed by the French Social Security system. Demand, though, has grown relatively modestly, and many spa centres have therefore tried to enlarge this health function, notably by developing related 'keep fit' and relaxation activities. Indeed certain towns such as Vichy have also sought to diversify their range of tourist attractions, notably by seeking to attract conferences or sporting events (for which the accommodation infrastructure already exists).

The desire to enhance a town's image and to encourage tourism are motives which lie behind the organization of numerous festivals and sporting events. There are now approximately 800 festivals held annually in France (*Le Monde* 1994e), although those which have a national or international reputation are limited in number. Their theme varies, but amongst the most popular are those relating to the cinema (e.g., Cannes and Deauville), to the theatre (e.g., Avignon), music (e.g., Antibes), dancing (e.g., Bordeaux) or local culture. In general such events are located in smaller and medium-sized towns rather than the major cities. Once again their impact on the local economy may be considerable, particularly where visitors stay for a number of days as in the case of the Cannes film festival. However, the costs of organizing a festival are frequently high, requiring an important subsidy from local authorities. Thus the net impact on an area may not always be substantial.

In the hope of raising the profile of a city, and therefore enhancing its attractiveness for investors or tourists, it has also become increasingly popular to host major sporting events. Taken to its extreme, such a strategy implies the organization of a competition with world-wide appeal as in the case of the Olympic Games. Indeed, Paris was an unsuccessful contender for the 1996 Games. France has, however, met with more success in the footballing sphere. The capital, as well as a number of large provincial cities such as Lyon, Marseille and Nantes, will play host to the 1998 World Cup. On a more modest scale there is a long tradition of towns being associated with sporting events. This might be illustrated in motor sport by the Le Mans 24-hour race and the Monaco Grand Prix, or in tennis by the international championships held at Roland-Garros in Paris. As in many other fields of tourist-related activity, the French capital has a clear lead over its provincial rivals in the organization of sporting events, benefiting as well from specialized facilities such as the complex at Bercy (Palais omnisports de Paris-Bercy) close to the Gare de Lyon. Here a series of prestige indoor events regularly take place, ranging from tennis to go-karting. Other cities have attempted to follow this lead; Lyon organizes an annual indoor international tennis competition, Bordeaux is the venue of the national ice-skating championship and both Lyon and Lille have hosted the Tour de France in recent years. Apart from the positive impact that such events may have on a city's image, the other main justification behind their organization concerns the related expenditure of visitors in the local economy. Again this is hard to assess, but as with other activities already discussed, there is also a cost. Hosting the Tour de France may have its attractions but this privilege costs each of the towns which are used as stop-over points 600,000 francs (which is paid to the organizers), for the different centres used each year for the start and finish (always Paris) the cost reputedly rises to 2 million francs (*Capital* 1993).

A number of other urban-based activities might be seen as featuring a tourist component. Concerts or operatic performances fall within this category, as do establishments such as casinos. Visits to factories and industrial sites have also developed as an additional form of tourism. Shopping has already been recognized as a factor which may not in itself stimulate tourism, but which is certainly an important accompanying pursuit. Certain towns have sought to push this logic further. The town of Troyes, for example, which has a long history of textile manufacturing, has developed an important activity of direct selling of clothes from shops linked to local factories. It is estimated that over 1.2 million people each year shop in this way, with nearly half of this clientele originating from outside the local area (Moret 1994). The major spin-off for the town relates to meals taken by outside visitors in local cafés and restaurants. Such expenditure is estimated to amount annually to 39 million francs (Moret 1994). A similar phenomenon has developed in the coastal ports of Boulogne and Calais, relating to day visitors from Britain. At Boulogne in 1993, for example, there were over 500,000 such visits; not all of these visitors necessarily used the local shops, but for those that did, daily expenditure (excluding the cost of the trip) was found to amount to 1,100 francs (Grosheitsch 1994). The challenge for these towns in the future is to convert these day visits into stays of a longer duration, for at present the impact on the local economy remains limited.

TOURISM IN MAJOR CITIES

More detailed consideration is now given to tourism in the country's three leading cities. The aim is to demonstrate both the nature of their tourist attractions and the contrasts which exist between them. Thus, the scale of activity is very different at Paris compared with Lyon or Lille. The capital is unrivalled in France as an urban tourist centre, and its major competitors are international counterparts such as London or Rome rather than other French cities. Tourist policy therefore, is very much related to enhancing the capital's competitive advantage with respect to such rivals, although at a regional level efforts are directed at devising a more coherent strategy which integrates better the different tourist sites both within and around Paris. Lyon and Lille are less well-established tourist centres and indeed suffer from being relatively little known in this capacity. A more varied range of opportunities for tourism is to be found at Lyon, while the city of Lille has belatedly sought to enhance its image as a centre for business tourism; this has occurred in conjunction with a major scheme of urban renewal. In both cases the promotion of tourism has become an integral part of wider strategies attempting to market the cities more effectively.

Paris

The French capital represents a major pole of tourist activity easily outclassing all other cities in the country. Even in a European context, with the exception of London, it has few rivals. Paris benefits not only from the wide range of its attractions, but also in many instances (such as the Louvre or Eiffel Tower) from their unique character and world-wide reputation. This diversity means that the motives for visiting Paris are equally varied. The capital is celebrated for its important national museums and galleries (e.g., Louvre, Orsay, Pompidou Centre) as well as its innumerable smaller and specialized museums, its historic quarters and monuments (e.g., Marais, Ile-de-la Cité, Notre Dame), its theatres and opera houses (e.g., Bibliothèque Nationale, Sorbonne). Other major attractions include the capital's parks and gardens, its waterways, its shops and its sporting venues. The dominance of Paris compared with provincial cities may be illustrated with reference to the country's national museums – the capital alone accounts for 61 per cent of all visitors to such museums (INSEE 1990).

Paris has an equally important function as a centre for business tourism. In part this derives from the strength and, above all, the influential role of the capital's economy in a national context. Paris houses, for example, 27 per cent of the country's value-added and 40 per cent of employment in banking and financial services as well as a high proportion of company head offices in this same field (Robert 1994). More generally, Paris is the focus of the majority of head offices of large national and multinational groups. This 'control' function inevitably generates a vast range of business activity. In the more specialized areas of conferences and exhibitions the capital's dominance is similarly apparent. Paris disposes of approximately 550,000 square metres of exhibition space spread over four main sites (Porte de Versailles, the CNIT at La Défense, Le Bourget and Villepinte), and is capable of welcoming up to 100,000 conference delegates each day; it also boasts the largest auditorium at the Palais des Congrès situated close to the Porte Maillot, which has the further advantage of a location close to the heart of the city.

The development of Paris as a tourist centre has also been facilitated by the ease of access to the capital both in a national and international context. Paris lies at the hub of the country's motorway, rail (including the TGV) and internal airline networks, and possesses Europe's second most important airport complex after London. The capital also benefits from a large and diverse range of possibilities for accommodation, including more than 70,000 rooms in over 1,400 classified hotels. Indeed, this latter figure accounts for the greater part of the region's hotel capacity which exceeds 2,100 hotels (Table 3.8). Within Paris itself the upmarket segment is particularly conspicuous, representing nearly a quarter of the capital's hotel capacity, with a strong concentration in the 1st and 8th *arrondissements* (Bensaïd 1989). This capacity has been increased significantly over recent years through the investments of major hotel chains, favouring both central and more peripheral locations served by motorway links (Mesplier 1993). In 1993, tourists spent over 40 million nights in the Paris region's hotels, representing more than 27 per cent of the total nights in French hotels (Direction du Tourisme 1994).

Table 3.8 Hotel capacity in the Paris region (Ile-de-France), 1994

Type of hotel	No. of hotels	No. of bedrooms
1 star	324	10,139
2 star	1,090	50,810
3 star	652	40,988
4 star and luxury	99	12,579
Total	2,165	114,516

Source: Direction du Tourisme (1994)

Together these different features result in a rather different profile for tourism in the capital compared with the major provincial cities. This may be illustrated by reference to three interrelated features. First, despite the importance of business tourism, leisure-based tourism is also strongly represented, unlike the situation in Lyon or Lille (Renucci 1991). Second, there is a far greater international component to tourism in the capital. The hotels of the region Ile-de-France welcome over 10 million foreign guests each year, representing more than 25.5 million 'hotel nights', a total which in turn accounts for more than 63 per cent of all tourist nights spent in the region's hotels (INSEE 1990; Direction du Tourisme 1994). Third the length of stay in the capital is generally longer than in provincial cities (Renucci 1991); the average stay in the capital's hotels lasts 2.5 days (Bensaïd 1989).

A further singular dimension has been given to tourism in the Paris region by the opening in 1992 of the extensive Disneyland complex. This project was first decided upon in the mid-1980s, following an intensive search by the Walt Disney Company (the American parent group) to find a suitable European site for a theme park similar to those already existing in the United States. The principal advantage of a location close to Paris resided in the access this would give to a vast potential visitor market, represented by the city region of Paris itself (above all for short-stay visits), and by the ease with which the French capital may be reached from other French and European cities. Following an official agreement signed in 1987 between the French authorities and the Walt Disney Company, the park subsequently opened in April 1992. It lies on a 2,000 hectare site, just over 30 kilometres to the east of Paris on the eastern outskirts of the new town of Marne-la-Vallée. The park is directly accessible from Paris via the A4 motorway as well as by the capital's high-speed metro system (RER), specially extended to serve Disneyland. Since 1994, the site has also been linked by a new station to the TGV network.

While the theme park itself represents the central element of the development, it is by no means the only feature. A series of hotels, offering 5,200 rooms (1994), have been built, as well as over 30,000 square metres of office floorspace. In addition, the presence of such an important investment within the new town of Marne-la-Vallée has resulted in the associated building of new homes and the provision of additional services (Lanquar 1992). Indeed, Disneyland has been viewed as an essential dynamic force behind the further expansion of the new town, not least as subsequent second and third stages of development were originally envisaged for the site. These were to include the creation of two new theme parks as well as a major conference centre and additional related hotel building; however, for the moment such plans have been shelved. The initial phase has represented an investment of over 23 billion francs by the Disneyland authorities, as well as an additional 3 billion francs of public investment in new infrastructure (*Le Monde* 1993g).

Much, therefore, was expected of this development, not least from the major interested parties – the owners, the local authorities, the French state and the various financial institutions which lent money for the operation. Their different hopes have not necessarily all been fulfilled. While Disneyland has attracted large numbers of visitors and created a substantial volume of employment, it has also made substantial losses in both its first two years of operation – 5.3 billion francs in 1992/3 and 1.8 billion francs in 1993/4 (*Les Echos* 1994d). As a result the company's share price fell dramatically, staff have been made redundant and in early 1994 investors were forced to agree to a major renegotiation of Disneyland's debt repayments.

These adverse features need to be balanced by a series of positive impacts, notably concerning the number of visitors. In 1994 their total amounted to 8.8 million, although this number had decreased compared with the previous year (*Les Echos* 1994d). This figure far exceeds those of other theme parks in France (including the Asterix park to the north of Paris), although so does the size of the initial investment. With respect to jobs, Disneyland itself has a permanent workforce of 11,000 people (*Le Monde* 1994f), this number increasing during the summer months through additional seasonal workers. In a wider context the park is estimated to have created, directly or indirectly, over 43,000 jobs in the local economy; furthermore, over 300 million francs are paid by the company each year in local taxes and more than 750 million francs are returned to the government in the form of VAT (Bouillot 1993). Disneyland's annual turnover amounted to 4.1 billion francs in 1994 (*Les Echos* 1994d).

Numerous difficulties, however, have characterized the park's early years of operation and help explain its financial problems. In part Disneyland has been a victim of its launching during a period of intense recession, provoking fewer visitors, lower levels of spending by the visitors (per capita spending in the park in 1994 averaged 248 francs – *Les Echos* 1994d) and difficulties in disposing of assets such as its hotels due to the associated collapse in the property market. This situation was aggravated by the high interest payments on the debts incurred to fund the development. Certain of these problems were accentuated by the marketing strategy of the company – entrance fees and hotel charges were shown to be unrealistically high and restaurant facilities ill-adapted to customer tastes. Similarly, the park and its attractions did not meet with universal approval in France, being seen as too 'American' and too little adapted to European, and particularly French, cultures (*Le Monde* 1994f); such a view appears partially confirmed by a lower proportion of visitors from France than anticipated.

Faced with such circumstances changes have been effected. Management has been restructured, shops and restaurants have been modified, greater contacts have been made with French tour operators and other tourist organizations and, significantly, prices have been reduced. One positive outcome is a slow rise in hotel occupancy rates which now average 60 per cent (*Les Echos* 1994d). However, it is still questionable whether the park in its present form is capable of inducing people to stay longer and spend more. This may not occur until other investments have been undertaken such as the conference centre, new attractions and sporting facilities.

Despite these various problems, Disneyland represents an important diversification of tourism in a region already rich in such attractions. The large number and extensive range of tourist activities suggest that their contribution to the regional economy is sizeable. Accurate measurement of this impact is, however, difficult due to the absence of reliable data. Estimates suggest, nevertheless, that tourism injects approximately 100 billion francs into the regional economy and employs, directly and indirectly, around 160,000 people (Mairie de Paris 1992). For certain activities, this influence is easier to assess. Paris, for example, is a major European focus for conferences and exhibitions; indeed, the city is the world's leading destination for international conferences, playing host to 361 such events in 1991 (Clary 1993). In the same year 1,130 conferences were held in Paris, involving 565,000 delegates whose expenditure amounted to nearly 3.5 billion francs; if seminars and promotional events are also taken into account then total spending by participants attending all these activities rises to nearly 5 billion francs (Clary 1993). A similar picture emerges with respect to exhibitions. Paris is the European leader for these events (ahead of Milan), attracting up to 6 million visitors each year (Office du Tourisme et des Congrés de Paris 1992). Associated expenditure is estimated to represent over 16 billion francs, although not all of this is necessarily spent in the local area; approximately a quarter of this total is accounted for by the costs of preparing the stands and setting up the exhibition and, as with conferences and seminars, spending on hotels and restaurants is also substantial (Clary 1993). On a smaller scale the important attractive power of tourism and the high potential benefits for the local economy may be illustrated by reference to the Eiffel Tower. In 1992 it was visited by 5.7 million people who spent 180 million francs on entry tickets alone; when other receipts are taken into account (such as expenditure on restaurants, souvenirs and television nights to use the Tower) total spending is estimated at over 300 million francs (*Le Monde* 1993h).

Paris, therefore, benefits from an extremely diverse range of tourist attractions which have a high drawing power and result in substantial expenditure; the capital has no rival in France. However, competition does exist from other world cities, implying the need for constant investment and innovation to sustain the capital's appeal. The extensive renovation of the CNIT exhibition and conference facilities at La Défense or the recent large-scale refurbishing of the Champs-Elysées might be seen as examples of this imperative (*Le Monde* 1994h). Yet maintaining a high level of tourist activity also implies other changes. Certain features of the capital still provoke a negative image, notably with respect to the quality of welcome – poor knowledge of foreign languages, high prices, too few taxis and insufficient sign posting (*Les Echos* 1990). Other problems such as insufficient capacity to meet certain demands also exist. This latter feature is particularly apparent in the central areas of the capital with respect to exhibition space and hotel accommodation.

In an attempt to rectify such shortcomings a number of initiatives have been taken, aiming, for example, to improve the promotion of Paris as a tourist destination, notably for short breaks and to extend the season to ensure that tourism becomes a year-round activity. To this end efforts have also been made to develop a tourist strategy for the capital (Lesage 1992). Not only is this designed to improve co-ordination between the different actors and provide a coherent response to changes in demand but also to achieve a better integration between Paris and the surrounding region of Ile-de-France (Plaisait 1992). At present the spin-offs for this hinterland from the numerous visitors to the capital are limited, whereas conversely the vast drawing power of peripheral attractions such as Disneyland is not yet fully exploited by the central areas of the capital.

Lyon

Unlike Paris, the city of Lyon does not possess a strong image as a tourist centre and until comparatively recently there was little concerted effort to market the city as a destination for tourism (Renucci 1988). On the contrary, Lyon was seen much more as an industrial centre with its attendant problems of congestion and pollution. Indeed, for many people passing through Lyon by motorway on their way to or from the South of France, this impression was only reinforced – in part by the invariable traffic jams at the entrance to the Fourviére tunnel under the city and in part by the view that the motorway offered of the concentration of oil refining and related chemical industries on the city's southern outskirts.

At the same time, Lyon has undoubted advantages for tourism. Its 'crossroads' position which has long encouraged the development of many economic activities has equally favoured the expansion of tourism. Despite the problems of congestion alluded to above, motorway access has improved progressively, a new international airport (Satolas) was opened on the city's eastern periphery in 1975 and now handles over 4 million passengers each year, and accessibility by rail has been greatly enhanced since the inauguration of the TGV in 1981; currently there is a daily average of twenty-two trains in each direction between the centres of Paris and Lyon. The site of Lyon offers various attractions due not least to the hills which lie to the north and west and to the Rhône and Saône rivers which traverse the city. Within Lyon there are numerous monuments including Roman amphitheatres, the Fourvière basilica and the twelfth-century cathedral, as well as the old town of 'Vieux Lyon'. A series of museums, together with concert halls and the recently renovated opera house, add a further cultural dimension to these attractions. With respect to business tourism, Lyon possesses a modern and well-equipped exhibition centre (Eurexpo) and by the end of 1995 will have a new conference centre. Finally, to support the development of tourism, hotel facilities have been substantially improved and enlarged, with the result that the city offers nearly 10,000 beds of which approximately 40 per cent are in three- and four-star hotels.

As a result, a substantial tourist activity now exists in Lyon. It is estimated that over 4.8 million people visit the city each year, spending more than 3.7 billion francs; in addition, tourism provides over 8,300 jobs within Lyon (*Lyon-Figaro* 1992). This follows increasing efforts to promote Lyon as a tourist centre. Such promotion has been led by the Tourist Office in conjunction with the Chamber of Commerce and Industry and Aderly (a specialized agency created to foster the economic development of the Lyon region). They have worked closely with professionals in the tourist industry to devise a distinctive strategy. This involves raising the city's status as a centre for festivals and cultural events, increasing the importance of conferences and exhibitions, exploiting the potential offered by the Rhône and Saône for cruises and excursions and using Lyon as a 'stopover' point for tourists exploring the surrounding region (Tuppen 1985; Renucci 1988). For visitors, however, Lyon appears best known for its gastronomy, the old quarters of the city, and for the relative ease of access to surrounding areas such as the Alps and Beaujolais (Renucci 1992). This latter feature is reflected in a number of local tour operators such as Hexatour developing specialized tours of these areas. However, many such tourists spend relatively little time in Lyon. Thus, for local hoteliers, business tourism is of far greater importance, accounting for between 70 and 80 per cent of their activity (Renucci 1988; Van den Berg 1994).

Yet despite the importance of tourism and its diverse character, Lyon still does not stand out as a major tourist centre in France (Brunet 1989). Various obstacles have so far limited the development of tourism. Despite its different attractions, Lyon lacks famous museums, major historic sites and monuments and world-class theatres or opera houses which would act as an important draw for tourists. Unlike Paris, therefore, Lyon is not endowed with internationally renowned attractions; as such the city remains relatively little known, especially outside France (Renucci 1992). This problem of image also applies to the different forms of tourism developed by the city. Lyon still appears to lack a clear identity as a tourist centre, with no leading attraction to bring in visitors. Even in the field of business tourism, certain handicaps exist. The absence of a large modern, conference centre may have depressed this activity over recent years, although the completion of a new convention complex as part of a major inner urban development scheme (Cité Internationale) which combines offices, shops and hotels should improve this position. With respect to exhibitions, the same drawback does not exist, given the recent development of Eurexpo and the high quality of its facilities. However, in both cases there remains the underlying problem of how to attract exhibition promoters and conference organizers away from Paris and generate a distinctive image for Lyon. Thus, although the future of Lyon as a tourist centre clearly depends on the quality and accessibility of its attractions, it is also dependent on changing the perception of the city itself.

Lille

Lille displays many similarities with Lyon, although at first sight the potential for tourist development might appear less. The city is the head of a region (Nord-Pas-de-Calais) marked by a long history of industrial decline affecting the majority of its staple industries. Coal, textiles, iron and steel, heavy engineering, shipbuilding and chemicals have all experienced large-scale closures and an attendant sharp fall in employment. Like many other urban centres in the region, the Lille conurbation has been faced with these economic problems. New investment, notably in the car industry, has sought to attenuate this decline, but unemployment remains high, income levels are depressed and, above all, in the context of developing tourism, deindustrialization has left a legacy of derelict land and disfigured urban landscapes.

More generally the north of France is perceived as a region which has little appeal for tourism – the physical landscapes lack variety, the climate is seen as inhospitable and the long association with heavy industry has created an unfavourable external image tending to repel rather than attract visitors. In addition, the region has long acted as a zone of transit for tourists rather than as an area to be visited in its own right.

At the same time, Lille possesses certain advantages for the development of tourism. The city has a rich cultural and architectural heritage, centred on the historic core of 'Vieux-Lille'. It is the focus of the region's major theatres, museums and art galleries, with the Musée des Beaux-Arts representing one of the leading such museums in provincial France (Dewailly 1985). Lille also hosts a series of festivals and concerts, while its symphony orchestra is widely renowned. Similarly, its long history as an industrial and commercial centre has favoured the growth of business tourism. Specialized facilities have long existed for exhibitions (Nordexpo) on the south-eastern outskirts of the city, whereas in 1983 a new conference centre was opened in the centre of the city (Palais des Congrés et de la Musique). Such developments have been accompanied by the progressive increase in hotel facilities both in central and peripheral locations, including a number of up-market hotels, a segment of the market which was previously poorly represented at Lille (Bruyelle 1991). More generally accessibility to the city (notably by motorway) has been improved, while movement within Lille has been facilitated by the development of the metro.

Tourism has thus long been an element of the city's economy, although traditionally its role and the priority accorded to its development have been of minor importance. Moreover, tourist activity has been associated with various weaknesses such as the short length of stay, the limited attractions of Lille as a holiday destination and the absence of a clearly defined development strategy. However, over recent years a change has become apparent following a series of major investments in new infrastructure. Such investment has been associated principally with the arrival of the TGV. This follows the success of the Lille local authorities in persuading the French government in 1987 to route the TGV services from Paris to London and Brussels through the city (Bruyelle 1991). As a result, Lille is destined to become a central pivot in the emerging European TGV network, while already the TGV Nord in the centre of the city is within an hour's journey time of central Paris.

This substantial increase in accessibility has been accompanied by the building of a second central station (Lille-Europe), to accommodate the TGV services (with the exception of trains to Paris), in association with a new, major business and commercial complex known as Euralille. This development, of which the first elements were completed in 1994, houses or will ultimately house a large shopping centre, extensive office accommodation, hotels, an urban park and a combined conference, exhibition and concert complex known as the Grand Palais. A similar project had been proposed around the existing mainline station in the early 1970s, but despite limited development it was never completed largely due to a lack of political will and clear conception of its role. By the late 1980s these conditions had changed. Euralille and the TGV became central features of the city's strategy (actively promoted by the mayor, Pierre Mauroy) to become a 'European business city' (*Le Monde* 1993i). At the same time these developments provided the opportunity to reinforce Lille's function as a tourist centre, notably for business tourism. This is the intended goal of the ultra-modern conference and exhibition complex (Lille Grand Palais) which supersedes pre-existing facilities, judged out-dated and ill-adapted to current demands (Dewailly and Marnot 1994). The centre's major advantage stems from both its technical sophistication and the ability to adapt its use to a wide range of events.

Lille, therefore, has adapted a bold strategy to develop this particular facet of tourist activity which relies heavily on the declared aim of reinforcing Lille's status as a business centre. Given the city's previous difficulties in attracting or retaining company head offices and high-level business functions this might appear an over-ambitious objective. Such a strategy also implies certain risks not least due to the size of the related investment. The Grand Palais represents an investment of 410 million francs, part of which has been directly supported by the city. To meet its operating costs, a further annual subsidy is also likely to be necessary. However, as in other urban centres, the justification for such investment is seen in the wider benefits which such a facility generates for the local economy. As an example, the Socialist Party Conference which was held in the city in 1987 was estimated to have injected 20 million francs into the city's business (*Le Monde Affaires* 1987), although this takes no account of the extra costs generated by an event of this scale.

CONCLUSION

French cities have long been variously labelled in terms of their functions as industrial or service centres, but it is only comparatively recently that they have been conceived as tourist attractions. With the growing realization that tourism might play an important role in the urban economy, an increasing range of potential tourist activities has been developed, with considerable emphasis given to business tourism. Similarly, the number of urban authorities seeking to give greater priority to tourism has also risen, although with the exception of Paris no other city may be considered to have achieved the status of a major tourist centre; as in many other aspects of French life, the capital still possesses an overwhelming dominance in this field. This has not prevented many municipal authorities from investing in prestigious projects ranging from conference centres to museums.

However, this interest in urban tourism and the related investment has not always been matched by a clear vision of how tourist activities should be developed. Effective co-ordination between the different actors involved in tourism is also often lacking. Numerous bodies and firms are directly concerned by tourist activities, ranging from individual hotel or restaurant owners and travel agencies to public or semi-public bodies such as Tourist Offices, Chambers of Commerce and Industry, and Departmental and Regional Tourist Committees. The responsibilities of each are not necessarily readily evident and may frequently overlap, while there is not always a well-defined overall framework within which to co-ordinate different actions. It is for this reason that cities such as Paris and Lyon have sought to develop a tourist blueprint outlining future policy.

Better co-ordination also implies the need for a coherent strategy which recognizes the relationship between different activities. A modern exhibition centre is unlikely to function efficiently if the city's hotel capacity is unable to meet its requirements in terms of the number, quality and location of rooms. Similarly, it is difficult to attract events if the city lacks a clear image as a tourist centre. Again it is only comparatively recently that many cities have sought actively to develop these interrelationships. Clear links also exist between tourism and urban renovation and rehabilitation schemes. They may take the form of reviving historic quarters of the city, as in Vieux-Lyon, or of redeveloping specific areas of the urban core as in the case of the Euralille scheme.

In the same way tourism itself has become a means of promoting the city, contributing to the growing trend of city marketing. This tendency has emerged with force over the recent years and may be illustrated by the efforts made by the two cities of Lyon and Lille to assert their 'European' and 'International' status. Similar strategies are also evident in smaller centres such as Nice and Strasbourg. The success of such an approach is also dependent, however, on effective communication, and in this field scope exists for considerable improvement, notably with respect to tourism and the relatively small budgets which are devoted to the promotion of this activity. French cities undoubtedly possess a wide range of attractions to woo tourists, but without an appropriate communication strategy this potential is unlikely to be fully realized.

REFERENCES

Bensaïd, S. (1989) '12 millions de visiteurs en 1987', *Regards sur l'Ile-de-France* 4, 7–12.

Bouillot, P. (1993) 'Fallait-il inviter Mickey?', *Espaces* 124, 4–8.

Boyer, M. and Viallon, Ph. (1994) *La Communication Touristique,* Paris: Presses Universitaires de France.

Brunet, R. (1989) *Les Villes Européennes,* Paris: La Documentation Française.

Bruyelle, P. (1991) 'La Communauté urbaine de Lille', *Notes et Études Documentaires* 4936.

Capital (1993) 'L'irrésistible ascension du Tour', July, pp. 28–32.

Cazes, G. (1993) *Le Tourisme en France* (4th edn), Paris: Presses Universitaires de France.

Chambre de Commerce et d'Industrie de Lyon (1992) *Région Urbaine de Lyon: repéres et tendances économiques,* Lyon: Chambre de Commerce et d'Industrie de Lyon.

Clary, D. (1993) *Le tourisme dans l'espace français,* Paris: Masson.

Dewailly, J.M. (1985) 'Tourisme en agglomération non touristique: le cas de la conurbation de Lille', in F. Vetter (ed.) *Big City Tourism,* Berlin: Reimer.

Dewailly, J.M. and Marnot, P. (1994) 'How to make use of the new opportunities arising from international links, for urban tourism; the case of Lille', Paper given to the Urban Tourism and City Trips Conference, World Trade Centre, Rotterdam, 28–29 April.

Direction du Tourisme (1994) *Mémento du Tourisme,* Paris: Direction du Tourisme.

Grosheitsch, J.M. (1994) 'Shopping à Boulogne-sur-Mer', *Espaces* 128, 24–7.

INSEE (1990) *Tableaux de l'Economie de l'Ile-de-France,* Paris: INSEE.

INSEE (1994a) *Tableaux de l'Economie de l'Ile-de-Française,* Paris: INSEE.

INSEE (1994b) 'Les dépenses pour les loisirs depuis 1960', *INSEE Premiére,* no. 306.

Jamot, Ch. (1992) 'Le tourisme culturel à Clermont-Ferrand: mythe ou réalite?', *Revue de Géographie de Lyon* 67, 49–56.

Lanquar, R. (1992) *L'Empire Disney,* Paris: Presses Universitaires de France.

Lefol, J.F. and Chaigneau, E. (1985) 'Les voyages touristiques de courte durée', *Espaces* 76, 16–27.

Le Monde (1986) 'Le tourisme d'affaires, première industrie de la capitale', 3 and 4 August.

Le Monde (1989) 'Des Parcs de loisirs à l'aventure', 27 July.

Le Monde (1992) 'Le parc de Villepinte expose sa réussite', 29 and 30 November.

Le Monde (1993a) 'La foire de Paris', 9 May.

Le Monde (1993b) 'Bilan mitigé pour la Foire de Lyon', 14 April.

Le Monde (1993c) 'La viévre des musées: les nouveaux temples de las consommation culturelle', 2 February.

Le Monde (1993d) 'Grand Louvre', 19 November.

Le Monde (1993e) 'Grenoble: comment faire tourner la machine?', 3 February.

Le Monde (1993f) 'Les trésors de Lourdes', 11 and 12 April.

Le Monde (1993g) 'Disney à la mode chez nous', 11 and 12 April.

Le Monde (1993h) 'Les bonnes affaires de la Tour Eiffel', 5 and 6 September.

Le Monde (1993i) 'Euralille à la mode hollandaise', 23 and 24 May.

Le Monde (1994a) 'Grenoble: l'art déployé', 29 January.

Le Monde (1994b) 'Les retombées économiques du grand stade', 15 and 16 May.

Le Monde (1994c) 'Futuroscope l'anti-Disney', 1 February.

Le Monde (1994d) 'Les travaux de rénovation du Centre Pompidou ne pourront commencer qu'en 1997', 7 April.

Le Monde (1994e) 'Supplément Art et Spectacles', 9 June.

Le Monde (1994f) 'Euro-Disney tente d'atténuer les effets de son plan social', 22 June.

Le Monde (1994g) 'La joconde et Michey', 31 August.

Le Monde (1994h) 'Champs-Elysées: un projet dénaturé', 28 September.

Le Monde Affaires (1987) 'Lille: les gros sous d'un congrés', 4 April.

Lesage, J.L. (1992) 'Plan d'aménagement du tourisme parisien', *Espaces* 116, 60–2.

Les Echos (1990) 'Paris se dote d'une véritable politique touristique', 5 December.

Les Echos (1993a) 'Le Futuroscope vise les 3 millions de visiteurs', 3 June.

Les Echos (1993b) *Entreprise et Implantation*, Dossier, hors série, October.

Les Echos (1994a) *Le Nord – Pas-de-Calais*, Dossier, hors série, May.

Les Echos (1994b) *Entreprise et Voyages d'Affaires*, Dossier, hors série, March.

Les Echos (1994c) 'Montpellier conforte sa place de ville de congrés', 3 March.

Les Echos (1994d) 'Euro-Disney affiche une perte nette de 1,8 milliards de francs en 94', 4 and 5 November.

Libération (1992) *Le grand chantier des congrés*, Supplément Economique Rhône-Alpes, 5 November.

Lyon-Figaro (1992) 'Lyon fait ses comptes', 29 April.

Mairie de Paris (1992) *Lettres de Paris 1991–92*, no. 20, Paris: Mairie de Paris.

Mermet, G. (1994) *Francoscopie 1995*, Paris: Larousse.

Mesplier, A. (1993) *Le Tourisme en France* (5th edn), Paris: Bréal.

Michaud, J.L. (1983) *Le Tourisme face à l'environnement,* Paris: Presses Universitaires de France.

Moret, D. (1994) 'Tourisme et commerce à Troyes', *Espaces* 128, 14–18.

Office du Tourisme et des Congrés de Paris (1992) *Lettre de Paris,* no. 20.

Plaisait, B. (1992) 'Plan d'aménagement du tourisme parisien', *La Lettre du Tourisme à Paris,* no. 2.

Py, P. (1992) 'Le Tourisme: un phénomène économique', *Notes et Études Documentaires,* no. 4951.

Ragu, D. (1989) 'Faut-il encore construire des palais des congrés en Ile-de-France?', *Les Cahiers de l'Institut d'Aménagement et d'Urbanisme de la Région d'Ile-de-France* 91, 9–20.

Renucci, J. (1988) 'Tourisme et produit touristique à Lyon', Revue de Géographie de Lyon 63, 191–205.

Renucci, J. (1991) 'Le tourisme urbain française en question: sous-exploitation et efforts d'impulsion', *Dossier de la Revue de Géographie Alpine* 6, 57–66.

Renucci, J. (1992) 'Aperçus sur le tourisme culturel urbain en région Rhônc-Alpcs: l'cxcmplc dc Lyon ct dc Vicnnc', *Revue de Géographie de Lyon* 67, 5–18.

Robert, J. (1994) *L'Ile-de-France,* Paris: Presses Universitaires de France.

Theumann, B. (1994) 'Le Phénomène de chaîne et de marque pour l'entreprise indépendante', *Espaces* 129, 12–16.

Thompson, I.B. (1994) 'The French TGV system: progress and projects', *Geography,* pp. 164–8.

Tinard, Y. (1994) *Le Tourisme: économie et management,* Paris: Ediscience.

Tirone, L. (1991) 'Marseille en 1990: crises et métamorphoses', *Méditerranée* 2(3), 59–65.

Tuppen, J. (1985) *Urban Tourism in France,* Urban Tourism Project Working Paper no. 3, University of Salford.

Tuppen, J. (1988) *France under Recession 1981–86,* London: Macmillan.

Tuppen, J. (1991) 'France: the changing character of a key industry', in A. Williams and G. Shaw (eds) *Tourism and Economic Development* (2nd edn), London: Belhaven Press.

Van den Berg, L. (1994) 'Urban tourism', Paper given to the Urban Tourism and City Trips Conference, World Trade Centre, Rotterdam, 29 April.

Wackermann, G. (1992) 'Le rayonnement touristique', pp. 157–92, in G. Wackermann (ed.) *La France dans le Monde,* Paris: Nathan.

Wermes, A. (1991) 'L'envol touristique des villes nouvelles', *Espaces* 108, 21–3.

4 Major city tourism in Germany

Peter Schnell

INTRODUCTION

During the past two decades city tourism has gained importance compared with other kinds of tourism. Several reasons can be adduced for this development: (1) the number of persons taking short breaks has increased considerably, and for this group of tourists cities are ideal destinations; (2) public transport organizations like German Rail and private coach enterprises have developed programmes of city tourism which attract demographic groups which in former years have not been participating in tourism to such a degree; and (3) new forms of tourism (e.g., 'cultourism' and 'histourism') have evolved where tourists are interested in cultural events or historical urban settings.

According to official German statistical data thirty-eight cities had 200,000 or more inhabitants at the end of 1992. Of these, thirty had populations of more than 250,000, making a total of almost 18 million; they are therefore included in this study. Their share of the German population amounts to 22 per cent. This figure may underestimate their importance as parts of these agglomerations may be outside the administrative boundaries of the city. The significance of these cities in the national context is reflected by the fact that nearly one-quarter of all tourist arrivals (24 per cent) come to these cities; however, only 14.3 per cent of all tourist nights spent in Germany are spent in these cities. These two percentages indicate that the tourist visiting the major cities does not stay in them very long; in fact, tourists spend only 2.1 nights in these cities compared with the national average of 3.5 nights and with the average of 3.9 nights for the other tourist regions outside the major cities.

For the cities with more than 100,000 inhabitants within the old Federal Republic, the period 1987–92 is characterized by an above average increase in the number of tourist nights until 1990. Although the increase continues after this date, rate of increase is below average. The reason for this change is considered to be the decrease of foreign tourists observed in the years 1991 to 1993. Since this group of tourists had a share of nearly 30 per cent of all tourist nights in cities with a population of more than 100,000, this general decrease is said to have had an above average impact (Statistisches Bundesamt 1995). Such statements about the development of city tourism suffer from the fact that older data are not available for the major cities in the eastern states of the Federal Republic – only since the political reunion has reliable statistical data been published. In addition to the decreasing numbers of foreigners visiting the major cities, the general falling-off in numbers of business-based trips during the last few years also affects the statistics.

MAJOR CITY TOURISM IN GERMANY

As far as major city tourism as a field of research is concerned, quite a lot of studies have been carried out. Most of them deal with smaller cities and towns which are attractive tourist destinations because of their historical buildings and their small size compared to the larger cities, or with special aspects of city tourism such as the economic impact of tourism or congress and conference tourism. In a publication dealing with city tourism in general, case studies from Hesse, Rhineland Palatinate and Saarland are presented, but none of the cities belongs to the major cities with 250,000 and more inhabitants (Akademie für Raumforschung und Landesplanung 1982). There are other publications which deal with city tourism in general or with special aspects of it, an example being the study of Münster (Hank-Haase 1992). Becker (1986) analysed Munich as a place of exhibitions and fairs from a social-geographic point of view, but he did not explicitly use the term 'city tourism' in the title. According to Schreiber (1990) major city tourism is composed of business-oriented tourism (business tours, congress tourism and exhibition tourism) and privately motivated tourism (sightseeing tourism). Those visits to the major cities which are connected with their role as central places and therefore mostly do not require overnight stays are excluded. One reason why day visits are not taken into consideration is that it is extremely difficult to record them quantitatively.

According to German statistical usage, major cities comprise all urban settlements with 100,000 or more inhabitants. At the end of 1992, eighty-four such major cities existed in Germany, holding a share of 32.2 per cent of the population. Their share of the tourist arrivals and tourist nights was 26.5 per cent and 18.1 per cent respectively. Among the major German cities are thirty (35.7 per cent) with 250,000 or more inhabitants. The city tourism of these and four other cities which have slightly fewer inhabitants (Kiel, Krefeld, Rostock and Aachen) is analysed in more detail in this chapter. The thirty-four cities are of dominant significance as far as city tourism is concerned, for their share of tourist arrivals amounts to 83.4 per cent and of tourist nights 81.2 per cent, respectively. Several reasons can be put forward for this dominance: (1) nearly all of these cities are university towns so there will usually be many conferences and symposia; (2) most have exhibitions and fairs; and (3) the historical character of most of these cities attracts many visitors who also often make use of the cultural facilities like theatres, operas, music halls, etc.

According to Schreiber (1990) city tourism has passed through four phases between 1960 and 1987:

Phase I (1960 to 1966): The first phase can be considered as the final phase of a positive development which started in 1952 and is characterized by a simultaneous increase of German and foreign tourist arrivals and nights. Between 1960 and 1966 the number of nights increased by 22.4 per cent and the accommodation capacity by 21.6 per cent.

Phase II (1967 to 1974): The second phase is a period of stagnation with visitor nights increasing by only 3.1 per cent. In the same period the major cities' accommodation capacity grew by 31 per cent. Due to this the bed occupancy rate dropped from 53 per cent in 1966 to 42 per cent in 1974. The reasons for this development are threefold: (1) a general decrease in business-based tourism; (2) an above-average decrease of foreign visitors; and (3) a strong increase in accommodation costs which caused many visitors to look for accommodation in smaller towns on the outskirts of the major cities.

Phase III (1975 to 1980): Due to tourism promotion a positive development characterizes this period: tourist nights increased by 21.8 per cent, while the accommodation capacity went up by only 11.7 per cent so that the bed occupancy rate improved to 46 per cent in 1980. One reason for this increase is said to be the creation of a congress and exhibition infrastructure. Thus by 1979 West Berlin held rank seven in the international congress statistics, while it had ranked only seventeenth in 1976. Congresses and exhibitions also add to the attraction of the major cities for foreign visitors so that they gain a greater share of the accommodation. In addition, this phase a growth in private city tourism occurs as major cities attract weekend tourists to spend short breaks for a shopping holiday and/or to participate in cultural events.

Phase IV (1981 to 1987): The development of tourist nights corresponds to that of phase III (+21 per cent), while that of the accommodation capacity (+30.1 per cent) and of the bed occupancy rate (43 per cent) is similar to that of phase II. It is a characteristic of this phase that an increase occurs in all fields of demand. This is demonstrated by the general growth of short breaks undertaken by the German population (1976: 11.8 millions; 1985: 18.8 millions), the growing interest in the city tour programme of German Rail, and the growing numbers of participants in exhibitions and conferences.

According to the official tourism statistics of the Federal Statistical Bureau the development of tourist nights characteristic of phase IV continued until 1990, after which the growth rates dropped below the average. The main reason given for this development is the decrease in the number of foreign guests who had a share of nearly 30 per cent of all guest nights spent in the major cities compared with an average of 12 per cent for all Germans until a downturn occurred after 1990 (Statistisches Bundesamt 1994).

In Germany, tourism geography had been established as an independent branch of the discipline by the end of the 1930s. Since then there have been unresolved problems with the definition of tourism – visits for business reasons not being accepted as belonging to tourism. Although there still is no general definition of tourism available, there is a general agreement that the movements of tourists involve, contrary to day tripping, at least one overnight stay away from home. It is also generally accepted that business-based travels are to be understood as part of tourism for it has been recognized that this segment of tourism, because of its economic importance, is of great significance for city tourism especially.

City tourism can be split up into four main areas as can be seen in Figure 4.1. These will be dealt with in turn. How detailed the analyses will be depends on the availability of statistical data. For example, there is quite a lot of information available as far as exhibitions and fairs are concerned, and to a lesser extent this holds true for congresses and conferences also; however, no exact statistical data are available concerning business travels and commercial tours. The situation for privately motivated sightseeing tourism is even worse. Official tourism statistics give information as to the numbers of arrivals and nights so that the length of stay can be calculated, but there is no information about the reasons for travelling or the demographic and socio-economic structures of the tourists. Such missing information can be drawn from case studies, but one cannot come to general conclusions from these studies. Schreiber (1990) quotes a travel statistic containing information about the bookings of the city tours offered by German Rail in 1985/6: in that year 42,664 bookings were counted for the cities of Hamburg, Munich, Berlin (West), Düsseldorf, Nuremberg, Bremen and Heidelberg; in 1986/7 the number of bookings for these cities had increased by 23.5 per cent to 52,697. It can therefore be concluded that city tourism represents a very attractive offer for private short-break holiday trips. However, the development characterized by these data may by no means be understood as presenting a comprehensive summary of the segment 'privately motivated city tourism' because, according to information from German Rail, data like those quoted above are not available for later years. Another reason why the information about this sector city tourism is incomplete and will remain so is that almost all those visitors arriving by car are not recorded systematically; therefore there are no complete and reliable data available. Thus Vetter argues that in the middle of the 1970s in West Berlin where all incoming visitors were recorded because of the political situation at that time, 75 per cent of the German city tourists preferred to stay with friends or relatives instead of choosing expensive hotels, the outcome being that they were not recorded in the official accommodation statistics (Vetter 1980).

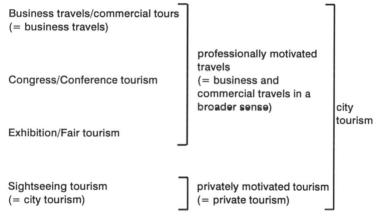

Figure 4.1 The main segments of city tourism in Germany
Source: Schreiber (1990: 21)

LOCATION, DISTRIBUTION AND TYPES OF CITY TOURISM

The locations of the thirty-four cities mentioned above are shown in Figure 4.2. Their distribution can be said to be remarkably uneven, for fourteen of these cities are concentrated in the state of North Rhine-Westphalia, and here in the densely populated and highly industrialized Rhine–Ruhr agglomeration. The uneven distribution is also seen in Table 4.1 which at the same time demonstrates some structural elements of major city tourism and allows comparisons with the German averages.

Figure 4.2 Major cities in Germany with 250,000 or more inhabitants

The data display some of the essential characteristics of major city tourism. The population of the major cities with 250,000 or more inhabitants represents nearly one-quarter (23.2 per cent) of the German population, and nearly three-quarters (72.2 per cent) of the population of all major cities with 100,000 and more inhabitants. The latter have 32.2 per cent of the German population. The significance of these cities as regards tourism is underlined by the fact that nearly one-quarter (23.7 per cent) of all tourist arrivals recorded statistically in Germany in 1993 took place in the thirty-four major cities, whereas the share of all major cities was only slightly higher (26.7 per cent). One feature typical of city tourism is that the share of tourist nights held by the major cities is much lower than that of the arrivals, so it can be argued that city tourists stay in these cities for a very short period of time only. The length of stay criterion marks major city tourism as a kind of tourism of its own because the length of stay is nowhere that low. The contrast between city tourism and other holiday regions and resorts can also be seen in Table 4.1. In Schleswig-Holstein, for example, tourists stay only 2.1 nights in Kiel, but 6.2 nights in the more rurally structured districts the most attractive of which are adjacent to the Baltic Sea and the North Sea. The same goes for Lower Saxony where, again, the coast and the islands of the North Sea attract many tourists; in this state there are also attractive midland regions like the Harz suited for holiday-making. Midland regions are also the holiday regions favoured most in Hesse and Baden-Württemberg (e.g., Black Forest, Odenwald, Taunus, Schwäbische Alb). Bavaria is the German state with by far the highest amount of tourist nights (see Table 4.2) of which only 15.8 per cent are spent in politically independent cities. Of these, however, 68.5 per cent fall to the three major cities of Munich, Nuremberg and Augsburg. The most popular holiday regions of Bavaria are, of course, the Alps, where the length of stay rises to more than eight nights in some areas.

It is very obvious from Table 4.2 that in Germany tourism is well developed in the states of the old Federal Republic, and that the new states in the former German Democratic Republic will have to make great efforts in order to catch up with the 'old' states. There are only five major cities with 250,000 and more inhabitants and another seven with populations of 100,000 to 250,000. According to information from German Rail, trips to cities and historic towns in the former GDR are very well booked at the moment, but there is a possibility that here the 'charm of novelty' is still at work – that is, that the interest in sightseeing tourism will decrease when the Germans have grown accustomed to the still new political situation and previously suppressed demand will be satiated.

City tourism, and especially major city tourism, plays an above average part in the city states of Berlin, Hamburg and Bremen, of course, and in the states of North Rhine-Westphalia, Saxony and Hesse. In all other states tourism is to a greater extent concentrated upon the counties (*Landkreise*). A differentiation according to the 128 tourist regions would not be desirable because the major cities are each a part of these regions so that the statistical data could not be interpreted; moreover, some of the new eastern states have not yet delimited tourist regions (Mecklenburg-Western Pomerania and Thuringia).

Table 4.1 Regional distribution and tourism structure of the major German cities

State ('Bundesland')	Major cities	% of population	% of arrivals	% of nights	Length of stay			Beds (1,000)	Beds/ enterpr.
					Maj. City	County	State		
North-Rhine Westph.	14	32.4	23.3	24.8	2.0	3.7	3.1	70,491	67
Bayern	3	10.7	20.7	19.2	2.0	4.8	3.9	49,865	114
Baden-Württemberg	3	6.4	5.5	5.5	2.0	4.0	3.5	17,904	73
Saxony	3	6.9	4.2	5.0	2.4	3.5	3.0	13,378	152
Hesse	2	5.0	10.7	10.1	2.0	4.1	3.4	25,731	113
Lower Saxony	2	4.2	3.4	3.2	1.9	4.2	3.9	12,172	108
Saxony-Anhalt	2	3.1	1.0	1.0	2.7	2.9	2.8	3,527	93
Berlin	1	18.6	15.0	17.3	2.5	–	2.5	43,219	99
Hamburg	1	9.0	10.5	9.4	1.9	–	1.9	22,933	96
Bremen	1	3.0	2.2	2.0	1.9	–	1.9	5,763	82
Meckl.-W. Pomerania	1	1.3	1.3	1.6	2.2	3.9	3.5	5,116	128
Schleswig-Holstein	1	1.3	1.5	0.9	2.1	6.2	5.6	2,541	77
Federal Republic	34	100.0	100.0	100.0	2.1	4.1	3.3	272,640	84

Source: Statistisches Bundesamt (1995)

Table 4.2 Tourism in the Federal Republic of Germany, 1993

State ('Bundesland')	Nights	%	% cities	% major cities	% counties ('Landkreise')
Bavaria	74,462.5	25.4	15.8	10.9	84.2
Baden-Württemberg	39,071.4	13.4	12.8	5.9	87.2
North Rhine-Westphalia	35,310.1	12.1	31.9	29.5	68.1
Lower Saxony	32,274.6	11.0	7.3	4.1	92.7
Hesse	26,870.5	9.2	19.5	15.7	80.5
Schleswig-Holstein	21,988.7	7.5	6.5	1.8	93.5
Rhineland-Palatinate	20,833.4	7.1	11.0	–	89.0
Mecklenburg-W. Pomerania	7,606.9	2.6	20.6	8.9	79.4
Berlin	7,322.3	2.5	100.0	100.0	–
Saxony	7,142.2	2.4	30.6	29.2	69.4
Thuringia	5,694.4	2.0	17.6	–	82.4
Brandenburg	4,007.0	1.4	15.5	–	84.5
Hamburg	3,960.1	1.4	100.0	100.0	–
Saxony-Anhalt	3,367.6	1.2	14.4	12.9	85.6
Saarland	1,869.9	0.6	–	–	100.0
Bremen	976.9	0.3	100.0	100.0	–
Fedferal Republic	292,758.5	100.0	19.6	15.4	80.4

Source: Statistisches Bundesamt (1995)

The accommodation capacity of the major cities with 250,000 and more inhabitants amounted to 272,640 in 1993 (Table 4.1), and that number represented 13.3 per cent of all tourist beds. Apart from the city-states Berlin, Hamburg and Bremen, of course, the highest share is reached in North Rhine-Westphalia (29.4 per cent) and Saxony (25.7 per cent).

It can be considered to be a typical feature of major city tourism that the bed occupancy rate is rather balanced over the year. The more exhibitions and congresses that take place, the more there are marked declines in the curves of the bed occupancy shown in the summer months (which are, of course, the main holiday months), and about the end of the year and the beginning of the new year, respectively.

Schreiber (1990) groups the major cities into four types using such criteria as bed capacity in hotels with 100 or more beds, the seating capacity (in rows) in congress and multi-purpose halls, the indoor exhibition space (square metres), and the visitor space (square metres) in museums and galleries. This classification was applied to twenty-nine major cities which recorded 300,000-plus tourist nights in 1987; all were located in the old Federal Republic. If one concentrates only upon the major cities with 250,000 and more inhabitants the number of cities is reduced to twenty-one. The following is a short presentation of the four types of city tourism:

Type A: Cities of this type are very well suited for sightseeing tourists because most of them have historic city centres. Nearly half of all tourist nights are spent in the months from June to September which can be understood as an indication of privately motivated tourism. Individual studies of cities of this type confirm that nearly 60 per cent of all tourist nights fall to private city tourism. Only three of the major cities with 250,000 and more inhabitants belong to this type: Aachen, Augsburg and Kiel. The other seven cities of this type have a size of 100,000 to 250,000 inhabitants.

Type B: The business-based city tourism is of dominant significance in these cities for 75 per cent of all tourist nights fall to this type of visitor. Contrary to type A, there is less demand for accommodation in the summer months June, July and August, with demand peaking in September, October and May. The share of foreign visitors amounts to more than 30 per cent, and no decrease of demand can be observed in the summer months due to the fact that foreign tourists attend exhibitions and congresses and come for sightseeing purposes. Major cities of this type are Bielefeld, Bonn, Bremen, Dortmund, Karlsruhe, Mainz, Mannheim, Münster and Wiesbaden. Of these only Mainz has less than 250,000 inhabitants.

Type C: The characteristic feature of major cities of this type is the huge supply of exhibition space when compared to the cities of the types A and B. Since exhibition and fairs take place to a large extent in the months February to May and September to November, there is a maximum demand for accommodation at these times of the year. In addition to this, there is also a strong accommodation demand generated through congresses and other business-based tourism so that about 80 per cent of all tourist nights are generated by business-related visits. Because of special exhibitions and fairs like the Christkindl Market in Nuremberg, the demand for accommodation in cities of this type is higher than in the cities of types A and B even in the months December and January. The major cities of this type – Düsseldorf, Essen, Hanover, Cologne, Nuremberg and Stuttgart – all have 250,000 or more inhabitants.

Type D: The subdivision into two types which Schreiber had developed for the year 1987 cannot be upheld for 1993, because the special situation of West Berlin has changed markedly since 1990. Schreiber (1990: 54) argued that the low percentage of tourist nights falling to foreigners and their above-average length of stay make West Berlin different from the other major cities of Type D. These arguments are no longer justified, although the share of nights falling to foreign visitors is still rather low (25.1 per cent) compared with that of Frankfurt/Main (56.9 per cent); length of stay, however (2.4 and 1.9 nights, respectively), has become rather similar.

The extremely high share of tourist nights falling to foreigners in Frankfurt/Main can be explained because of the existence of the Frankfurt airport – a lot of foreigners arriving at Frankfurt by airplane spend one night in Frankfurt before continuing their travel in Germany or central Europe. The average share of tourist nights spent by foreigners in the cities of this type amounted to 34.5 per cent in 1993; Hamburg and Berlin stay below the average, while Frankfurt and Munich exceed it. In 1987 the share of nights falling to foreigners in Frankfurt, Munich and Hamburg reached 45 per cent (Schreiber 1990: 56), the difference in percentages reflecting the already mentioned general decrease of foreigners visiting Germany. The increased share in Berlin mirrors the nomalization of the political situation since 1991.

In Table 4.3 the classification data used by Schreiber have been compiled in an as updated version as possible. The only characteristic where that was possible for all major cities is the number of tourist nights. A comparison of the 1986 and 1993 data shows an increase in all major cities with 250,000 or more inhabitants, and that there are considerable differences depending upon the type of city tourism. Thus the type A cities had a growth of 13.8 per cent between 1986 and 1993, those of the type B of 27.7 per cent, those of the type C of 24.1 per cent and those of type D of 4.3 per cent. Taking the new political situation into consideration, however, the D-type cities have an increase rate of 14.7 per cent because of the inclusion of East Berlin.

To include the five major cities located in the new eastern states of the Federal Republic into the major city tourism classification is no easy task, for only when the phase of adjustment has finished will comparisons between major cities in the western and eastern states become possible. Under the condition that the same threshold values can be applied today as at the time the above-quoted classification was carried out, the cities Chemnitz and Halle/Saale could not be included because the number of tourist nights does not reach 300,000. Leipzig is certainly a city which could preserve its fame as a long-established exhibition and fair city, but this function has been reduced and the city has not yet regained its old position. Limitations like that can be adduced for the other major cities of the eastern states (Dresden, Magdeburg, Rostock), too, and one should perhaps wait another five years for a classification of these five cities.

EXHIBITIONS AND FAIRS

The segment 'exhibitions and fairs' is the statistically best documented of all segments of city tourism because it was realized very early that cities can profit from the kind of tourism generated through such events.

Leipzig is the most famous German exhibition and fair city, such events having taken place since the thirteenth century, mainly because of its extraordinarily good location within central Europe. In Cologne exhibition tourism has developed only since 1924 (Knoll 1988). For Leipzig and Cologne (and for other exhibition and fair centres) their geographical positions as traffic junctions (railways, ships, roads, etc.) were very important for the origin of exhibitions and fairs: both exhibitors and visitors could easily reach these places.

Table 4.3 Types and structural characteristics of selected major cities

Major city	Tourist nights	Bed capacity in big hotels	Seating capacity in congress halls	Indoor exhibition space (sq. m)	Museums/ galleries (sq. m.)	City tourism type
Aachen	647,340	1,000*	3,500*	–*	8,427	A
Augsburg	448,577	1,000*	7,130	18,500	12,130	A
Kiel	390,064	1,000*	6,500*	9,300*	6,507	A
Bielefeld	388,838	1,000*	3,600	20,000*	2,886*	B
Bonn	1,107,313	2,500*	5,200*	–*	26,585	B
Bremen	828,840	2,600*	7,500*	35,700*	24,750	B
Dortmund	496,467	1,100*	18,975	41,215	27,870	B
Karlsruhe	517,788	1,800*	18,000	20,000	22,296	B
Mannheim	517,212	1,600*	4,100*	45,200*	18,421	B
Münster	1,140,934	500*	6,900*	22,000*	21,166	B
Wiesbaden	1,013,818	2,500*	6,800*	20,000*	6,804	B
Düsseldorf	1,906,228	6,300*	5,013	198,400	27,530	C
Essen	821,539	1,800*	12,500	90,000	33,489	C
Hanover	969,164	3,800*	5,220	474,470	24,232	C
Cologne	2,492,942	5,700*	11,808	260,000	36,095	C
Nuremberg	1,532,237	3,600*	7,550	101,000	71,617	C
Stuttgart	1,285,811	3,100*	8,973	59,500	40,791	C
Berlin	7,292,337	14,700*	13,219	103,500	144,381	D
Frankfurt	3,215,722	11,400*	14,311	273,757	48,650	D
Hamburg	3,960,104	10,700*	11,206	62,500	77,951	D
Munich	6,094,976	20,200*	6,994	125,000	144,691	D

Sources: Schreiber (1990: 50); Statistisches Bundesamt (1995); Deutscher Städtetag, Köln (1994); Gruner & Jahr & Co. (1992)
Note: * Update impossible because of lack of data

One of the basics of modern city tourism, especially for the major cities, is the existence of exhibitions and fairs. This element of city tourism has been gaining importance since the 1960s because it was realized that exhibitions – especially those with international participants – are of very high importance for the accommodation industry. This development is documented by the fact that in the statistical yearbook for the Federal Republic there are listed only three cities (Frankfurt/Main, Hanover, Cologne) with five exhibitions in 1963. Thirty years later the number of cities involved increased to fifteen and the number of exhibitions and fairs to 102. The new political situation hasn't had much influence upon this development for in 1993 Leipzig was the only major city of the new eastern states to be included in the uplisting of exhibition and fair cities. The five-year period 1983 to 1988 is one of stagnation, with the number of cities with fairs or exhibitions remaining stable at twelve, and the number of events increasing just by one from fifty-seven to fifty-eight. The number of visitors amounted to 6.571 million in 1983, decreased by 7.6 per cent in 1988 and then rose sharply by 50.2 per cent to 9.121 million in 1993. In the latter year the share of foreign visitors was 17.5 per cent. It is obvious from these figures that exhibition and fair tourism will have a strong influence upon the bed-occupancy rates of the major cities. There are, of course, two categories of attendants: the exhibitors, who come for professional reasons and stay in the city for the whole exhibition or fair period, and visitors, who mostly come for one day only, attend the event for professional reasons, too, but also visit for sightseeing and/or entertainment reasons. The first category of attendants usually stay in middle- and upper-class hotels and are of great importance for the city tourism because of the economic effect; the second category consists mostly of day visitors who don't make use of the tourism infrastructure to a very large extent.

In the AUMA handbook of exhibitions and fairs in Germany for 1995, 307 exhibitions and fairs are listed for twenty-two of the major cities with 250,000 and more inhabitants. Of these, 47 per cent are said to have a mostly regional catchment area and 53 per cent to be of national and international importance. The top-ranking cities for exhibitions with a regional catchment area are Leipzig (21), Hamburg (20), Stuttgart (18), Dortmund (16) and Nuremberg (13). The leading cities for exhibitions and fairs of the second kind are Düsseldorf (30), Frankfurt/Main (22), Cologne (21), Munich (21), Nuremberg (15), Hanover (13) and Berlin (11). From 1990 to 1993 the number of visitors to exhibitions and fairs of the first type increased by 3.3 per cent and reached nearly 9 million; for the second type the figures are 9.4 per cent and, again, nearly 9 million.

A necessary condition for the organization of exhibitions and fairs is, of course, the existence of facilities, i.e., indoor and outdoor space. In Germany, cities, and not only major ones, began to build exhibition and congress facilities in the 1970s; later this development was supplemented by the trend to extend the existing facilities – for example, to enlarge the exhibition space, to build new indoor facilities or modernize old ones. This trend was partly caused by competition pressure and the growing numbers of German and foreign exhibitors: the square metres of rented exhibition space grew by 43.7 per cent between 1983 and 1993, and at the same time the number of exhibitors increased from 81,638 to 131,015 (+60.5 per cent) of whom 39.9 per cent and 44.0 per cent, respectively, were foreigners. For seventeen cities, four of which have less than 250,000 inhabitants, the indoor exhibition space was extended from 659,848 square metres in 1971 to 1,812,333 square metres in 1991 (+174.7 per cent) (Gruner & Jahr 1992).

For the year 1991 there is some information available for exhibitions and fairs in selected major cities. The exhibitions and fairs organized by the AMK in Berlin were attended by 8,616 exhibitors, 56.4 per cent of these coming from abroad. Of the visitors, 21.9 per cent came for professional reasons, and 51.2 per cent were not residents of Berlin; another important feature for that year was the high share of visitors coming from the new states of the former GDR. The economic effect of the exhibitors and visitors coming from outside Berlin is estimated at about DM 575 million. In Frankfurt 36,300 exhibitors were counted at twenty-five exhibitions and fairs (+ 12 per cent compared with 1989); 49 per cent of the exhibitors were foreigners, and the 2.6 million visitors represented 138 countries. In Cologne 21,000 exhibitors from ninety-seven countries were visited by 979,811 professionals from 149 countries. In Cologne, as in Berlin, the abolition of the Iron Curtain had strong effects upon the structure of the exhibitors and the professional visitors, for in 1991 more than 300 exhibiting enterprises and 400 professional visitors from the new states in Eastern Germany were recorded compared to a maximum of twenty exhibitors and about 500 professional visitors in former years. The same goes for participants from Eastern European countries: 300 instead of 100 exhibitors and about 12,999 instead of nearly 2,500 visitors (all data from Gruner & Jahr AG & Co 1992).

In Table 4.4 data about the exhibition and fair situation in major cities with more than 250,000 inhabitants are collected from several sources. The significance of the major cities as locations of exhibitions and fairs is emphasized by the fact that in 1992 63.6 per cent of all such events took place in them. The correlation between city size and number of exhibitions and fairs is underlined by the fact that the share of the major cities with a population of 500,000 and more amounted to 49.2 per cent of all events and 77.3 per cent of all exhibitions and fairs having taken place in the major cities with 250,000 and more inhabitants.

Using the example of Munich the economic effect of exhibition and fair tourism for major cities was analysed by Becker for the year 1985. In order to take into consideration all components of this segment of city tourism, he calculated the expenditures for two main groups of persons: first, the exhibitors and their employees, and second, the visitors. Detailed information about the daily expenditures were gathered for all persons attending the exhibitions and fairs and spending at least one night in Munich and its surroundings. The average total expenses of the visitors amounted to DM 302 each and those of the stand employees to DM 271 each. The percentages for six different categories of expenses were as follows (visitors/employees): accommodation 49/51, food 27/30, entertainment 7/5, shopping 9/5, transport 3/2, and other items 5/7 (Becker 1986). In addition, Becker analysed the impact of fairs and exhibitions on other economic branches (e.g., transport and the catering trade).

Table 4.4 Exhibitions and fairs in German cities with more than 250,000 inhabitants

Major city	Population (Dec. 1992)	*Exhibitions and fairs 1992*		*Exhibitions and fairs 1995* International /national		Regional	
		No.	%	No.	%	No.	%
Berlin	3,446,031	40	11.1	11	6.8	9	6.3
Hamburg	1,668,757	33	9.1	5	3.1	20	13.9
Munich	1,229,052	22	6.1	21	9.2	2	1.4
Cologne	956,690	19	5.2	21	12.9	1	0.7
Frankfurt	654,079	28	7.8	22	13.5	7	4.9
Essen	629,989	16	4.4	7	4.3	7	4.9
Dortmund	601,007	21	5.8	0		16	11.1
Stuttgart	591,946	32	8.5	9	5.5	18	12.5
Düsseldorf	577,561	27	7.5	30	18.4	1	0.7
Bremen	552,999	9	2.5	2	1.2	1	0.7
Duisburg	537,441	1	0.3				
Hanover	517,476	17	4.7	13	8.0	6	4.2
Leipzig	503,191	15	4.2	5	3.1	21	14.6
Nuremberg	497,498	30	8.4	15	9.2	13	9.0
Dresden	485,132	6	1.6	0		4	2.8
Bochum	398,578						
Wuppertal	385,463						
Bielefeld	322,132	3	0.8				
Mannheim	314,685	3	0.8	0		1	0.7
Halle	303,019	1	0.3				
Bonn	296,244						
Gelsenkirchen	293,839	1	0.3				
Chemnitz	287,511	8	2.2				
Karlsruhe	278,579	9	2.5	1	0.6	6	4.2
Magdeburg	275,238	1	0.3	0		2	1.4
Münster	264,181	2	0.5			3	2.1
Wiesbaden	264,022	11	3.0	0		1	0.7
Mönchenglad-bach	262,581						
Augsburg	259,884	5	1.7	1	0.6	3	2.1
Braunschweig	259,127	1	0.3	0		1	0.6
		361	100.0	163	100.0	143	100.0

Sources: Deutscher Städtetag (1994); m & a Messen (1991); AUMA (1995a, 1995b)

CONGRESSES AND CONFERENCES

Congresses, conferences and other meetings are rather well documented as far as the distribution of locations and facilities is concerned; as to the number of such events, however, the situation is less satisfying because many such meetings are not recorded statistically and numbers of participants are also not known for all congresses and conferences. Generally speaking, the statistical basis for statements about congress and conference tourism with respect to major cities can be said to be rather insufficient because there is no comprehensive and detailed data about congresses and their participants available. Hank-Haase (1992) points out that in the recent past a new trend can be observed which seems to be very logical. There is a growing number of congresses which take place in combination with exhibitions and fairs and vice versa, because congress participants can also visit the exhibition or fair if there is a thematic connection. One reason why this kind of combination is very successful is that such events show above-average increases in rates of participation compared with the traditional exhibition or congress.

Hank-Haase (1992) also emphasizes that there are some locational factors which strongly influence the decision as to whether a city is acceptable as a congress and conference place or not. The concentration of conference places is to a very high degree identical with the population density (see the Ruhr in North Rhine-Westphalia). A comparison of Figure 4.3 with Figure 4.2 demonstrates that nearly all major cities are at the same time congress and conference cities.

It can be gathered from Figure 4.3, however, that another category of conference place plays an important role, especially in the southern and south-eastern parts of Germany. This is the health resort and spa where often conference and congress facilities are available and normally all types of accommodation as well as sufficient bed capacity do exist. As far as overall conference capacity is concerned, these places cannot compete with the major cities. Another very important locational factor is accessibility by public and private transport. In this respect, the major cities are normally much better located than other communities because in many cases such locational advantages have been the reason why these communities became major cities. The shorter a congress or a conference is, the more significant the factor of 'accessibility' becomes. The attractiveness of the surrounding landscape plays a much more important role outside the densely populated and economically important regions.

Another positive locational factor has been mentioned already: cities where exhibitions and fairs take place are preferred as congress and conference locations because of the good technical and accommodation infrastructure. Hank-Haase lists ten criteria which are said to be favourable for the present situation and future development of congress and conference tourism in major cities. With reference to the year 1992, twenty-four cities, of which only four have less than 250,000 inhabitants (Darmstadt, Freiburg, Heidelberg, Mainz), were checked and a rating was carried out as to their suitability as congress places (Table 4.5). City tourism, especially as far as exhibitions and fairs as well as congresses and conferences are concerned, exerts a strong direct and indirect economic impact.

Major cities
● (> 100,000 inhabitants)
o Spas
• Other conference places

Figure 4.3 Conference places in Germany
Source: Hank-Haase (1992: 26)

Studies about the expenditure of participants in congress and conference tourism allow relatively exact calculations about income received from such tourism. The average expenditures for ten major cities with a population of 250,000 or more (Berlin, Hamburg, Bremen, Frankfurt, Hanover, Cologne, Düsseldorf, Munich, Stuttgart, Bielefeld) amounted to DM 134 per person per day. Of this 36.3 per cent was spent on accommodation, 45.2 per cent on food, 13.7 per cent on shopping and 4.8 per cent on entertainment and sport (Koch 1980). According to Henseling (1984) about 60–70 per cent of the total expenditures are spent on accommodation and food, and this percentage varies depending on the duration of the event, the type of city the congress takes place in, socio-economic and demographic variables and the source of financing the participation. Schreiber points out that the character of the congress will also influence the total of the daily expenditures. Thus at a medical congress the average expenditure of each participant who stayed overnight was DM 282, at a business-oriented congress DM 238, and at a cultural event DM 179. Comparing this data with that quoted first (see p. 105), one has to take into consideration the increase in prices and the higher costs of living. The average daily expenditure rose to about DM 260 in 1986; since the accommodation costs nearly quadrupled from 1980 to 1992, while the cost of food remained relatively stable, the share for the different categories would also have changed. According to Hank-Haase (1992), in 1986 the average daily expenditure amounted to DM 173 in major cities, while the overall average for all congress places amounted to only DM 147. Leyers (1993) summarizes the factors influencing the expenditure behaviour of congress participants in major cities: (1) size of the community where the congress takes place: in major cities more money is spent because of a broader and more attractive spectrum of offers; (2) kind of congress: international congress participants spend more than those attending working meetings; (3) duration: the shorter the congress, the higher the expenditure per day; (4) socio-economic position of the participants: the higher the position, the higher the expenditure; and (5) origin of the participants: foreign participants spend about 50 per cent more per day than national participants. Thus in Münster the congress participant spent on the average DM 248 per day in 1992, an amount similar to that in Mainz. Of this amount, 50 per cent was spent on accommodation, 17.7 per cent on food, 12.5 per cent on shopping, 6.5 per cent on cultural events and entertainment, and 13.3 per cent on other items (e.g., public transport) (Leyers 1993). Although the expenditure total per day is distinctly higher in Wiesbaden (DM 369.95 in 1991/2) than in Münster, the percentages of the expenditure categories mentioned above (Koch and Leyers) are rather similar: accommodation 47.4 per cent, food 23 per cent, shopping 17.9 per cent, leisure and cultural events 4 per cent, other items 7.6 per cent (Hank-Haase 1992).

Taking into consideration the multiplier effect, congress tourism induced an income of about DM 24 millions in Münster which corresponded to an additional income per inhabitant of DM 92 in 1991 (Leyers 1993). The income effect of congresses and conferences per inhabitant of sixty-eight major cities amounted to DM 48; in Frankfurt it was DM 96 (1990), in Berlin DM 137 (Hank-Haase 1992), and in Wiesbaden DM 155 (Hank-Haase 1992). It becomes obvious from this data that the economic effect of congress and conference tourism must not be underestimated in the economy of the major cities.

Table 4.5 Criteria of suitability of selected major cities as conference and congress places

City	Direct Motorway Connection	IC Stop	Distance to Airport max. 50 km	Fairs	University	Accomm. Cap. ≥ 5,000	Tourist Intensity ≥ B 250 n/100 i	Average Acc. Size > 70 beds	Largest Congress Hall > 2,500	Hotels of Internat. Chains	Points
Aachen	x	x	o	o	x	o	x	o	x	x	6
Berlin	x	x	x	x	x	x	x	x	x	x	10
Bonn	x	x	x	o	x	x	x	o	o	x	7
Bremen	x	x	x	x	x	o	x	x	x	x	8
Cologne	x	x	x	x	x	x	x	x	x	x	10
Darmstadt	x	x	x	o	x	o	x	o	o	x	6
Dortmund	x	x	o	x	x	o	o	o	o	x	6
Düsseldorf	x	x	x	x	x	x	x	x	x	x	10
Essen	x	x	x	x	x	o	o	o	x	x	7
Frankfurt	x	x	x	x	x	x	x	x	x	x	10
Freiburg	x	x	o	o	x	o	x	o	x	x	6
Hamburg	x	x	x	x	x	x	x	x	x	x	10
Hanover	x	x	x	x	x	x	x	x	x	x	9
Heidelberg	x	x	o	o	x	x	x	o	o	x	6
Karlsruhe	x	x	o	x	x	o	o	o	x	x	6
Leipzig	x	x	x	x	x	x	x	x	o	x	8
Mainz	x	x	x	x	x	o	x	x	o	x	9
Mannheim	x	x	o	x	x	o	o	x	o	o	5
Münster	x	x	o	o	x	x	x	x	x	x	8
Munich	x	x	x	x	x	x	x	x	x	x	10
Nuremberg	x	x	x	x	o	x	x	o	x	x	8
Saarbrücken	x	x	x	x	x	o	o	o	x	x	7
Stuttgart	x	x	x	x	o	x	o	o	x	x	8
Wiesbaden	x	x	x	x	o	x	x	x	x	x	9

Source: Hank-Haase (1992: 47–8)

SIGHTSEEING TOURISM

While exhibition and fair tourism as well as congress and conference tourism can both be considered as kinds of professional tourism, sightseeing tourism can be said to be city tourism strictly speaking (see Figure 4.2). This kind of tourism comprises several variants such as shopping, visiting museums, galleries and historical buildings, attending cultural events, etc. It is very difficult to get exact and reliable data about this type of tourism because the recording of data is extremely problematic. If it is accepted that city tourism must be connected with at least one overnight stay, many activities or visitors can be excluded.

The booking figures for city tours offered by German Rail mentioned previously can be considered as indicators of the increasing popularity of city tourism. The analysis of the 1995 catalogues of seven enterprises offering city tours gives evidence of the obvious appeal of this kind of tourism. Seventy-four destinations are offered of which more than one-fourth (twenty = 27 per cent) belong to the major towns dealt with here. Another eighteen destinations, among which Kiel, Rostock and Aachen are to be found, belong to the major cities with 100,000 to 250,000 population so that the share of the major cities of all city tour destinations amounts to 51.4 per cent. 'Ameropa' alone offers sixty-two different city tour destinations, of which 25.8 per cent are to major cities with ⩾ 250,000 inhabitants; another 19.4 per cent are to major cities of the smaller category. In the 'Ameropa' programme smaller towns and cities, of which quite a few are health resorts and spas, are of marginally greater significance than the major cities. Several of the smaller major cities one can go to with German Rail were classified by Schreiber as type A cities – that is, cities which are visited by tourists mostly for sightseeing reasons. There are other travel agents, however, who offer only large major cities as tour destinations (ADAC: seven out of ten; Wolters: seven).

In his 1987 study of city tourism in Mainz Schreiber emphasizes the difficulty with this segment of city tourism because very few reliable large studies have been carried out. The data collected by Schreiber appear to be characteristic of major city tourism, so they will be referred to here.

As stated before, most sightseeing tourists visit cities because of the cultural, historical and architectural attractions they have to offer. Other visitors include those who live in the surrounding areas and come only to shop or to make use of the facilities Mainz has to offer; Schreiber excluded these from his study. Contrary to the business-based tourist, sightseeing tourists were not necessarily expected to stay in Mainz for one night.

The first interesting result of Schreiber's study is that 34 per cent of the business-based tourists also participated in sightseeing activities while in Mainz. There are, however, some significant differences between the business-based tourists on the one hand, and the privately motivated sight-seeing visitors on the other. With the latter the gender proportions are nearly even, whilst with the first males are predominant. Another typical feature of the sightseeing tourists is that only about one-quarter are travel-ling alone; the highest percentage falls to groups consisting of two per-sons (51 per cent), so that the average group size is 2.18 persons. The age structure of the sightseeing tourists is much more balanced than that of the professional tourists, who reach their highest shares (more than 20 per cent) in the age groups 26 to 35, 36 to 45, and 46 to 55 years; the sightsee-ing tourists, on the other hand, reach shares of about 20 per cent in the age groups 16 to 25, 26 to 35, 36 to 45, 46 to 55 years, older persons having a greater share than in the business-based tourist category.

A high percentage of the sightseeing tourists have attended grammar schools, colleges or universities (Mainz 67 per cent), 37 per cent are employed as civil servants in leading positions, and another 20 per cent are pupils or students. About one-third of these tourists are foreigners, 84 per cent of which stop only for a short break in Mainz. Thirty-eight per cent of the German tourists, many of whom come as day visitors, only start their trip in the surrounding and neighbouring states of Rhineland-Palatinate and Hesse. The densely populated agglomerations of the Ruhr (North Rhine-Westphalia) and of the Rhine-Main (Hesse) are significant regions of visitor origin. Most sightseeing visitors come by car (56 per cent) and train (29 per cent). Coach travel is not very important (7 per cent), but this mode of transport has gained in importance during the last decade, especially in city tourism.

According to Schreiber's survey most of the sightseeing tourists stay in the city only for a few hours, just 31 per cent of them spending one night or more in Mainz. Two-thirds of those who spend one or more nights stay with relatives or friends, another 20 per cent staying in youth hostels or in smaller hotels; only 15 per cent choose more expensive hotels. Sixty per cent of all sightseeing visitors to the city would consider spending a short holiday in Mainz. The average length of stay amounts to 5.2 hours. Since most visitors arrive in the morning and leave in the afternoon, the catering enterprises do profit from the sightseeing city tourism to some extent. For many of the tourists coming to Mainz, either as the tour destination or in the course of a round trip, 'major city tourism' is the leading motivation for the visit. For those visitors who stay for more than one night sightsee-ing tours in the surroundings of Mainz are an important activity. The same probably goes for Münster, which can be used as a starting point for cycling tours in surrounding areas in the course of which visits to castles and historic small towns are very popular.

A very problematic point is the calculation of the economic effect of sightseeing tourism. Schreiber points out that expenditure correlates with length of stay, a result which is not very surprising. However, since there is little reliable data about the economic impact of sightseeing city tourism available, Schreiber's calculation of the economic effect seems to be very interesting. The sum total of all expenditure by sightseeing tourists for one year amounts to DM 38.8 million: 60.6 per cent of this is spent on shopping (predominantly by the day visitors), 23.5 per cent on food and beverages, 5.9 per cent on accommodation, and 10.1 per cent on other items such as transport, admission fees, etc. This spending data emphasizes the economic significance of sightseeing tourism which is an important part of major city tourism. In other cities like Berlin, Hamburg, Stuttgart, Munich, Bochum and Frankfurt expenditure on cultural events would have to be added; when booking city tours with Ameropa one can book the accommodation, the railway ticket and a theatre or musical performance ticket at the same time.

According to tourists, the most attractive sight by far in Mainz is the cathedral (96 per cent). Other sights are the Gutenberg Museum, St Stephan's church and the historic city centre. Knoll quotes a study of 1972 in which 58 per cent of tourists interviewed said that their main reason for coming to Cologne was to see the cathedral. Other important reasons were the positive image of Cologne (19 per cent), professional and business contracts (17 per cent), the river Rhine (12 per cent) and shopping (8 per cent). For three out of four foreign visitors the city of Cologne was the main reason for coming, but the same was true only for one of four German visitors for whom the fame of the city and the visit to relatives or friends is an important reason to come to Cologne. For 47 per cent of all tourists coming to Cologne the city itself was the only place visited. Cologne is the main tour destination for 80 per cent of the German, 60 per cent of the European and 25 per cent of the visitors from other continents (Knoll 1988).

A comparison of the economic effect of the three segments of major city tourism dealt with so far demonstrates that privately motivated sightseeing city tourism cannot compete with business based exhibition/fair and congress/conference tourism. It must not be underestimated, however, especially as far as the multiplier effect is concerned. It has to be pointed out, however, that to date not enough studies have been carried out so that there is a lack of knowledge in many respects.

CITY TOURISM AND CITY PLANNING

In Germany, major city tourism has had no great direct influence upon the city planning process. Knoll reports that in Cologne after the Second World War the reconstruction of the bombed area around the cathedral, which was traditionally the main location area of visitor accommodation, was carried out taking into consideration the demands of tourism (Knoll 1988). Cologne probably can be considered as an exception to the rule, because in other major cities the accommodation enterprises were usually not concentrated into such a small area.

In most other major cities tourism represents just one aspect of the urban economy and of urban life. Since tourism has become a booming economic branch of business – a trend which it is thought will continue – tourism development and promotion is used as an instrument of improving the economic structure, not only of peripheral regions but also of towns and cities. In the planning policies of major cities tourism certainly does not take a primary position, but neither is it completely neglected.

Since the 1970s, cities have tried to improve their images in order to make themselves attractive as locations for economic enterprises, and tourism is just one of the many branches which have helped to improve the economic situation and to create new jobs. In her introductory remarks about the term 'image', May (1986) points out that a positive attitude towardss a city can have the effect of making negative features less obvious.

For many cities the creation of a new image, or the improvement of an existing one, can lead to an increase in appeal. As far as city tourism is concerned that can mean that the cities gain appeal as trip destinations. In a time when the challenge of high unemployment rates requires special job creation strategies, city tourism can be one means of partly overcoming such difficulties. Apart from that, city tourism can contribute to the urban economy to a considerable degree.

CONCLUSION

City tourism, especially in the major cities, has undergone a very positive development since the Second World War. It did of course exist before that time as Knoll has demonstrated, but only with the expansion of exhibitions and fairs as well as of congresses and conferences. Although the major cities cannot compete with the other German tourist regions, as far as tourist arrivals and nights are concerned they nowadays represent a branch of the urban economy that is of growing importance since other economic branches depend on it to some extent.

The major cities are interested in promoting and developing city tourism because they can thus improve their images. From the economic point of view, exhibitions and fairs as well as congresses and conferences are the most important variants of city tourism because the average expenditures of business-based tourists are much higher than those of the sight-seeing city tourists. It would be a mistake, however, to underestimate the significance of this segment of city tourism, and it will certainly be necessary in the future to analyse this part of the city tourism more thoroughly in order to get information as reliable as that on the other two segments.

ACKNOWLEDGEMENT

The author would like to thank Andrea Leyers very much indeed for assistance and help with the passages on exhibition and fair tourism as well as on conference and congress tourism.

REFERENCES

Akademie für Raumforschung und Landesplanung (ed.) (1982) 'Analysen und Fallstudien aus Hessen, Rheinland-Pfalz und Saarland', *Forschungs- und Sitzungsberichte* 142 (Hannover).

Ausstellungs- und Messeausschuβ der Deutschen Wirtschaft e.V. (AUMA) (1993) *Tätigkeitsbericht 1993,* Köln.

Ausstellungs- und Messeausschuβ der Deutschen Wirtschaft e.V. (AUMA) (1995a) *Handbuch Messeplatz Deutschland 1995*, Köln.

Ausstellungs- und Messeausschuβ der Deutschen Wirtschaft e.V. (AUMA) (1995b) *Handbuch Regionale Ausstellungen 1995*, Köln.

Becker, W. (1986) 'Messen und Ausstellungen – eine sozialgeographische Un tersuchung am Beispiel München', *Münchner Studien zur Sozial- und Wirtschaftsgeographie* 31 (Kallmünz/Regensburg).

Deutscher Städtetag (ed.) (1994) *Statistisches Jahrbuch Deutscher Gemeinden. 80. Jahrgang 1993,* Köln.

Gruner & Jahr AG & Co (eds) (1992) *Messen, Ausstellungen, Kongresse*, Branchenbild Nr. 8, Hamburg.

Hank-Haase, G. (1992) 'Der Tagun- und Kongreβreiseverkehr als wirtschaftlicher Faktor in deutschen Groβstädten unter besonderer Berücksichtigung von Wiesbaden', *Materialien zur Fremdenverkehrsgeographie*, no. 27 (Trier).

Henseling, E. (1984) 'Der Fremdenverkehr in der Stadt Münster unter besonderer Berücksichtigung des Kongress- und Tagungsverkehrs', *Arbeitsgemeinschaft Angewandte Geographie Münster*, Arbeitsberichte 05 (Münster).

Knoll, G.M. (1988) 'Herausbildung, Dynamik und Persistenz von Standorten und Standortgemeinschaften im Groβstadttourismus der Innenstadt von Köln im 19. und 20. Jahrhundert – Eine historisch-geographische Untersuchung', *Geostudien*, Sonderfolge 1 (Köln).

Koch, A. (1980) 'Die Ausgaben im Fremdenverkehr in der Bundesrepublik Deutschland', *Schriftenreihe des Deutschen Wirtschaftswissenschaftlichen Instituts für Fremdenverkehr an der Universität München*, no. 35 (München).

Leyers, A. (1993) 'Kongreßtourismus in Münster – Eine Studie der Angebots- und Nachfragesituation und der Entwicklungstendenzen', Unpublished thesis, Münster.

May, M. (1986) 'Städtetourismus als Teil der kommunalen Imageplanung, dargestellt am Beispiel der kreisfreien Städte im Ruhrgebiet', *Materialien zur Fremdenverkehrsgeographie* no. 14 (Trier).

m & a Messen, Ausstellungen und Kongress GmbH. (ed.) (1991) *m & a messeplaner* 91/92, Frankfurt.

Schreiber, M. (1990) 'Großstadttourismus in der Bundesrepublik Deutschland am Beispiel einer segmentorientierten Untersuchung der Stadt Mainz', *Mainzer Geographische Studien*, no. 35 (Mainz).

Statistisches Bundesamt (ed.) Statistisches Jahrbuch der Bundesrepublik Deutschland, vols 1964, 1969, 1974, 1979, 1984, 1994, 1995, Wiesbaden.

Statistisches Bundesamt (ed.) (1994) *Tourismus in Zahlen 1993*, Wiesbaden.

Vetter, F. (1980) 'Strukturelle Veränderungen des mittelheuropäischen Großstadttourismus', pp. 209–14, in P. Schnell and P. Weber (eds) *Agglomeration und Freizeitraum*, Münstersche Geographische Arbeiten 7, Paderborn.

5 City tourism in Spain

A recently discovered potential

Gerda K. Priestley

INTRODUCTION

In Spain according to the most recent census (Instituto Nacional de Estadística 1992) there were twenty-one major cities in 1991 (see Table 5.1). Of these only seven had more than 400,000 inhabitants and only three (Madrid, Barcelona and Valencia) had over one million. In a country where tourism, mainly based on the sun/sand/sea trilogy, plays a leading role in the economy, and where fifteen of the twenty-one major cities have coastal locations (see Figure 5.1), the task of distinguishing between seaside resorts and true urban tourism destinations is not always an easy one. Las Palmas de Gran Canaria, for example, a busy port and provincial capital, has a kilometre-long beach-front lined with hotels. It is, at the same time, both a seaside resort and an industrial and commercial centre. Moreover, as a result of the rich cultural and architectural legacy of the different civilizations which have inhabited Spain, certain bustling cities are also museums and living monuments. The most noteworthy examples are Cordoba and Granada. Hence, a priori, it would appear inadvisable to exclude any of the existing twenty-one major cities from this analysis.

THE FRAMEWORK FOR PLANNING AND POLICY-MAKING

The importance which tourism has acquired in Spain's economy since the early 1950s has never been paralleled by political and legislative measures. There has never been a government Ministry to deal exclusively with tourism, and legislative measures have been limited, only partially implemented and tardy. For example, a truly effective law to regulate development on the coastal fringe was introduced as late as 1988 (Ley 22/1988). No medium- or long-term planning was undertaken by the central government under Franco. Under the democratic regime which was established after 1975, responsibility for tourism was transferred to the regional autonomous government bodies, thus encouraging the introduction of planning only at regional level. The central government retained jurisdiction over hotel prices (price control was eventually abolished in 1979) and the promotion of tourism.

Table 5.1 Population in major cities in Spain, 1991

Metropolitan area	No. of inhabitants
Madrid	4,531,648
Barcelona	3,133,845
Valencia	1,343,760
Seville	952,700
Bilbao	874,294
Malaga	638,470
Zaragoza	615,770
Palma de Mallorca	376,371
Valladolid	363,046
Granada	361,052
Murcia	358,912
Las Palmas	347,668
Alicante	336,528
Santa Cruz de Tenerife	316,556
La Coruña	314,481
Cordoba	309,212
Cadiz	277,920
Vigo	276,573
San Sebastian	275,116
Gijon	260,254
Jerez de la Frontera	253,681

Source: Instituto Nacional de Estadística de España (1992)

Town planning has always been a responsibility of the municipal authorities in Spain. Urban master plans ('Plan de Ordenación General') were drawn up in the 1980s to replace outdated plans existing since the early years of the Franco regime. However, the main instrument of tourism promotion today is the 'Patronato de Turismo', a body which has been set up in each of the municipalities where tourism is considered to play an important role in the local economy. An initiative of the municipal councils, these bodies are financed wholly by them or jointly with companies involved in the tourist sector and business organizations such as Chambers of Commerce ('Cámara de Comercio') as in Barcelona. The 'Patronatos' are responsible for organizing activities to promote tourism, serve as information centres, and co-ordinate promotional and publicity campaigns.

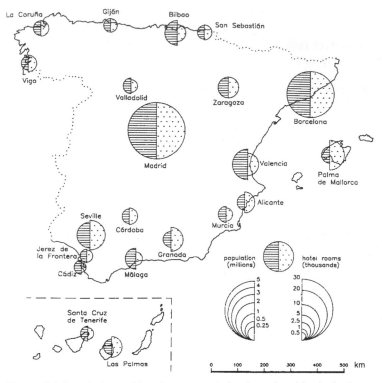

Figure 5.1 Population and hotel accommodation in major cities in Spain
Source: Ministerio de Comercio y Turismo

It is understandable, within this framework of lax regulations and the absence of medium- and long-term objectives in tourism development and of planning mechanisms, that the pattern of supply and demand throughout the period of rapid growth was based almost exclusively on the sun/sand/sea product, very much in fashion and offering assured returns on investment in boom conditions. A fall-off in growth rates in the years following the 1973 international economic crisis, together with an interest in developing other forms of tourism (partly in response to market trends, partly in an effort to protect the already deteriorated coastal fringe, and partly as a result of an increasing awareness on the part of municipal authorities of the economic benefits of tourism), stimulated the development and promotion of city and especially convention tourism after 1980, a subsector of tourism hitherto largely neglected. In an effort to plan for future growth, some municipalities have produced strategic plans in recent years, which have included strategies for the development of the tourist sector.

Serious difficulties, however, faced these new initiatives for the development of city tourism. For thirty years, government investment in infrastructures had been oriented towards the needs of coastal tourism (Cals 1987). As a result, airports serving coastal resorts were much better equipped than those serving inland cities (with the obvious exception of the capital city of Madrid). Likewise, in the early 1980s, the motorway network provided little more than rapid access from France along the Mediterranean coast, and much of the rest of the road network was of low quality. In fact, it was not until 1993 that the motorway between Madrid and Barcelona was completed. The railway network was, and still is, also inadequate, the main inconvenience being that the tracks are not standard European gauge. Even today, single tracks exist on many stretches, some of which serve major cities, and the development of TGV lines is slow. The first line, joining Madrid and Seville, was inaugurated for the World Exhibition of 1992 ('Expo 92'), and a second line extending the French TGV as far as Barcelona is scheduled for construction between 1997 and 2001.

Central government policy has, until recently, demonstrated a marked bias towards coastal tourism. The White Paper ('Libro Blanco del Turismo Español') published in 1991 (T.H.R. *et al.* 1991) and the four-year restructuring plan ('Plan Marco de Competitividad del Turismo Español', known as 'Plan FUTURES') which followed in 1992, placed emphasis on measures designed to improve and remodel existing coastal resorts (Ministerio de Comercio y Turismo 1993c). Marketing and promotion placed the accent on the sun. Even recent campaigns designed to diversify demand have followed the same pattern. Examples include: 'Spain: everything under the sun' and 'We have many ways to tempt you out of the sun' accompanied by images of shops offering local products, and ending up with 'but the beach, the golf course, the tennis courts, the sailboats are waiting. How can you possibly go in, out of the sun?' The bias is clear. Recently some attempts have been made to promote historic cities through, for example, a poster of a panoramic view of Toledo and the caption 'A view with a room'. In all, the Spanish government dedicated 77 million dollars (2.15 dollars per tourist) in promotion in 1993, but the major cities were largely neglected in their campaigns. However, there were signs of a change in policy in May 1994 with the signing of an agreement between the Ministry of Culture and the General Secretariat for Tourism ('TURESPAÑA'), a section of the Ministry of Commerce and Tourism, to launch a 'City Circuit' in Spain, beginning with a pilot project involving Madrid.

In recent years, the promotion of conference centres and congresses on any scale has become the goal of most large cities. One of the main contributions to the development of this subsector has been the establishment of the 'Spain Convention Bureau', an initiative of the Spanish Federation of Municipalities and Provinces ('Federación Española de Municipios y Provincias'), set up in 1982 to help promote the tourism subsector of congresses, conventions and incentive trips. It is financed by its members (initially sixteen and now twenty-six), is non-profit making, and offers its services to any group interested in organizing an event of this nature in Spain. Fifteen of the major cities are members, together with five important coastal tourist resorts and six medium-sized cities.

In 1992, the nomination of Barcelona as the venue for the XXIV Olympic Games, of Madrid as European Cultural Capital, and Seville as the site for the World Exhibition, provided an important stimulus not only to tourism in these cities but also to the promotion of city tourism in Spain in general, as potential visitors began to realize that Spain had something more to offer than sun-drenched beaches (Carandel Robuste 1992; Marchena Gómez 1992; Vila Fradera 1992). Moreover, the occasion generated an important process of improvements and additions to the supply of urban hotels in Barcelona and Seville, mainly within the four- and five-star categories. To a lesser degree, this process has spilled over to other cities with a high level of economic activity but an insufficient lodging supply available (Horváth 1991).

As far as hotels were concerned, after the events of 1992 tourism in major cities had to face the problem of the difference in VAT rates applied in different categories of hotels. Five-star hotels are subject to a 15 per cent service charge, whereas only 6 per cent VAT is charged on services provided in all other categories. As five-star hotels are largely concentrated in the major cities, these are the most adversely affected by the measure. Indeed, several hotels have opted to be downgraded to four-star status to enable them to be more competitive. In the face of the possible disappearance of maximum category hotels in Spain, a 6 per cent VAT charge will be applied in all hotels from 1 January 1995.

THE ROLE OF URBAN TOURISM IN SPANISH TOURISM

The greatest obstacle to analysing the role of cities in Spanish tourism as a whole is the absence of comparable statistics. TURESPAÑA, responsible for data collection, does not distinguish city tourism from other forms of tourism. Data are registered at provincial or autonomous region level. Data collection carried out by municipal authorities is voluntary, and its quality and detail vary greatly according to the importance each individual authority attaches to the tourist sector. Statistics are generally based on small samples, on visitor counts at museums or enquiries at information offices. They are therefore often incomplete or unreliable, and certainly inapplicable for comparative purposes.

Nevertheless, the share of urban tourism in tourism in general can be estimated through calculations based on accommodation supply. In Spain in 1994, the total number of hotel rooms was 533,880 of which 94,600 (17.7 per cent) were located in the twenty-one major cities (Ministerio de Comercio y Turismo 1993b, 1994a). Such statistics must, however, be contextualized, as they do not take into account the fact that a large proportion of Spanish tourists (both international and domestic) are lodged in non-hotel accommodation on the coast and in rural areas. According to 1992 government estimates, this type of accommodation provided approximately 24 million additional beds (Ministerio de Comercio y Turismo 1993a).

Statistics of accommodation capacity or overnight stays do not, however, reveal the important contribution day-trippers make to city tourism. This is certainly the case of the cities located on the Mediterranean coast and on the Balearic island of Mallorca. As all are within easy reach of coastal resorts which are major destinations for mass tourism, they attract large numbers of day-trippers from such resorts, with the consequent positive repercussions on the local micro-economy. Day-trippers are also numerous in the historic cities of inland Andalusia. In Cordoba only 35 per cent of all visitors to the city stay overnight, and in Granada, in 1993, the total number of visitors to the Alhambra (over 2 million) was 2.5 times the total number of hotel visitors.

THE STRUCTURE OF ACCOMMODATION SUPPLY AND ATTRACTIONS

In the absence of reliable and comparable statistics of demand, accommodation supply can serve as an indication of the spatial distribution of city tourism (see Figure 5.1 and Table 5.2). The predominance of Madrid and Barcelona is evident, as together they provide 40 per cent of the total supply and 50 per cent of four- and five-star category rooms. Only two other cities, Seville and Palma de Mallorca, with approximately 7,000 hotel rooms, provide a total of over 5,000 rooms, and nine of the twenty-one major cities have less than 2,000 hotel rooms. Moreover, some one- and two-star guest houses (*pensiones*) serve as permanent homes for immigrant city workers and do not constitute part of the tourist accommodation market. It is therefore evident, at the outset, that city tourism, with the exception of Madrid and Barcelona, is not a major tourist subsector in Spain, although it plays a significant role in the economy of some specific cities.

Table 5.2 Hotel rooms according to category rating, 1994

	5 & 4 star	3 star	2 & 1 star	Total	Average size
Madrid	12,674	5,962	6,659	25,295	48.5
	50.1%	23.6%	26.3%		
Barcelona	8,374	4,031	5,224	17,629	52.8
	47.5%	22.9%	29.6%		
Valencia	1,327	1,426	1,191	3,944	54.8
	33.6%	36.2%	30.0%		
Seville	4,051	1,954	1,094	7,099	82.5
	57.1%	27.5%	15.4%		
Bilbao	1,011	806	429	2,246	77.4
	45.0%	35.9%	19.1%		
Malaga	470	309	653	1,432	46.2
	32.8%	21.6%	45.6%		
Zaragoza	1,419	859	1,125	3,403	55.8
	41.7%	25.2%	33.1%		
Palma de M.	1,955	2,142	2,755	6,852	77.9
	28.5%	31.3%	40.2%		
Valladolid	342	482	494	1,318	43.9
	25.9%	36.6%	37.5%		
Granada	1,786	1,281	1,497	4,564	53.1
	39.1%	28.1%	32.8%		
Murcia	518	352	472	1,342	58.3
	38.6%	26.2%	35.2%		
Las Palmas	1,655	1,167	698	3,520	70.4
	47.0%	33.2%	19.8%		
Alicante	869	1,692	839	3,400	65.4
	25.6%	49.8%	24.7%		
Santa Cruz	298	336	450	1,084	72.3
	27.5%	31.0%	41.5%		
La Coruña	691	327	914	1,932	37.9
	35.8%	16.9%	47.3%		
Cordoba	940	451	768	2,159	51.4
	43.5%	20.9%	35.6%		
Cadiz	296	155	298	749	49.9
	39.5%	20.7%	39.8%		
Vigo	474	452	1,257	2,183	31.6
	21.7%	20.7%	57.6%		
San Sebastian	944	369	518	1,831	44.7
	51.6%	20.2%	28.3%		
Gijon	230	555	639	1,424	39.6
	16.2%	39.0%	44.9%		
Jerez	673	155	365	1,193	54.2
	56.4%	13.0%	30.6%		
Total	40,997	25,263	28,339	94,599	53.9
	43.3%	26.7%	30.0%		

Source: Ministerio de Comercio y Turismo (1993b)

Several of the major Spanish cities constitute the principal points of entry by air and sea for foreign visitors to Spain, although these cities are often not the destination of arriving visitors (see Table 5.3). Madrid, and in some cases Barcelona, receives inter-continental arrivals, some of whom do not stop over before continuing their journey. Visitors arriving at other cities are often distributed along the adjacent coastlines, especially on the island archipelagos and on the Andalusian coast (from Malaga) and, to a lesser extent, on the Valencian, Alicante and Catalan coasts. Seville serves as a distribution centre for the Andalusian interior (see Figure 5.2).

Table 5.3 Visitor entries from abroad, 1992[a]

	Airports	*Seaports*	*Distribution points*[b]
Madrid	2,803,745		*
Barcelona	1,034,000	159,044	*
Valencia	144,655	8,394	*
Seville	247,952	5,209	*
Bilbao	65,501		
Malaga	1,675,014	63,178	***
Zaragoza	22,258		
Palma de Mallorca	3,993,601	61,992	***
Valladolid	3,282		
Granada	1,656		
Murcia	19,313		
Las Palmas	1,830,209[c]	32,183	***
Alicante	980,649	34,459	**
Santa Cruz de Tenerife	2,081,542	133,547	***
La Coruña	450	13,906	
Cordoba			
Cadiz		105,258[d]	
Vigo	916	33,262	
San Sebastian			
Gijon	3,855	3,157	
Jerez de la Frontera	18,633		
Total	14,927,231	653,589	
% total Spain	82.2	38.6	

Source: Ministerio de Comercio y Turismo (1993a)
Notes: [a] Figures include all visitors entering from abroad;
[b] Importance as a distribution point for surrounding tourist region;
[c] The airport is actually 30 km from the city;
[d] Mostly composed of North African immigrants travelling through Spain without stopping in the region

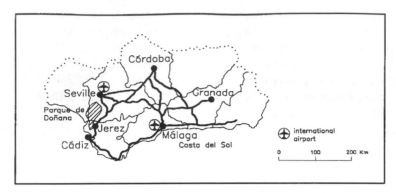

Figure 5.2 Tourism circuits in Andalusia

The majority of Spain's major cities offer a wealth of attractive architectural styles. As a result, the old quarters and historic buildings generally constitute major attractions, even in cities not renowned as historic cities (see Table 5.4). Predominating forms are Gothic and Baroque cathedrals, such as Zaragoza's 'Basílica del Pilar', and buildings of Islamic architecture, especially numerous in the Andalusian cities of Granada, Cordoba and Seville. Museums and art galleries are also important, but most of the best exhibitions are confined to Madrid and Barcelona. Notable exceptions are the various examples of Goya's work which can be seen in Zaragoza. Another common denominator in many Spanish cities is the celebration of traditional cultural events, usually known as 'Ferias' and often associated with local festivals. The most renowned constitute important tourist attractions, for example, Seville's 'Feria de Abril', 'Las Fallas' in Valencia in March, 'Carnaval' in Cadiz in February, Cordoba's 'Romerías', the 'Feria del Caballo' in Jerez de la Frontera in May and the Easter Processions in all Andalusian cities. More modern cultural and sporting events also help promote tourism, such as the annual Film Festival in San Sebastian and various motor cycle and racing car competitions held at the International Racing Circuit at Jerez de la Frontera, which is also the seat of the Andalusian Equestrian School ('Real Escuela Andaluza del Arte Ecuestre').

Many of the cities with fewer than 400,000 inhabitants are provincial or regional capitals which serve as distribution centres for visitors to the surrounding region. This is true in the case of the north-west coastal cities: Vigo and La Coruña offer accommodation and urban services to visitors to Galicia, where the main attractions are the picturesque rural scenery, the ria coastline, local gastronomic specialities (based on fish and

Table 5.4 Principal attractions in Spain's major cities

	Architecture and historic buildings	Museums and art galleries	Culture and sports events	Trade fairs, conventions, congresses	Regional centre^a	Other attractions
Madrid	**	***		***B^b	***	
Barcelona	***	**		***B	*	Olympic venue
Valencia	*	*		***B	*	Gastronomy
Seville	***		**	**B	***	Expo venue
Bilbao	*			**		Univ./Eur. cap.^c
Malaga			*	B		
Zaragoza	˙ **	*		**B		
Palma de M.	**			*B	*	
Valladolid	*	*		*		University
Granada	***	*	*	**B		
Murcia						
Las Palmas				*B		Beach resort
Alicante				**B		Sport/Eur. cap.^d
Santa Cruz						
La Coruña				*B	**	Gastronomy
Cordoba	***	*	*	*B		Gastronomy
Cadiz			*			
Vigo					**	Gastronomy
San Sebastian				*B	*	Beach/gastronomy
Gijon	*			*B	*	Beach resort
Jerez	**	*	***	*B	*	Equestrian centre/ sherry cellars

Source: Author, based on information provided by municipal authorities
*** Major source of attraction
 ** Important source of attraction
  * Source of attraction
Notes: ^a Provides accommodation for visitors to the surrounding region;
 ^b B = member of Spanish Convention Bureau;
 ^c University/European capital (Trademark, Design and Model Harmonization Office);
 ^d Sports training facilities/European capital (European Agency for Health and Safety at Work)

sea-food) and the cathedral city of Santiago de Compostela, declared a World Heritage City by UNESCO (see Figure 5.3). The north-coast cities serve not only as regional centres but also as coastal holiday resorts, mainly for the population of Madrid and other inland provincial capitals. These include Gijon and San Sebastian, where the tradition as a holiday resort goes back to the late nineteenth century. Jerez de la Frontera is also, in part, a distribution centre for visitors to the surrounding coast, notably the National Park of Doñana. Some of the major cities on the Mediterranean coast and island archipelagos have been developed as distribution centres for adjacent tourist regions and as sun/sand/sea destinations in their own right. Demand for these resorts has decreased since 1980 as beach resorts have developed on their coastal hinterlands. As a result, attempts have been made to maintain visitor levels through the development of congress and conference tourism. Cities with these characteristics include Alicante, Palma de Mallorca and Las Palmas. The latter has, in fact, suffered such a marked decline in demand in the face of competition from more modern resorts on the island that accommodation capacity has fallen to almost half of 1973 levels, and visits for business purposes now constitute the principal motive (75 per cent) of visits. Finally, the long-standing tradition of Valladolid as a university town has encouraged its development as a destination for educational tourism.

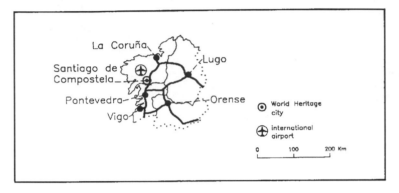

Figure 5.3 Tourism circuits in Galicia

THE ROLE OF CONFERENCE AND EXHIBITION BUSINESS

Spanish major cities offer certain advantages for the development of conference and exhibition tourism. On the one hand, these cities are, in general, attractive, and the Mediterranean coast and island archipelago cities have the added advantage of a pleasant climate for most of the year. On the other, the existence of well-developed air transport networks linked to coastal tourism makes travel from a wide range of points of departure both easy and relatively inexpensive. Madrid has the obvious advantages of any capital city.

Three cities – Madrid, Barcelona and Valencia – clearly dominate the trade fair and exhibition market, with a calendar of exhibits and fairs that extends throughout the year (see Table 5.5). The three largest cities in Spain, they have the most complete exhibition premises and also the highest capacity for conventions and congresses (see Table 5.6). At a second level are the cities of Bilbao, Seville, Alicante, Zaragoza and Valladolid, all of which have ample premises for exhibitions but a lower level of demand, followed by Gijon, Granada and Jerez de la Frontera. Palma de Mallorca, Las Palmas and Cordoba also have small premises.

Table 5.5a Exhibition floor space, major cities, 1993

| | Gross area (sq. m.) | | Net area (sq. m.) | |
	Covered	Open air	Covered	Open air
Madrid	102,600	30,000	56,430	16,500
Barcelona	117,252	14,500	72,350	8,700
Valencia	215,000	20,000	110,000	15,000
Seville	21,600	12,000	12,300	6,000
Bilbao	105,000	25,000	45,000	25,000
Zaragoza	48,522	48,572	32,270	32,300
Palma de M.ˑ	10,000	4,000	7,500	3,000
Valladolid	34,237	66,608	15,833	21,174
Granada	10,000	45,000	10,000	45,000
Las Palmas	12,300	8,000	5,000	3,500
Alicante	40,302	4,000	18,000	2,500
Cordoba	10,000	20,000	7,000	8,000
Gijon	12,138	110,360	9,572	47,286
Jerez	12,000	34,000	6,000	10,000

Source: Author, based on information provided by Asociación de Ferias Españolas and municipal authorities

Table 5.5b Exhibition activities, major cities, 1993

	No. of events	Net exhibition space used ('000 sq. m.)	No. of exhibitors	Paying visitors ('000)
Members of AFE				
Madrid	41	404.7	8,715	623.1
Barcelona	33	496.6	8,985	1,718.4
Valencia	25	291.5	4,386	296.9
Seville	18	77.7	1,213	311.1
Bilbao	22	82.1	1,169	288.9
Zaragoza	5	81.5	1,590	270.9
Palma de M.	6	16.2	437	137.7
Valladolid	8	63.6	1,054	418.4
Las Palmas	2	5.0	135	31.7
Alicante	17	76.1	1,465	89.6
Gijon	4	112.4	699	796.9
Non-members of AFE				
Granada	5	42.4	n/a	189.6
Cordoba	3	6.2	n/a	130.0
Jerez	5	24.4	205	150.0

Source: Author, based on Asociación de Ferias Españolas (1994 – for its members) and information provided by trade fair institutions (for non-members of AFE)
Note: n/a = not applicable.

Table 5.6 Conventions and congress facilities in Spain

	Congress centre(s)			Other lecture halls	Hotel facilities	
	Largest hall (capacity)	*Auxil. hall (capacity)*	*Ownership/ management*		*Hotels (no.)*	*Meeting rooms (no.)*
Madrid	1,924[a]	814	Turespaña	174	45	282
	1,900[b]	1,500	Turespaña			
	600	–	tfi[c]			
Barcelona	1,650	300	tfi	136	48	314
Valencia	1,793	420	municipal	41	12	67
	500[b]	–	tfi			
Seville	1,100	435	tfi	8	16	79
Bilbao	500	–	tfi	–	3	21
Malaga	–	–	–	–	4	11
Zaragoza	640	200	tfi	8	9	37
	402[b]	265	private			
Palma de M.	1,739	331	private	2	8	25
	1,200[b]	800	private			
Valladolid	–	–	–	–	2	10
Granada	2,000	1,000	tfi	14	15	46
Murcia	–	–	–	–	2	7
Las Palmas	800	300	tfi	8	7	25
	400	350	tfi			
Alicante	536	–	private	13	10	32
Santa Cruz	–	–	–	–	1	7
La Coruña	1,550	425	mun./priv.[d]	–	6	18
Cordoba	590	200	aut. govt.[e]	15	5	13
	350	–	tfi			
Cadiz	–	–	–	–	1	7
Vigo	–	–	–	–	1	1
San Sebastian	–	–	–	25	10	38
Gijon	900	202	tfi	7	7	18
Jerez	1,890[f]	360	municipal	5	6	29

Source: Author, based on Ministerio de Comercio y Turismo (1994b) and information provided by municipal authorities
Notes: [a] Halls which can be joined;
[b] Second independent congress centre;
[c] Trade fair institution;
[d] Municipal ownership/private management;
[e] Autonomous regional government;
[f] Open air facility

There is a clear link between exhibitions and the convention market, as the same cities offer facilities for both types of events. Interest in the development of this sector of tourism became evident especially after 1980, when congress centres financed by public authorities (national, regional or municipal) were built in several cities to add to those already existing in Madrid and Barcelona. All of the cities with trade fair complexes have become members of the Spain Convention Bureau. Malaga, La Coruña and San Sebastian are also members of the Bureau, which shows their interest in developing the sector, but, of the three, only San Sebastian is already considered an important destination for this type of activity. One indication of the interest in development is the amount invested in tourist promotion directed towards the congress market in Cordoba, one of the least important congress destinations, in 1993. The total was 39.5 million pesetas, an average of 648,000 pesetas per congress and almost 4,300 pesetas for each delegate who attended. However, as the average expenditure of the 9,230 delegates, who stayed an average of 2.7 days in the city, was 40,000 pesetas per day, the investment represents only 4 per cent of the 1,000 million pesetas of income generated.

It is extremely difficult to assess the precise dimension of this sector in the different destinations, and it is especially confusing to make comparisons, as the efficiency of data collection and the criteria used in classification vary from one city to another. The most complete statistics available are those collected by the Spain Convention Bureau referring to 1990 (Spain Convention Bureau 1991), and even these include certain contradictions, such as the data for San Sebastian which refer to congresses with fifty or more delegates, whereas all other data refer to congresses with a minimum of a hundred participants (see Table 5.7). The predominance of Madrid and Barcelona is marked and especially so for international congresses. Other noteworthy characteristics are the impor-

Table 5.7 Conventions and congresses held in major cities, 1990

| Cities which returned data to SCB | Events | | | Delegates | | Income |
	Total no. >100 deleg.	% of all cities	International no. = (%)	Total no.	% of all cities	(million pesetas)
Madrid	499	27.9	235 (47)	167,920	38.4	22,040
Barcelona	375	20.9	196 (52)	105,424	24.1	11,481
San Sebastian	298[a]	16.6	42 (14)	57,470	13.2	4,700
Alicante	174	9.7	26 (15)	37,015	8.5	–
Seville	171	9.6	32 (19)	10,622	2.4	–
Granada	164	9.2	43 (26)	33,000	7.6	3,000
Zaragoza	79	4.4	16 (20)	17,767	4.0	1,546
Cordoba	30	1.7	3 (10)	7,565	1.7	567
Total	1,790	100.0	593 (33)	436,783	100.0	

Source: Author, based on Spain Convention Bureau (1991)
Note: [a] Events with fifty or more delegates

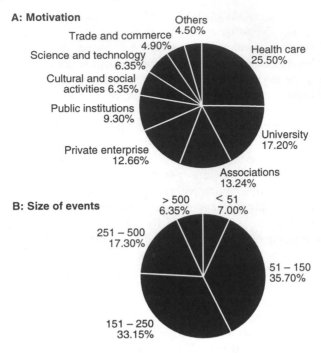

A: Motivation

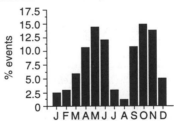

B: Size of events

C: Monthly distribution

D: Venues

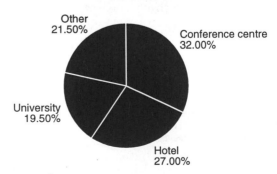

Figure 5.4 Characteristics of conferences in Spain
Source: Spanish Convention Bureau

tance of congresses linked to the medical professions and to the university (see Figure 5.4a); the predominance of medium-sized events (51–250 delegates) (see Figure 5.4b); and the concentration of the celebration of congresses in spring (38 per cent) and autumn (40 per cent) (see Figure 5.4c). The high share of hotels (27 per cent) as venues, only slightly exceeded by conference centres (32 per cent) (see Figure 5.4d), is an indication of the trend to add such facilities in hotels in recent years. Congresses are also held in cities other than those mentioned, but all cities seriously interested in promoting this sector become members of the Spain Convention Bureau (Ministerio de Comercio y Turismo 1994b). Such is the case of Jerez de la Frontera, which joined the organization in 1993, when congresses were already generating considerable tourist flows in the city. By 1991, a total of 23,229 hotel guests had attended 356 activities of this nature, lasting for 621 days.

Incomplete statistics from the same source and referring to 1992, give the total number of congresses of the same dimensions as follows: Barcelona 310 (159 of which were of an international nature); Zaragoza 99 (23); Alicante 99 (6); San Sebastian 88 (7); Seville 64; Granada 61. In that same year, 487 (252) congresses were held in Madrid (according to statistics supplied by the 'Patronato'). Smaller cities tend to attract local or regional events which are not reflected in these statistics. Figures for Cordoba are illustrative of this tendency which has become more marked each year since 1990 (see Table 5.8). Madrid and Barcelona are becoming increasingly important in the international market for large meetings (see Table 5.9). According to the International Congress and Convention Association, in 1993 Barcelona occupied fourth place in the celebration of congresses with a hundred or more participants, rising from eighth place in 1992 and fifth in 1991. For the same years, Madrid was fourteenth, third and ninth respectively. (This classification refers to congresses held at regular intervals, though not necessarily annually, at venues in at least four different countries on a rotatory basis.) However, the International Union of Associations ranked Madrid nineteenth (with fifty-seven events) and Barcelona twelfth (with seventy-two events) in 1993 in the organization of international congresses with 300 or more delegates, and both cities were placed sixteenth (with eighty-seven events) in the classification which included national congresses with international participation. Despite the predominance of Madrid and Barcelona, other cities are now registering an increasing demand as venues for congresses. The case of Zaragoza serves to illustrate this trend. In 1986, the twenty-five congresses held there attracted 6,230 delegates. By 1991, the number of events peaked at 102 before falling to sixty-six in 1993. The number of delegates, however, continued to rise, reaching a total of 31,569 in 1993 –

a reflection of the increasing size of congresses. It was estimated that the total income from congress tourism for the same year was almost 3,536 million pesetas, with a daily average expenditure of 35,000 pesetas per delegate. These statistics would indicate that congress tourism makes an important contribution to city tourism in general.

Table 5.8 Size of congresses in Cordoba, 1990–3

No. of participants	1990 (%)	1991 (%)	1992 (%)	1993 (%)
Less than 50	10.0	8	21	37.2
50–149	26.6	60	20	23.5
150–299	30.0	24	34	25.5
300–499	23.4	8	20	11.8
500 or more	10.0	0	5	2.0

Source: Author, based on information provided by the Oficina Municipal de Congresos e Información Turística, Cordoba

Table 5.9 UIA[a] International congress ranking, Madrid and Barcelona, 1986–93

	Inter. + national meetings[b]		International meetings[c]	
	Madrid	Barcelona	Madrid	Barcelona
1986	5	9	–	–
1987	5	17	–	–
1988	3	27	11	25
1989	6	24	12	28
1990	7	19	15	18
1991	11	16	17	18
1992	5	10	6	7
1993	16	16	19	12

Source: Author, based on information provided by Spain Convention Bureau and Turisme de Barcelona
Notes: [a] UIA International Union of Associations;
[b] Meetings of international organizations and national meetings with international participation;
[c] Meetings of international organizations
Criteria of ranking: delegates = 300 min.
foreign participants = 40% min.
participating countries = 5 min.
duration of meeting = 3 days min.

TOURISM DEMAND

In spite of the lack of standardized statistics, there is sufficient data available to enable certain general characteristics and trends to be distinguished. For the most part, the following analysis is necessarily based on statistics provided by individual municipal authorities without adhering to any unified criteria.

Madrid and Barcelona overwhelmingly predominate the city tourism market in Spain, and are dealt with separately at some length. In the remaining cities visitor levels vary, mainly according to the economic dimension of the city and the amount of fair and congress facilities available (see Table 5.10). In fact, it could be said that the fundamental characteristic of city tourism in Spain is that it is composed principally of Spanish nationals on visits related to their work. In most cities short-stay (1–2 days) business trips and congresses constitute the motive for between 60 per cent and 70 per cent of all visits, and domestic demand reaches similar percentages (see Table 5.11). This is true not only in cities with low visitor levels but also in those where the number of visitors is higher. In this case, congresses and fairs generally constitute the principal differentiating factor which accounts for higher visitor levels.

Table 5.10 Hotel visitors in selected cities

	Year	No. of visitors	No. of overnight stays	Annual occupancy rate (%)	Average length of stay
Madrid	1993	3,335,264	6,648,126	45.00	1.99
Barcelona	1993	2,503,838	4,256,524	44.6	1.7
Valencia	1992	N/A	700,167	38.53	N/A
	1993	N/A	585,888	32.24	
Seville	1991	818,983	1,566,690	50.09	1.91
	1992	959,790	2,070,969	50.04	2.16
Zaragoza	1993	N/A	1,071,068	86.23	N/A
Valladolid	1993	45,955	N/A	N/A	N/A
Granada	1994	997,926	2,084,430	43.06	2.09
Murcia	1990	N/A	448,057	45.25	N/A
	1993	N/A	405,015	39.13	N/A
Las Palmas	1992	288,230	N/A	N/A	N/A
Santa Cruz	1993	120,053	308,199	34.0	N/A
Cordoba	1993	372,759	573,948	36.7	1.54
San Sebastian	1993	365,500	657,900	60.0	1.8
Jerez	1991	N/A	269,984	45.57	N/A
	1993	N/A	261,300	30.0	N/A

Source: Author, based on information provided by municipal authorities
Note: N/A = statistics not available

A second differentiating factor is the existence of numerous buildings of historic or architectural interest, which not only attract visitors *per se*, but also make the cities more attractive as venues for congresses (for example, Seville, Granada and Cordoba). The case of Jerez de la Frontera is somewhat unique, as it offers a wide range of contrasting attractions to visitors (see Table 5.12). In the cities on the northern coast summer holiday visitors constitute the principal sector of demand. For example, in San Sebastian leisure was the motivation of 70 per cent of all visitors in 1993. Figures for Vigo clarify this situation even further: in August 1993 leisure was the motive declared by 78 per cent of its visitors, while business accounted for 89 per cent of the visits made between November 1993 and January 1994.

Table 5.11 Origin of hotel visitors in selected cities

	Year/ period	Spanish (%)	Principal nationalities of foreigners
Madrid	1993	60.5	USA, UK, Fra, Ita, Ger, Jap
Barcelona	1993	37.9	Fra, Ita, USA, Ger, UK, Jap
Valencia	1992	80.35	Ita, Fra, UK, Ger
Seville	1991	57.65	N/A
	1992	63.38	N/A
Zaragoza	1993	88.62	N/A
Palma de Mallorca	1992	40.6	UK, Ita, Ger, Swe
Granada	1994	58.34	USA, Fra, Ita, Jap, Ger, UK
Las Palmas	1992	83.91	Ger, UK, Fra, Ita
Santa Cruz	1993	89.85	Ger, Swe, UK
Cordoba	1993	63.73	Fra, UK, Ger, USA, Jap, Ita
Cadiz	6.93/5.94	75	UK, Fra, Ger, USA, Ita
Vigo	2.93/1.94	85 (76 – summer)	Por
San Sebastian	1993	72 (68 – summer)	Ger, USA, Ita
Gijon	6.94/9.94	83	S.Amer, Fra, Ger
Jerez	1990	61	Fra, UK, Ger, USA

Source: Author, based on information provided by municipal authorities
Note: N/A = statistics not available

The origin of visitors from within Spain is closely related to population size and distance (see Table 5.11). Hence, the highest percentage of visitors to most destinations is from Madrid, followed at some distance by Catalonia, where intra-regional tourism predominates. Visitors from other European countries are predominantly German, French and British, although the number of Italian visitors has also risen rapidly in recent years. Tourists from the United States and, to a lesser extent, from Japan are also numerous in Madrid and in the Andalusian cities. The presence of North American visitors in San Sebastian is partly related to the Film Festival, and of South Americans in Gijon to ancestral family relationships. It is, in fact, noteworthy that visitors from Germany, the United Kingdom and France, who constitute the overwhelming majority of tourists at Spanish coastal resorts, play a much less significant role in city tourism (see also Tables 5.20 and 5.24).

Table 5.12 Visitors at principal attractions, 1993, and future projections, Jerez de la Frontera

	No. of visitors 1993	Future projections Strategic Plan (1990)
Racing circuit	284,500	250,000
Equestrian school	112,645	110,000
Sherry cellars	107,359	110,000
'Feria del Caballo'	N/A	350,000
Easter week	N/A	75,000
Congresses	98,699	50,000

Source: Author, based on information provided by the Ayuntamiento de Jerez
Note: N/A = statistics not available

Table 5.13 Monthly hotel occupancy rates in selected cities

	B 1994	S 1991	S 1992	P 1992	G 1994	M 1993	LP 1992	Co 1993	Ca 93/94	J 1991	J 1993
Jan	35.0	31.1	29.0	29.2	31.9	26.4	57.8	25.7	27	32	22
Feb	39.4	36.4	32.4	33.6	42.4	39.5	61.9	29.2	43	44	25
Mar	50.8	49.8	37.4	45.0	50.2	47.2	51.6	41.2	43	50	29
Apr	52.3	68.3	51.6	51.7	48.5	43.0	47.4	46.6	41	57	41
May	49.4	61.1	66.4	54.5	50.3	45.6	35.7	48.0	44	60	43
Jun	46.1	49.0	65.2	49.7	40.2	45.7	35.9	35.9	59	46	32
Jul	44.0	40.7	62.7	50.2	39.3	30.5	38.2	30.1	52	43	25
Agu	45.9	41.5	65.4	66.0	46.3	22.2	47.0	38.5	79	50	31
Sep	55.4	56.3	86.1	59.2	51.8	44.4	44.4	46.1	53	49	31
Oct	56.2	65.7	50.1	47.8	47.9	52.4	46.2	43.7	39	44	30
Nov	45.1	55.2	25.0	32.7	32.0	40.7	46.5	29.5	24	43	26
Dec	40.1	46.0	28.9	28.6	35.8	32.4	45.1	26.2	25	30	23
Average	46.6	50.1	50.0	45.7	43.1	39.2	46.5	36.7	44	46	30

Source: Author, based on information provided by municipal authorities
Key: B = Barcelona; S = Seville; P = Palma de Mallorca; G = Granada; M = Murcia; LP = Las Palmas; Co = Cordoba; Ca = Cadiz; J = Jerez de la Frontera

Hotel occupancy rates serve as indicators both of the number of visitors and of the motivations of their visit. Occupation levels are, in general, low, normally no more than 50 per cent as an annual average; in some cases this falls to a 20 per cent monthly minimum (see Table 5.13). In fact, considerable monthly fluctuations are registered in most cities. December and January are the months when demand is lowest. In the north-coast cities, summer holiday demand prevails, while in the remainder of the cities peak demand is registered in spring and autumn. This is a reflection of the predominance of business and congress tourism in a country where economic activity is disrupted in July and August. Moreover, the extreme heat registered at the height of the summer in the southern cities discourages tourism for leisure purposes in this season. Occupation levels at weekends also tend to be much lower than on weekdays, clearly a consequence of the high degree of dependence on business tourism.

Nevertheless, tourism makes an important contribution to the economy in most of the major cities. For example, a survey carried out in Vigo in 1993 calculated daily average expenditure per person at 8,500 pesetas per day. A comparable survey carried out in Gijon put daily expenditure at just over 7,000 pesetas per day, and total income from tourism at 6,475 million pesetas for the three-month period from mid-June to mid-September 1993. In the same year, municipal authorities in Granada calculated that the contribution of tourism to the city's GDP was 16.7 per cent of the total.

THE EVOLUTION OF DEMAND

City tourism grew during the 1980s, but fluctuations in demand began to occur in 1990, coinciding with the Gulf crisis (see Table 5.14). In some cities a negative growth was registered in 1990, while in others it was delayed until the following year and, in fact, signs of recovery are already visible.

Several factors help to explain not only the existence of these fluctuations but also their temporal variations. In the first place, the predominance of Spanish nationals in the demand for city tourism means that this type of tourism is much more sensitive to trends in the Spanish economy than in the European or world economy. As a result, the deep economic recession affecting Spain in the early 1990s had marked repercussions on city visitor levels. Not only did the number of visitors fall but stays were also shortened, with a consequent drop in occupation rates.

Where foreign visitors or motivations other than business are important the pattern of visitor levels has followed a slightly different trajectory. Moreover, the mega-events contributed to disguise the general downward trend, not only in the three cities where these were held, but in nearby cities, notably the Andalusian cities near Seville, namely Cordoba, Granada and Jerez de la Frontera.

Table 5.11 Evolution of hotel visitor numbers in selected cities

	Peak	Decline	Stabilization	Recovery
Madrid	1990	1991, 1993	1992	N/A
Zaragoza	1991	1992, 1993	N/A	N/A
Murcia	1991	1992, 1993	N/A	N/A
Santa Cruz	1989	1990, 1991		1992, 1993
San Sebastian	1989	1990, 1991, 1992	1993	1994
Jerez	1989	1990, 1991		1992, 1993

Source: Author, based on information provided by municipal authorities
Note: N/A = no clear indication of stabilization/recovery in 1994

The low participation level of foreigners in Spanish city tourism is indicative of the limited extent of promotion of this sector outside Spain. The creation of the Spain Convention Bureau has contributed to developing demand, and after 1985 some cities designed strategic plans which included tourism development objectives. This has occurred not only in major cities such as Barcelona and historic cities such as Cordoba, but also in smaller cities including Vigo and Jerez.

Most planning and promotion measures, however, date from the 1990s, and were introduced partly as a response to the drop in demand at this time and only partly because of a growing awareness of the potential contribution of tourism to urban economies. Measures include city-centre rehabilitation plans, such as those implemented in Las Palmas and Malaga. Campaigns to stimulate city tourism have been launched by the Andalusian regional government ('Junta de Andalucía'), and by the municipal councils in Seville, Valencia and Bilbao. It is noteworthy that even industrial cities, such as Bilbao, have begun to promote themselves as tourist destinations. In Spain, Bilbao is traditionally renowned for its damp and misty climate, ugly port and industrial landscape. However, in 1989, under the auspices of the Basque autonomous government and the provincial organization ('Diputación Foral de Bizkaia'), a 'Strategic Plan to Revitalize Bilbao' was designed. The public administrative bodies involved joined forces in the society 'Bilbao Ría 2000' and with the private sector in an association 'Bilbao Metropoli-30' to implement specific projects. The refurbishing of the historic sector of the city, already undertaken, and the proposed almost total redevelopment of the derelict waterfront port facilities are the main elements of the plans for urban improvement. Obviously the basic objective is the economic resurgence of the city, but the expansion of business tourism is intended to play a significant role. The main assets which are being promoted as tourist attractions are the Guggenheim Museum (scheduled for completion in 1997); cultural activities and festivals; congresses, to which the prestigious University of Deusto and the new Congress and Concert Hall planned for construction on the waterfront will contribute; exhibitions and fairs, and Bilbao's fame for traditional Basque cuisine.

The most recent efforts have been directed towards the correction of existing defects: an excessive reliance on the domestic market, and low hotel occupation levels especially at weekends. With these objectives in mind three types of measures have been implemented by the municipal authorities in many of the cities. These measures are: the enhancement of the city's image abroad in order to increase foreign participation in demand; the improvement of installations for the reception of congress and convention tourism; and the promotion of weekend leisure tourism for both the domestic and international market through special offers in complete packages or in hotel prices and specific attractions (such as free or reduced prices for entrance to cultural events, museums, sightseeing tours, etc.)

MADRID AND BARCELONA

Undoubtedly, the metropolises of Madrid and Barcelona are the principal destinations of urban tourism. This is in no way surprising as, traditionally, a large share of tourism has always been for business purposes. However, in recent years tourism for pleasure has begun to play an important role in motivation. In fact, already in the 1980s, a well-consolidated leisure tourism sector existed in Madrid, and the city was included in some of the European capital city circuits organized with North American, South American and, more recently, Japanese tourists in mind. Barcelona, at this time, relied mainly on day-trippers from coastal resorts.

The turning point was the build-up to the mega-events celebrated in Spain in 1992. The publicity generated served not only to promote these events but also as a boost to city tourism in Spain in general and the cities directly involved in particular. This is demonstrated in the International Union of Associations' ranking of cities for congresses, in which Barcelona has literally jumped up the scale (see Table 5.9). Moreover, the theme of the respective events coincided with major long-term sources of attraction. In Madrid, European Cultural Capital, its museums are considered one, and probably the most important, of its assets. In Barcelona, the architectural wealth and diversity and the Olympic venues so publicized in 1992 are, likewise, major permanent attractions.

This contrasts with the situation in Seville, where the city's main attractions are its historic buildings and traditional Andalusian culture, whereas Expo 92 was an exhibition in which modern technology played a major role. Many of the pavilions were dismantled immediately afterwards, while a technological park and modern leisure complex have remained, together with an excessive supply of hotel accommodation.

THE CHARACTERISTICS OF TOURISM IN MADRID (see Figure 5.5)

The basic structure of the hotel accommodation now existing in Madrid was already established in 1974, the main change in the following twenty years being the concentration of supply in the four-star category (see Table 5.15). During this period, Madrid's functions as political, administrative and financial capital dominated the motivations of visitors to the city (Gutiérrez Ronco 1984). As a result, Spanish nationals on short stays for business purposes made up a large percentage of hotel clients. A natural extension of this sector of demand was the gradual development of congress and convention tourism, which was consolidated during the 1980s. Leisure tourism, based on cultural attractions, developed alongside. In this respect, Madrid's role at that time as the only entry point in Spain for inter-continental air traffic was an important factor.

Table 5.15 Hotel accommodation in Madrid, 1974–94

Category	1974			1994		
	Establishments	No. rooms	% total (rooms)	Establishments	No. rooms	% total (rooms)
Hotels						
5-star	14	3,568	15.9	7	1,371	5.4
4-star	26	4,138	18.5	48	11,303	44.7
3-star	36	3,734	16.7	46	5,004	19.8
2-star	20	1,390	6.2	13	1,052	4.2
1-star	19	1,110	5.0	4	185	0.7
Total hotels	115	13,940	62.3	118	18,915	74.8
Guest-house						
3-star	34	1,352	6.0	27	958	3.8
2-star	178	2,886	12.9	164	2,872	11.4
1-star	388	4,192	18.7	213	2,550	10.1
Total guest-houses	600	8,430	37.7	404	6,380	25.3
Total	715	22,370	100.0	522	25,295	100.0

Sources: Ministerio de Comercio y Turismo (1993b) and Ministerio de Información y Turismo (1973)

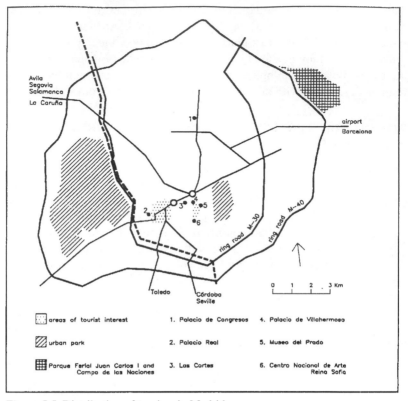

Figure 5.5 Distribution of tourism in Madrid

With regard to planning and promotion, Madrid has certain advantages over other cities, as there is a coincidence of interests and corporative effort between city authorities, the autonomous regional government (which comprises only the province of Madrid), and the relevant government organizations, principally TURESPAÑA and the Ministry of Culture, whose headquarters are located in Madrid. The maintenance and management of monuments is shared – the royal palace ('Palacio Real') forms part of the National Patrimony and, as such, is managed by the Presidency Ministry, while the remaining monuments are the responsibility of the Autonomous Regional Government. The main municipal organizations with responsibility for tourism are the 'Patronato Municipal de Turismo' founded in 1980, and the Madrid Convention Bureau, founded in 1984 and integrated within the Patronato. The Autonomous Community has full legislative powers over the trade fair installations, but its management and promotion are channelled through IFEMA ('Institución Ferial de Madrid'), a consortium created in 1979 with the participation of public institutions (the Municipal Council and the Autonomous Government) and private enterprise (the 'Cámara de Comercio' and Madrid Savings Bank – 'Cajamadrid'). In addition, a public company ('Tourmadrid SA'), dependent on the Autonomous Government, was founded in 1990 to promote the trade fair complex.

In fact, Madrid's facilities for congresses and fairs are one of its main assets (Valenzuela Rubio 1992). Its first (and Spain's second) congress hall ('Palacio de Congresos'), including a 2,738-seat auditorium, was built in the early 1970s. It is state-owned, and is situated in the financial centre of the city and close to the area designated for the expansion of government offices. In 1979, Madrid's present trade fair complex ('Parque Ferial Juan Carlos I') was built on the outskirts of the city and close to the airport. It comprises eight large pavilions sized between 5,400 and 16,200 sq. metres, an auditorium with seating capacity for 600 people, car-parking facilities for 14,000 vehicles, and is located next to the 'Campo de las Naciones', Madrid's largest service and leisure area, which includes two four- and five-star hotels, two golf courses and extensive gardens. In this area a second congress hall ('Palacio Municipal de Congresos'), with seating capacity for 3,400 people in two auditoriums, was inaugurated in 1992.

However, in the present decade, conscious efforts to expand the tourist market in Madrid have been made by municipal and regional government authorities together with the Ministry of Culture. The objective is to enhance the image of Madrid as a 'City of the Arts', based mainly on its numerous museums, but especially on its permanent art exhibitions. In fact, the three major art exhibits, located moreover in close proximity, constitute a History of World Art. The 'Museo del Prado', opened to the public in 1819, houses exhibits of the most important European schools of painting from the twelfth to the nineteenth century. Plans to expand the museum to incorporate the contiguous museums of the 'Casón del Buen Retiro' and the 'Museo del Ejército' are well advanced. The second museum is the 'Centro Nacional de Arte Reina Sofia', inaugurated in 1986, which offers a varied selection of twentieth-century Spanish art, together with temporary exhibitions of both Spanish and foreign artists. The restored 'Palacio de Villahermosa' completes this triangle of art exhibitions. It houses the Thyssen-Bornemisza collection, one of the largest private art collections in the world, with more than 700 masterpieces dating from the seventeenth century to the post-vanguardists (see Table 5.16). A varied calendar of opera, light opera ('Zarzuela'), orchestra and chorus music, dance and theatre performances and bull-fighting, completes the arts attractions. Obviously the numerous buildings associated with Madrid's capital functions (for example, the 'Palacio Real' and the seat of Parliament – 'Las Cortes') and the historic centre of Madrid are additional attractions for visitors.

Table 5.16 Visitors to principal museums and monuments in Madrid, 1993

	No. of visitors[a]
Museo del Prado	1,500,299
Centro Nacional de Arte Reina Sofia	1,194,370
Palacio Villahermosa (Thyssen)	625,000
Palacio Real	635,267
Museo Arqueológico Nacional	237,644
Museo de Cera (Wax Museum)	200,000
Museo de la Ciudad (City Museum)	118,101

Source: Information provided by Madrid Patronato Municipal de Turismo
Note: [a] Museums with less than 100,000 visitors are excluded

The city also plays a significant role as the distribution centre for tourists making excursions to monuments and historic cities within the surrounding region (see Figure 5.6). These include the Monastery of El Escorial, the monument to Civil War victims ('Valle de los Caídos'), the typical Castillian village of Chinchón, the historic cities of Aranjuez and Cuenca, and the UNESCO World Heritage Cities of Avila, Segovia, Toledo and, to a lesser extent, Salamanca.

The pattern of demand is clearly a reflection of the attractions available in the city. Business and congress tourism still accounts for 70 per cent of demand. In 1992, the Trade Fair complex housed fifty events which attracted over 2 million visitors. The increase in the number and size of such events since the construction of the complex has been continuous (see Table 5.17). There are also clear indications of an increase in the number of congresses held in Madrid, in spite of a drop in 1991 (see Table 5.17). In 1992, 487 congresses, involving almost 200,000 participants, generated 36,100 million pesetas in income for the city. In 1993 the number of congresses held increased to 589, but they were attended by only 168,000 delegates with a total income of 31,100 million pesetas. This is a reflection of the decrease in demand from Spanish nationals, in turn related to the economic recession affecting Spain particularly after 1990. Not only was there a reduction in domestic tourism for pleasure but also of trips for business purposes and saving on expenses on such trips by shortening stays or completely avoiding overnight stop-offs. Statistics corroborate these assertions, for, while the number of foreign visitors rapidly showed signs of recovery towards pre-recession levels after 1991, the domestic market has not yet recovered (see Tables 5.18 and 5.19).

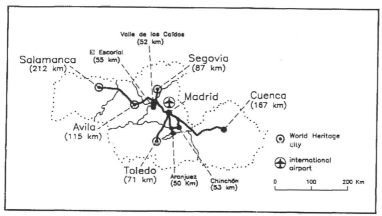

Figure 5.6 Tourism in the Madrid region

The growth of commercial and political relations with the European Community has given rise to an increase in the number of visitors from EC countries (see Table 5.20). The long-standing market of North American and South American visitors, joined more recently by tourists from Japan, most of whom follow the European capital city route (mainly in summer), also suffered losses in 1991, but has rapidly recovered since. Demand could therefore be characterized as consisting of 70 per cent short stay (one to two days) business tourism in which Spaniards still predominate, although to a lesser extent than before. The remaining 30 per cent are visitors for pleasure purposes, consisting mainly of foreigners (mostly non-Europeans) who visit in summer for periods of three to four days. Statistics also indicate that approximately 40 per cent of all visitors organize their trips through tour operators.

Obviously, Madrid's cultural capitality in 1992 could have disguised general downward trends. Only incomplete figures for 1993 are available, but these appear to confirm the gradual recovery of the foreign market on the one hand, and a further drop in the domestic market, which has had serious negative repercussions on hotel occupation levels, on the other. Preoccupation caused by these trends culminated in the campaign to promote Madrid as the 'City of the Arts'. The attractions exist, but the campaign has just been launched. There are attempts to reactivate domestic demand, especially through the incentive of price reductions in hotels at weekends. But obstacles exist which must be overcome – the main one being the Sunday closing of most of Madrid's museums and art galleries.

Table 5.17 Madrid: trade fairs (1979–93) and congresses (1986–93)

		Trade fairs		Congresses	
	No. of fairs	Floor space ('000 sq. m.)	Visitors ('000)	No. of events	Participants ('000)
1979	1	18	108	–	–
1980	15	93	1,076	–	–
1981	18	130	1,638	–	–
1982	26	175	1,967	–	–
1983	21	180	2,081	–	–
1984	20	252	2,637	–	–
1985	31	245	2,202	–	–
1986	30	265	1,606	408	148.5
1987	26	250	1,965	417	160.9
1988	38	335	2,219	463	128.8
1989	34	327	2,159	462	137.8
1990	39	349	1,267	499	167.9
1991	41	474	1,974	403	152.8
1992	52	600	2,075	487	199.9
1993	41	405	1,108	589	168.2

Sources: Trade fairs: Valenzuela Rubio 1992 (for 1979–88); information provided by IFEMA (for 1989–92); Asociación de Ferias Españolas 1994 (for 1993).
Congresses: no statistics available (1979–85); information provided by Madrid Convention Bureau (1986–93)

Table 5.18 Hotel visitors and overnight stays in Madrid, 1986–93

	Hotel visitors				Overnight stays				Annual occupancy rate
	Spanish ('000)	%	Foreign ('000)	Total ('000)	Spanish ('000)	%	Foreign ('000)	Total ('000)	
1986	1,922	60	1,259	3,180	4,726	60	3,089	7,815	67.64
1987	2,064	60	1,362	3,426	4,934	60	3,231	8,165	66.40
1988	2,159	60	1,431	3,590	5,155	60	3,374	8,529	69.32
1989	2,326	60	1,524	3,850	5,632	61	3,587	9,219	74.30
1990	2,520	63	1,456	3,976	6,035	64	3,447	9,482	71.00
1991	2,462	67	1,213	3,675	5,766	66	2,962	8,728	65.00
1992	2,289	61	1,490	3,779	4,475	58	3,242	7,717	51.30
1993	1,915	57	1,420	3,335	3,586	54	3,062	6,648	45.00

Source: Information provided by Madrid Patronato Municipal de Turismo

THE CHARACTERISTICS OF TOURISM IN BARCELONA (see Figure 5.7)

Prior to 1992 Barcelona suffered from a deficit in hotel accommodation to such an extent that demand for business purposes alone frequently out-stripped supply. The vast majority of tourists for pleasure purposes were day-trippers, and few were inclined to stay overnight. The image of the city was that of an important commercial and industrial centre, only worth a superficial visit. The celebration of, and the build-up to, the Olympic Games, however, had important consequences for the city, and have been fundamental in modifying the structure of its tourism (Alos *et al.* 1991; Chalkley *et al.* 1992; De Forn 1992). On the one hand, the transformation of urban infrastructures carried out in conjunction with the Games has not only greatly enhanced the city but also improved access to it and provided additional accommodation (Patronat de Turisme de Barcelona 1991). On the other hand, the publicity given to the city revealed assets hitherto unknown internationally and proved an incentive to potential visitors.

Table 5.19 Length of stay of hotel visitors in Madrid: annual average 1986–93 (nights stayed)

	Spanish visitors	Foreign visitors	Total
1986	2.46	2.45	2.46
1987	2.39	2.37	2.38
1988	2.39	2.36	2.38
1989	2.42	2.35	2.39
1990	2.39	2.37	2.38
1991	2.34	2.42	2.38
1992	1.95	2.18	2.04
1993	1.87	2.16	1.99

Source: Author, based on information provided by Madrid Patronato Municipal de Turismo

Table 5.20 Nationality of foreign visitors in Madrid, 1991–3

Nationality	%	1991 Average length of stay (nights)	1992 (%)	1993 (%)
USA	15	2.38	15	10
Japan	9	2.06	8	4
UK	8	2.44	11	10
Italy	10	2.42	9	7
France	7	2.18	8	8
Germany	5	2.46	6	8
Rest of Europe	10	2.23	_[a]	_[a]
Latin America	19	2.79	_[a]	_[a]
Rest of world	17	2.55	43	53

Source: Author, based on information provided by Madrid Patronato Municipal de Turismo
Note: [a] Included in rest of world

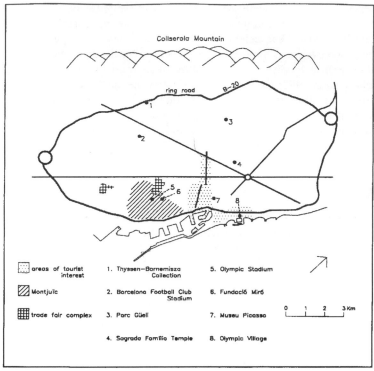

Figure 5.7 Distribution of tourism in Barcelona

The first major change associated with the Olympic Games was the construction of a large number of hotels and the refurbishing of many more. At the time of Barcelona's nomination in 1986 there was already a serious shortage of accommodation, notably in higher category ratings, at a time of economic resurgence and also as a result of the impulse to tourism that this nomination meant. In view of this necessity, the municipal authorities designed a Hotel Plan in 1986, involving both public and private initiatives, to encourage and ensure the construction of a sufficient number of hotel establishments to cover existing and foreseeable shortages. The urban planning regulations (Decret Legislatiu 1/1990) and the Land Use Law (Real Decreto 1/1992) were modified in order to permit the designation of suitable sites and the provision of land by the municipal authorities. Eight sites were selected with the objective of adding 2,600 new hotel rooms to reach a total of 18,000 rooms in three-, four- and five-star categories before the Olympic Games. Not all these sites were eventually used and some of the hotels were completed after the event, but the plan served to discourage speculation. Certainly, these hotels and others constructed under private initiative added over 4,700 beds to the 36,000 already existing (see Table 5.21). If guest houses are excluded, the increase is even more spectacular: from approximately 15,700 beds in 1987 to 25,000 in 1992 (59 per cent in five years).

Table 5.21 Hotel accommodation in Barcelona, 1974–94

	1974	1985	*No. of hotels* 1992 *(July)*	1994	1974	1985	*No. of rooms* 1992 *(July)*	1994
Hotels								
5-star	5	6	12	6	1,078	1,601	2,509	1,556
4-star	15	19	34	46	1,641	2,357	3,854	6,818
3-star	21	27	48	54	1,368	2,192	3,287	4,031
2-star	9	14	14	22	517	863	853	1,087
1-star	25	13	24	25	1,416	774	952	828
Total hotels	75	79	132	153	6,020	7,787	11,455	14,320
Guest-houses								
3-star	6	9	2	–	186	310	66	–
2-star	65	50	49	62	1,810	1,444	1,171	1,281
1-star	147	112	164	119	2,906	2,661	2,706	2,028
Total guest-houses	218	171	215	181	4,902	4,415	3,943	3,309
Total	293	250	347	334	10,922	12,202	15,398	17,629

Sources: Ministerio de Información y Turismo 1973 (for 1974); Servei d'Estadística . . . 1986 (for 1985); information provided by Turisme de Barcelona (for 1992); Ministerio de Comercio y Turismo 1993b (for 1993)

Nevertheless, the physical transformation which has affected Barcelona most profoundly has been the total redevelopment of a large section of the waterfront. It had often been said that Barcelona 'lived with its back to the sea' on account of the dilapidated industrial, rail and port installations that occupied the seafront, together with the polluted water and uncared-for beaches. This is no longer so. The railway line has been put underground and the old buildings demolished and replaced by the Olympic Village, a complex of spaciously laid-out apartment blocks with public parks lining a wide seafront promenade. Amenities are provided on the restored beach which, together with the sea, has been cleaned and provides safe bathing. The beach already attracted more than 1.5 million bathers in the summer of 1993 and this figure rose to over 2 million in 1994. A new marina, originally built for the Olympic sailing events, and two twin skyscraper towers (a hotel and an office block) complete the seafront redevelopment. Improvements have also been made in the existing commercial port, including the refurbishing of buildings and the construction of port-front promenades, and a walkway extending over the port waters (opened to the public in September 1994). The project also involved the construction of the largest aquarium in Europe, opened in September 1995. The entire complex constitutes a major commercial, leisure and tourist attraction.

Surprisingly, the physical modifications made for the actual sporting events have had less impact as, for the most part, they entailed the reconstruction, refurbishing or embellishment of existing installations. Visitor levels to the main sports complex (including the Olympic athletics stadium) on Montjuíc overlooking the port have undoubtedly risen, although this hill, which offers a magnificent viewpoint, was already a tourist attraction. In fact, even before these transformations, Barcelona was already an attractive city, as a result of the wealth and variety of its architecture, including its historic centre ('Barri Gòtic'), its numerous 'modernist' buildings and Gaudi's unique architecture (in particular the 'Sagrada Familia' Temple and the 'Parc Güell'). Permanent art exhibits were a further incentive for visitors, notably the 'Museu Picasso' and the 'Fundació Miró'.

But Barcelona was, above all, a business centre, in which trade fair and congress tourism played an important role (see Table 5.22). While in the leisure tourism sector Madrid and Barcelona could be considered complementary, in this sector they are, to a certain extent, direct competitors. By 1992, Madrid's installations were modern and ample, whereas Barcelona's fair and congress centre, built in 1963, was inadequate for present-day needs. The problems were twofold. As preparations for the Olympic Games had taken priority, no investment had been forthcoming for modernization, and indeed the use of the premises was somewhat restricted because of their proximity to the Olympic Stadium at the foot of Montjuíc, with the consequent danger of a loss of clients. The second problem was its situation, an enclave in the centre of the city without the possibility of expansion. A proposal for the total transfer of the premises to the outskirts of the city was shelved in favour of a less expensive and more immediate alternative solution. The 'Fira', the governing body responsible for the management of the installations, together with the city's Chamber of Commerce ('Cambra de Comerç, Indústria i Navegació'), have invested 5,750 million pesetas in the construction of additional premises (111,500 square metres) on a site at a distance of 2.5 kilometres. The project ('Montjuíc 2') includes the construction of various intercommunicated pavilions, the largest of which (27,000 square metres) will be the biggest in Spain. There will also be an 11-hectare public park. The first phase (42,000 square metres of floorspace) is scheduled for completion early in 1995.

Table 5.22 Barcelona: trade fairs (1979–93) and congresses (1987–93)

		Trade fairs			Congresses[a]	
	No. fairs	Floor space ('000 sq. m.)	Visitors ('000)		No. events	Participants ('000)
1979	14	231	1,590		–	–
1980	15	250	1,430		–	–
1981	21	336	1,833		–	–
1982	21	262	1,820		–	–
1983	28	311	2,109		–	–
1984	31	303	2,097		–	–
1985	31	346	2,297		–	–
1986	32	283	2,005		–	–
1987	33	508	2,412		279	80.4
1988	32	445	1,318		218	60.3
1989	42	739	2,450		330	95.3
1990	33	534	1,550		373	105.4
1991	33	657	2,203		324	169.0
1992	32	417	1,663		310	108.5[b]
1993	33	497	2,063		422	159.2

Sources: Trade fairs: author, based on information provided by Barcelona Fira; congresses: information provided by Turisme de Barcelona
Notes: [a] Congresses with 100 or more participants; [b] 15 July–15 August excluded from statistics

Similar plans to construct a new congress hall in the Olympic Village have been abandoned due to the excessive cost. As a temporary measure, the 'Fira' invested 500 million pesetas in 1994 on improvements to the existing building, including the extension of the main auditorium from 1,450 to 1,650 seats, of total capacity to 2,800 people, and the provision of a new entrance to allow independence from the fair installations. In spite of such shortcomings, congresses held at the Fira Hall in 1993 attracted 40,000 people to Barcelona and generated an income of 18,000 million pesetas.

Visitor levels have risen constantly over the last decade. It is calculated that a total of 10,000 day-trippers, mostly from tourist resorts on the coast, visit the city daily during the summer. In 1993, 100,000 people used the municipal sightseeing bus service ('Bus Turístic') to visit the city and, in summer, approximately eighty coaches enter Barcelona on sightseeing visits. The places most frequently visited by tourists are the 'Sagrada Familia' Temple, the Picasso Museum and the Barcelona Football Club Stadium (which received 230,000 visitors in the three summer months of 1994).

However, in spite of the rising number of visitors, hotel occupation levels fell considerably after the Olympic Games in the face of the now evident economic recession which had been disguised by the pre-Olympic business activity in the city. Moreover, the hotels which had been constructed in the cities and towns around Barcelona to supplement the supply at the time of the Olympics afterwards filtered off part of the clientele visiting the region for business purposes. In addition, hotels originally scheduled to open prior to the Games were completed afterwards, thus adding a further 2,000 beds to supply. The category rating mix of hotels constituted another difficulty. The short-term need for a large quantity of luxury hotel accommodation for the 'Olympic Family' had led to an excessive supply of five-star hotels for long-term needs (see Table 5.23). To combat low occupancy levels after 1992, eight of the thirteen five-star hotels have since chosen to downgrade their status to the four-star category in an attempt to offer more competitive prices.

Table 5.23 Accommodation in high-category hotels in Barcelona, 1989–94

| Hotel category | *% of total no. of rooms in hotels* | | |
	1989	*1992*	*1994*
5-star	15	20	7
4-star	33	39	60
3-star	35	27	26
Total	83	86	93

Source: Author, based on information provided by Turisme de Barcelona

Before 1992, occupancy rates had constantly been maintained above 60 per cent (see Table 5.24). In 1993, the level had dropped to 44.6 per cent, although signs of recovery were visible by the summer of 1994. An average of 57.5 per cent was registered in June, 52.6 per cent in July, 49.2 per cent in August and 63 per cent in September, although the more economic hotels and guest-houses in the gothic quarter reached 60 per cent and even 70 per cent rates. The average for the entire year is expected to be about 50 per cent, a considerable improvement on 1993. The composition of visitors has also changed, with a significant increase in the number of foreign visitors.

The 'Patronat de Turisme', aware of the dangers of an oversupply of accommodation to meet short-term needs, and in an attempt to take advantage of the good image and publicity derived from the Olympic Games, had already designed a Strategic Plan for Tourism Development in 1991. The plan identified, as strong points to be developed, the city's historic and monumental patrimony, its commercial structure and the association of the city with famous people (especially connected with the Arts). It did, however, recognize the lack of adequate promotion infrastructures of a unique image and of stategic definition for the city's tourism – in fact, the nonexistence of a well-structured tourist product. Obviously there had been no need to promote tourism in a city without the capacity to lodge potential visitors other than those coming for business purposes.

Table 5.24 Tourism in Barcelona before and after the Olympic Games (selected criteria)[a]

		Before		After
Visitors				
First visit	1989	17.4%	1993	25.9%
	1990	20.9%		
Hotels				
Hotel visitors	1989	1.62 m	1993	2.46 m
	1991	1.73 m	1994	2.66 m
Overnight stays	1989	3.80 m	1993	4.26 m
	1991	4.09 m	1994	4.70 m
Av. length of stay	1989	2.4 nights	1993	1.7 nights
	1991	2.7 nights		
Hotel occupancy rate	1989	62.6%	1993	44.6%
	1990	61.4%	1994	46.6%
	1991	60.2%		
Av. out-of-hotel				
spending	1989	15,700 ptas	1993	16,200
	1991	13,200		
Origin				
Spain	1989	48.6%	1993	37.9%
(principal regions)		(13.4 Madrid)		(15.1 Madrid)
		(4.4 Valencia)		(4.8 Valencia)
Foreign	1990	51.4%	1993	62.1%
(principal countries)		(11.1 France)		(9.0 France)
		(10.3 Italy)		(8.6 Italy)
		(9.4 UK)		(6.0 UK)
		(4.5 Germany)		(7.0 Germany)
		(3.4 N. Amer.)		(7.8 N. Amer.)
		(2.2 Japan)		(3.9 Japan)
Motivation				
Leisure	1990	22.7%	1993	28.4%
Business		53.8%		57.1%
Fairs		10.8%		3.2%
Congresses		4.5%		3.4%
Attractions				
Museu Picasso	1991	378,000	1993	580,000
Fundacío Miró		175,000		354,000
Thyssen-Bornemisza Collection				
(opened 1993)		–		76,000
Sagrada Familia Temple		700,000		660,000
Barcelona FC Stadium		429,000		337,000
Columbus Monument		44,000		131,000
City Tour Bus		24,000		102,000
Congresses				
National	1990	177	1993	354
International	1990	196	1993	356
Participants	1990	105,000	1993	175,000

Source: Author, based on information provided by Turisme de Barcelona
Note: [a] Statistics refer only to hotel visitors

Diverse initiatives have ensued, especially after the celebration of the Games. Already in 1992, the municipal council had produced an Economic and Social Strategic Plan for the following years. Within the framework of this Plan, the Tourism Commission identified several strategic objectives, which included: the promotion of Barcelona's newly gained image; the positioning of the city's tourist product in an international context; an increase in the number of visitors, in expenditure per person and in the number of repeat visitors. In order to achieve these objectives, a series of fourteen specific programmes – or sub-products – were designed. The underlying philosophy was that by diversifying the sources of demand, dependence on a limited number of markets would be reduced, thus making it possible to maintain higher occupancy levels throughout the year. The programmes included the traditional sectors of fairs and congresses, and aimed to expand Barcelona's market as a port of call for cruises, as a medical centre, a centre for cultural and sports events, of design and for shopping, and a destination for educational visits (such as summer university courses). Traditional attractions were to be marketed through promotional programmes grouped under the name 'Barcelona Turística', mainly consisting of special offers to encourage visitors on business trips to prolong their stay, especially over weekends.

The municipal authorities and the 'Cambra' co-operated, in 1993, in setting up a consortium denominated 'Turisme de Barcelona', to execute the plan. The considerable budget allocated (800 million pesetas for 1994) demonstrates the interest which has been taken in the project. Similarly, the 'Patronato' has been replaced by the 'Oficina de Turisme de Catalunya', in which the 'Cambra' also participates together with the 'Fundació Promoció Internacional de Barcelona', a municipally sponsored body. In 1994, the Barcelona Convention Bureau set up an office in the USA with obvious promotional objectives, and the city council offered collaboration with initiatives to construct a mosque with a view to stimulating incipient demand from Arab countries. The most recent initiative is the launching of the candidature of Barcelona as European Cultural Capital in the year 2001, to reinforce the image gained in 1992. To judge by statistics, the campaign to reap long-term advantage from the megaevent is beginning to be successful.

CONCLUSIONS

The most frequently recurring characteristic of tourism in the majority of Spanish major cities is the predominance of business as the motivation for visits (see Figure 5.8). As a result, the volume of tourism demonstrates, in most cases, a considerable degree of proportionality to population size. In addition, the largest cities are also the best equipped to attract trade fairs and congresses, thus emphasizing the differences. This is especially true of Madrid and Barcelona, unequalled in population, economic development, facilities for the celebration of fairs and congresses and accessibility, but also outstandingly attractive for tourism for leisure purposes

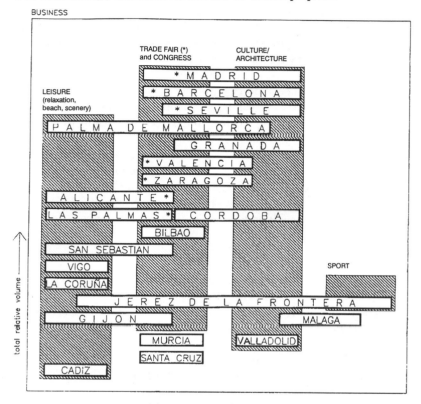

Figure 5.8 Volume and motivation of tourism, Spain

Apart from business and congress tourism, two other recurring motivations can be distinguished. In the first place, several major cities serve the additional function of coastal holiday resorts. These include the east and south coast and island cities of Alicante, Palma de Mallorca and Cadiz. The north and west coast cities of San Sebastian, Gijon, La Coruña and Vigo are resorts for long-stay holidaymakers and stop-off points for visitors to the surrounding region. The second motivation encountered in several cities, notably the Andalusian cities of Seville, Cordoba and Granada, is their cultural and architectural wealth. Jerez de la Frontera is somewhat unique, as its attractions offer considerable diversity and contrast.

Tourism is least developed in Murcia, a relatively isolated city; in the port of Cadiz; and in Malaga and Santa Cruz de Tenerife, where the respective airports serve as the entry points for large numbers of tourists who are transferred directly to nearby coastal resorts. These cities do not fulfil the requisites of the other cities sufficiently to be able to transform them into important tourist destinations. The evolution of tourism in Las Palmas is unique, and evidently related to trends in mass sun/sand/sea tourism, even though visits for business purposes now constitute the principal motive.

A serious effort to develop city tourism was not made until the mid-1980s, and the process only gained momentum in the present decade. In this respect, the publicity gained through the nomination of Madrid, Barcelona and Seville for the celebration of the three mega-events of 1992 made a significant contribution. Most major cities in Spain have, without doubt, many attractions to offer to visitors. In view of the interest which the national government tourist organizations and the authorities in most municipalities are showing in the development of tourism, considerable growth of the sector can be envisaged in the foreseeable future.

REFERENCES

Alos, E., Fabre, J. and Huertas, J.M. (1991) *La Barcelona del 1993*, Barcelona: Ajuntament de Barcelona.

Asociación de Ferias Españolas (1994) *Datos Estadísticos de las Manifestaciones Feriales 1993*, Madrid: Asociación de Ferias Españolas.

Cals, J. (1987) 'Turismo y política turística en España', in J. Velarde, J.L. García Delgado, and A. Pedreño, (eds) *El Sector Terciario de la Economía Española*, Madrid: Economistas Libros.

Carandel Robuste, L. (1992) 'Viaje al Madrid de la cultura', *Estudios Turísticos*, no. 113, Madrid: Instituto de Estudios Turísticos, pp. 41–54.

Chalkley, B., Jones, B. and Sims, P. (1992) 'Barcelona, urban structure of an Olympic city', *Geography Review* 6(1), 2–6.

Decret Legislatiu 1/1990 (text refos de los textos legals vigents a Catalunya en materia urbanística).

De Forn, M. (1992) 'Barcelona: development and internationalization strategies', *Ekistics* 59(352), 65–71 (Athens Center of Ekistics of the Athens Technological Organization).

Gutiérrez Ronco, S. (1984) *La Función Hotelera de Madrid*, Madrid: Consejo Superior de Investigaciones Científicas.

Horváth, G. (1991) *Industria Hotelera en España*, Madrid: Horwath International.

Instituto Nacional de Estadística de España (1992) *Censos de Población y Viviendas de España 1991, muestra avance – principales resultados*, Madrid: Instituto Nacional de Estadística.

Ley 22/1988 de 28 de julio de Costas. Real Decreto 1471/1989 de 1 de diciembre por el que se aprueba el Reglamento general para el desarrollo y ejecución de la ley de Costas.

Marchena Gómez, M.J. (1992), 'El turismo, una experiencia de descubrimientos', *Estudios Turísticos*, no. 113, 9–24 (Madrid: Instituto de Estudios Turísticos).

Ministerio de Comercio y Turismo (1993a) *Anuario de Estadísticas del Turismo*, Madrid. Ministerio de Comercio y Turismo, Secretaría General de Turismo, TURESPAÑA, Dirección General de Política Turística.

Ministerio de Comercio y Turismo (1993b) *Guía de Hoteles Oficial España 1994*, Madrid: Ministerio de Comercio y Turismo, Secretaría General de Turismo, TURESPAÑA, Subdirección General de Medios de Promoción.

Ministerio de Comercio y Turismo, Secretaría General de Turismo (1993c) 'Plan FUTURES: Memoria de Incentivos 1992', *Estudios Turísticos*, no. 119–20, 83–109 (Madrid: Instituto de Estudios Turísticos).

Ministerio de Comercio y Turismo (1994a) *Movimiento Turístico Año 1993*, Madrid: Ministerio de Comercio y Turismo, Secretaría General de Turismo, TURESPAÑA, Subdirección General de Medios de Promoción.

Ministerio de Comercio y Turismo (1994b) *Spain, Land of Congresses*, Madrid: Ministerio de Comercio y Turismo, Secretaría General de Turismo, TURESPAÑA, Subdirección General de Medios de Promoción.

Ministerio de Información y Turismo (1973) *Guía de Hoteles España 1974*, Madrid: Dirección General de Empresas y Actividades Turísticas.

Patronat de Turisme de Barcelona (1991) *Barcelona Proyectos de Infraestructura*, Barcelona: Ajuntament de Barcelona, Patronat de Turisme.

Real Decreto 1/1992 (modificación de la Ley de Suelos de 1975).

Servei d'Estadística, Ajuntament de Barcelona (1986) *Estadística Municipal: Butlletí 1985*, Barcelona: Ajuntament de Barcelona.

Spain Convention Bureau (1991) *El Mercado de Reuniones en el Spain Convention Bureau*, Madrid: Federación Española de Municipios y Provincias.

T.H.R. *et al.* (1991) *Libro Blanco del Turismo Español*, Madrid: Secretaría General de Turismo.

Valenzuela Rubio, M. (1992) 'Turismo y gran ciudad. Una opción de futuro para las metrópolis postindustriales', *Revista Valenciana d'Estudis Autonòmics*, no. 13, 103–38 (Valencia: Generalitat Valenciana).

Vila Fradera, J. (1992) 'La gran aventura de los Juegos Olímpicos de 1992 y el sector turístico de Barcelona', *Estudios Turísticos,* no. 113, 25–40 (Madrid: Instituto de Estudios Turísticos).

6 The London tourism complex

Paul Bull and Andrew Church

INTRODUCTION

London, with a population in excess of 6.5 million at the end of the 1980s, is not only the largest and most important city in the UK, it is also a major world city. It is the locus of decision-making for the British state, the top of the country's retail and cultural hierarchies, as well as the location of one of the world's most important financial and commercial command and control centres (HMSO 1991; Hamilton 1991). Because many of these qualities have endured in the capital for centuries the city has constantly attracted visitors: to begin with merchants and emissaries, and more recently business travellers and true recreational tourists coming to gaze on the buildings and institutions which attracted the very first visitors, the royal and ecclesiastical palaces, castles and cathedrals. Over a very long period of time, therefore, London has developed a complex interdependent web of facilities to attract, accommodate, feed and entertain its many tourists, of whatever kind they may be.

One important consequence of this evolutionary process is that London is the dominant tourist location in the UK.[1] For example, in 1992 London accounted for 9.98 million staying visits, or 66 per cent of all those to the twenty most popular towns in the UK (BTA 1994). What is equally significant is that of all overseas visitors to England in 1992, 51 per cent came to London only, with just 38 per cent choosing not to visit the capital at all (BTA 1993). Furthermore these overseas visitors to London consumed 68.7 million bed nights (37 per cent of the UK total) and spent £4,152 million (58 per cent of the UK total) (BTA 1993). For 1984 Horwath and Horwath (1986) estimated that 64 per cent of all visitors to the UK came to London. And for almost a decade earlier in 1976 Eversley (1977) suggested that only 25 per cent of visitors to the country did not spend at least one night in the capital. On the supply side of the industry London dominates the British entertainment industry, possessing over

11,000 arts organizations and companies and 40 per cent of its workforce (London Arts Board 1994). Yet at the same time it may be surprising to discover that in the mid-1980s London accounted for only 20 per cent of the nation's hotel bed spaces (Shaw and Williams 1994), and in 1989 had only 174,000, or 14.3 per cent, of the country's hotel and catering employees in employment (Bull and Church 1994). While these figures certainly indicate a concentration of tourist demand in London, they also demonstrate that for a conurbation with 12.1 per cent of the country's population and 15.2 per cent of its employment at the start of the 1990s, such a concentration was far less apparent on the supply side. This may indicate the efficiency and productivity of some aspects of the capital's tourist sector (Buck *et al.* 1986).

As one would expect from London's pre-eminence in the UK tourist scene, it has come to form a significant element of the London economy too. For example, it is estimated to have been responsible for 5 per cent of the city's GDP in 1992 (Reid 1994), while in terms of employment, hotel and catering alone increased by one percentage point of the capital's stock between 1981 and 1989 to stand at 174,000. Furthermore, if all arts-related jobs are included then this figure should be doubled to be almost 10 per cent of the capital's workforce; an importance likely to increase as other service industries in the capital, such as financial services, begin to shed jobs during restructuring (Hoggart 1995). But it is important to realize that the tourist-related industries in London do not just cater for the transient tourist population, they also provide food, shelter (for the homeless) and recreational opportunities for the capital's resident population, and for many others who live within commuting or day-tripping distance. Indeed it has been suggested that day-trippers to London during the early 1990s, a period of economic recession in the UK, may have been as large as 65 million per annum (Reid 1994). The very success of the tourist complex in London therefore depends on continually satisfying this varied cocktail of demand.

The significance of tourist-related industries in London to national tourism on the one hand and to the capital's economy and society on the other, makes the study of its development and geography particularly important. However, what is evident from a review of the most recently published research overviews of London is the limited reference to the tourist industry. For example, in *The Crisis of London* (Thornley 1992) and *London 2001* (Hall 1989) only tourist transportation problems within the city are noted. In the edited collection by Hoggart and Green (1991) only Hebbert makes brief reference to the tourist industry in terms of borough responses to the London Tourist Board's 1987 strategy document. What is most surprising is that even in the HMSO's *London: World City* the tourist industry is not treated in any consolidated way. It has to be inferred from sections on the cultural sector's contribution to the capital's wealth creation and quality of life.

This chapter will begin by looking at the growth of demand for tourism in London by means of visitor numbers, and go on to consider the growth of hotel bed spaces to accommodate them, and their use of the principal attractions in the city. This will be followed by a discussion of tourist-related employment. What will become clear is that this large industry is spatially highly concentrated in the west-central part of the capital, creating a distinct tourist complex. Such a concentration has created, and helped to exacerbate, a number of planning issues in the city. These will be discussed in terms of the role of the state and the development of policies for tourism in the final sections of this chapter.

DEMAND: VISITOR NUMBERS

'Tourism is an entirely new phenomenon', claimed Eversley (1977: 188). There had, of course, always been visitors to the capital, especially merchants and business travellers, with the wealthy and the leisured classes staying in distinguished hotels. There have also been for many decades boarding houses and hostels for long-term residents, students and workers. But large numbers of people travelling to London to stay at least one night for recreation and leisure was entirely new. In the first few years after the Second World War with major reconstruction required to London's infrastructure and rationing still in place in the UK, there was little opportunity or demand for recreational trips to the capital. Thus in 1950 as few as 500,000 foreign visitors stayed at least one night in London.

During the following decade, however, with the Festival of Britain in 1951 and the opening of Heathrow and Gatwick airports, the atmosphere and environment for visits to London changed substantially, both for British residents and foreign tourists. Following the work of Eversley (1977) the best guess for the number of foreign visitors to London in 1960 is 1 million, with 3 million by the middle of the decade and 6 million by the early 1970s. However, as can be seen from Table 6.1, this rate of growth was not to be sustained either during the 1970s or the 1980s. Between 1973 and 1983 barely one million more foreign visitors came to London, and by the early 1990s just over another 2 million had been added.[2] The 1960s, therefore, has been the period of most rapid growth in the number of visitors to the capital. The slowdown in visitor numbers after this decade may be understood in terms of trends in the world economy; a general deceleration after the long period of sustained growth in the 1950s and 1960s. The variation between particular years may be seen to be the result of, individually and collectively, the volatility of exchange rates, costs of living, levels of disposable incomes, the costs of travel (especially aviation fuel), the expanding range of international tourist destinations, and special factors such as air disasters, terrorist campaigns, military conflicts and royal weddings.

Table 6.1 Origin of overseas visitors to London, 1973–92

	Number of foreign visitors (millions)	*% from W. Europe*	*% from USA*
1973	6.0[a]	–	–
1974	6.3[a]	–	–
1975	7.1[a]	–	–
1979	7.6	47.7	18.8
1980	7.6	46.8	18.7
1981	6.4	43.9	20.6
1982	6.6	44.4	20.7
1983	7.0	39.3	26.8
1984	7.8	36.8	28.4
1985	8.5	36.0	30.4
1986	7.6	41.9	23.0
1987	8.6	41.8	25.3
1988	8.4	41.9	24.1
1989	9.1	42.1	23.3
1990	9.6	39.2	23.5
1991	8.2	46.5	19.0
1992[b]	9.9	–	21.0

Sources: LRC, *Annual Abstract of London Statistics*, various dates; [a] Eversley (1977); [b] BTA (1994)
Note: Excludes visitors from Republic of Ireland

At the beginning of the 1980s and in the early 1990s the proportion of visitors from both mainland Western Europe and the USA remained surprisingly constant at about 47 per cent and 19 per cent respectively, although following significantly different trends between these two points in time. The former slumped to 36 per cent in 1985 while the latter grew to 30 per cent in the same year (Table 6.1). Following the opening of the Channel Tunnel to passenger travel in 1994 the number of tourists from the near continent, including day-trippers, is expected to rise substantially in the latter half of the 1990s (Essex 1994). However, it was the downward trend of American tourists during the latter half of the 1980s and again at the beginning of the 1990s that was of particular concern to the capital's tourist industry, since US visitors, along with the Japanese, tend to stay longer and spend more per day than any other nationality group (Reid 1994).

The number of tourist nights spent in London, which includes both foreign and domestic demand, shows an even more stagnant picture than visitor numbers, with the number increasing by less than 2 per cent between 1978 and 1990. Between these dates there were over 30 million visits to London from within the UK, more than 30 per cent of the total to the capital. By 1991 this had slumped to only 19 million, 22 per cent of the total. It would appear that the recession in Britain at the beginning of the 1990s was significantly affecting the ability and willingness of British tourists to stay overnight in London. By contrast, and very fortunately for the capital's tourist-related businesses, foreign bed nights actually peaked in 1989/90 at over 76 million. From the temporal pattern of such visits it is clear that these two years were quite exceptional (Table 6.2).

Table 6.2 Tourist nights spent in London, 1973–92

	All visitors (millions)	Overseas visitors (millions)	Domestic visitors (%)
1973[a]	76.8	48.6	36.7
1974[a]	84.2	52.2	38.0
1975[a]	83.1	56.5	32.0
1978	94.8	62.8	33.7
1979	91.7	60.7	33.8
1980	88.4	56.4	36.2
1981	84.8	51.8	38.9
1982	87.5	53.5	38.9
1983	93.2	55.1	40.8
1984	95.8	61.8	35.5
1985	104.5	67.8	35.4
1986	97.1	63.1	35.0
1987	108.1	72.1	33.3
1988	100.1	69.1	30.9
1989	100.2	76.2	23.9
1990	95.8	76.8	19.8
1991	86.4	67.4	22.0
1992[b]	88.1	68.7	22.0

Sources: LRC *Annual Abstract of London Statistics,* various editions; [a] Eversley (1977); [b] BTA (1994)

There are three main reasons for visiting London: holidays, friends and relatives (VFR) and business. Of these the dominance of true recreational holidays is particularly significant in this case. They accounted for 51 per cent (around 5 million) of all overseas visits to London in 1992, compared with 44 per cent of all visits to the UK and 39 per cent of domestic visits to the capital (BTA 1993). London must be regarded therefore as an important location for mass tourism. VFR was the main reason for only

16 per cent of overseas visits, but for the domestic market it was over twice as important at 33 per cent. Business was responsible for 22 per cent of overseas visitors and 23 per cent of UK ones (BTA 1993).

ACCOMMODATION

In 1966 there were 44,000 bedrooms in the hotels and boarding houses of London. By 1970 this had risen to 80,000, 3,500 added in that year alone (Eversley 1977). Within four more years London possessed over 130,00 bed spaces in its 1,400 accommodation establishments, and 76 hotels with at least 200 rooms. What is more, much of this accommodation was heavily spatially concentrated in the three centrally located boroughs of Westminster, Kensington and Chelsea and Camden: over 1,000 of the hotels and boarding houses, and 64 of the largest ones with 200 or more bedrooms in 1974. The only other borough in the city at this time with a hotel concentration was Hillingdon with seven big hotels (3,591 rooms). This was due to the location of Heathrow airport in the borough.

One of the most important reasons for this frantic growth of interest in hotel construction in the early 1970s was the Development of Tourism Act (1969) which provided grants for bedroom completions by early 1973, at a time of property speculation on redevelopment sites in the inner city (Ambrose and Colenutt 1975). Furthermore there were another sixty-two hotel schemes in an early phase of development or awaiting planning permission at this time (Eversley 1977). However, the profitability of such tourist-related schemes was soon brought to an end by the increase in oil prices following the Yom Kippur War of 1973. A net increase of only ten large hotels took place in the capital by 1983, followed by a net decline of one, to eighty-five in total, by the early 1990s. Even the strong economic growth experienced by the South-East of England during the latter half of the 1980s was not enough to overcome the over-capacity in the large hotel sector set in train almost two decades earlier, although by the end of the decade there had been a number of warnings that this was indeed about to happen, diverting potential visitors to other cities either in the rest of Britain or, more worryingly, on the mainland of Europe (Horwath and Horwath 1986; Jeffrey and Hubbard 1988). By contrast, confidence amongst the smaller hotel operators at this time was much higher. As a result the total number of hotels in London between 1986 and 1992 increased by 10 per cent to 477, and the number of bed spaces by 8 per cent to 112,621.[2]

The locational pattern of hotel capacity in London at the start of the 1990s was very similar to the one for the early 1970s. The three boroughs of Westminster, Kensington and Chelsea and Camden still dominated, with 58 per cent of the hotels and boarding houses, and 73 per cent of all bed spaces. However, on the outskirts of the city a second important cluster grew to rival and then exceed Hillingdon. This was Croydon with twenty-eight hotels and almost 10,000 bed spaces by the end of 1992, benefiting from rapid commercial growth in a relatively cheap out-of-town location with easy access to the M25 and Gatwick airport on an important southern axis route to the south coast.

THE ATTRACTIONS

For the tourist, day-tripper, or local resident, London offers a vast array of attractions and activities: celebrated cultural establishments, famous buildings and architecture, the West End theatre quarter, parks and promenade areas, many different kinds of shopping, pub and club areas, as well as specific attractions such as Madame Tussaud's and London Zoo. Any visit to the city will almost certainly involve the use of a combination of these facilities. Unfortunately in many cases it is simply not known how often a particular facility has been frequented; how many people after visiting the Victoria and Albert Museum relax in Hyde Park, or before going to the theatre in Shaftesbury Avenue, visit a restaurant in Soho, listen to the street entertainment in Covent Garden and window shop in Oxford Street?

There are, however, a number of specific attractions for which visitor numbers are available, although it must be pointed out that the data has not always been collected with equal accuracy. They demonstrate quite starkly the dominance of London nationally and the importance of central London within the capital (see Figure 6.1). For example, of the top twenty tourist attractions in the UK charging for admission in 1993, nine were in Greater London, and a further two, Windsor Castle (state rooms) and Thorpe Park (Surrey) were in its immediate vicinity. What is more, in these eleven attractions, seven of the top UK eight were to be found! At this time the most visited attractions in London were Madame Tussaud's at almost 2.5 million and the Tower of London with 2.3 million (BTA 1994).

When attractions are subdivided into specific categories London's pre-eminence in certain areas becomes clear. In 1993 London possessed the most visited historic monument (Tower of London), cathedral (Westminster Abbey at 2.5 million, with St Paul's fourth at 1.9 million), Zoo (London with 0.9 million), garden (Hampton Court, 1.1 million, with Kew third with 0.9 million), and the top seven museums and galleries (British Museum 5.8 million, National Gallery 3.9 million, Tate Gallery

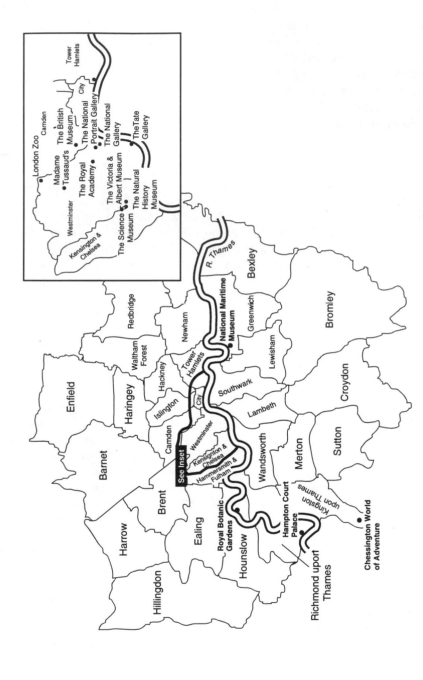

Figure 6.1 Tourist attractions in London, 1991

1.8 million, Natural History Museum 1.7 million, Science Museum 1.3 million, Victoria and Albert Museum 1 million and the Royal Academy 0.9 million) (BTA 1994). As Townsend (1992a) pointed out, inner London at the end of the 1980s accounted for 34 per cent of all nationally recorded visits to museums and galleries; a result which can only be understood in terms of their national and international importance and attraction to visitors of all kinds to the capital.

Table 6.3 Visits to selected tourist attractions (greater than 500,000 in 1991) in London

	1978	1983	1988	1991
British Museum	4,034,431	2,844,684	3,838,848	5,061,287
Chessington World				
of Adventure	792,000	667,724	1,151,000	1,410,000
Hampton Court Palace	659,600	504,400	537,955	502,377
London Zoo	1,606,634	1,239,210	1,326,027	1,116,247
Madam Tussaud's[a]	3,143,648	2,674,934	2,704,547	2,248,956
National Gallery	2,500,109	2,896,676	3,228,153	4,280,139
National Maritime				
Museum[b]	1,260,653	500,000	707,399	587,876
National Portrait				
Gallery	425,000	467,736	639,795	590,382
Natural History				
Museum	2,788,824	2,500,000	1,367,197	1,571,682
Royal Academy				
of Arts	800,000	560,000	987,018	807,962
Royal Botanic				
Gardens (Kew)	1,210,449	1,038,529	1,181,245	988,000
Science Museum	3,486,228	3,345,822	2,436,048	1,327,503
Tate Gallery	1,080,956	1,200,000	1,581,467	1,816,421
Tower of London	3,004,700	2,182,100	2,181,707	1,937,857
Victoria & Albert				
Museum	1,594,137	1,817,757	997,000	1,066,428

Source: LRC, *Annual Abstract of London Statistics*, various editions
Notes: [a] Includes Planetarium and Laserium; [b] Various systems of counting employed

During the recent past attendances at London's principal attractions have been far from constant (Table 6.3 shows the top fifteen in 1991). Between 1978 and 1991 some of the biggest museums such as the Natural History Museum and the Science Museum recorded significantly fewer attendances, by more than 50 per cent in the case of the former. Even Madam Tussaud's, the figures for which include the Planetarium and the Laserium, lost visitors. By contrast, the British Museum, the National Gallery and Chessington World of Adventure grew substantially. The latter achieved success by changing its product profoundly from a zoo to an adventure park. Explaining the trends in the other attractions is much more difficult, but each must in some way be related to the recession in the early 1990s, which hit the South-East of England particularly severely (Martin 1993), budgetary cutbacks in organizations traditionally taking group visits, and increased entry charges. The latter included some museums which began to charge for the first time. This not only helped to reduce attendances but also led to far more precise counts of their numbers, thereby revealing the optimism of earlier estimates.

Table 6.4 West End theatres and attendances, 1983–91

	Number of theatres	Paid attendances
1983	37	8,867,986
1984	42	10,014,769
1985	43	10,795,331
1986	42	10,236,362
1987	42	10,880,791
1988	43	10,897,384
1989	42	10,944,760
1990	40	11,321,288
1991	39	10,905,395

Source: LRC, *Annual Abstract of London Statistics*, various editions

Also probably indicative of the economic recession in the early 1990s is the slump in West End theatre attendances between 1990 and 1991 by over 400,000 (Table 6.4). Nevertheless, annual attendances at the forty or so theatres exceeded 10 million for the 1984–91 period, peaking at over 11.3 million in 1990. Of these approximately 30 per cent would be accounted for by overseas visitors to the city (Reid 1994). Furthermore, according to the London Arts Board (1994), of the 82.8 million individuals who on average attended arts-based events each year during the early 1990s, 45 per cent cited the arts event itself as their principal reason for visiting the city. Thus the capital's theatre and arts-related activities are not only an integral part of the tourist experience of London, they are also a vital attraction for the success of the tourist complex.

EMPLOYMENT IN TOURISM

This analysis of employment in tourism adopts a very broad definition of the sector which has been used in other investigations (Townsend 1992b). Following the categories of the British Standard Industrial Classification (1980) it includes restaurants and other eating places; fast food outlets;

public houses and bars; nightclubs; canteens and messes (contract cater-ing); hotels; other tourist accommodation; tourist offices and other com-munity services; libraries, museums and art galleries; sport and other recreational services. In September 1991 this group of activities recorded 287,000 employees in employment in Greater London, 8.8 per cent of the city's total, having grown by over 12 per cent since 1981.

Between the individual activity headings which constitute the tourist-related sector in the capital there was a great deal of variation in employ-ment growth (Table 6.5). Two groups, take-aways (152 per cent) and tourist/community services (115 per cent), grew spectacularly quickly. Both, interestingly, followed UK employment trends in these activities very closely indeed, indicating the importance of a national growth of interest in recreation and eating outside the home as a major stimulus for expansion in the tourist industry in London during the 1980s.

Table 6.5 Employment change in tourist-related industries in Greater London, 1981–91

	1981	*1991*	*Change*	*% change*
Eating places	38,663	50,558	11,895	30.8
Take-aways	3,346	8,429	5,083	151.9
Pubs	27,184	29,129	1,945	7.2
Night clubs	10,172	11,975	1,803	17.7
Contract catering	33,013	28,582	−4,431	−13.4
Hotels	39,394	37,056	−2,338	−5.9
Other tourist accommodation	868	494	−374	−43.1
Tourist offices/ community services	6,792	14,569	7,777	114.5
Radio/TV, theatres	35,114	39,887	4,773	13.6
Libraries, museums, galleries	13,686	14,044	358	2.6
Sport, other recreation services	47,562	52,169	4,607	9.7
Total	255,794	286,892	31,098	12.2

Source: NOMIS

In contrast to the employment successes of most of the tourist activity headings three groups actually shed labour during the 1980s. For contract catering, which lost almost 4,500 jobs, this was during a period of very rapid rationalization of capacity following merger and acquisition activity as the dominant firms became even more assertive. In the hotel sector job losses of almost 6 per cent indicate the competitive pressures faced by the

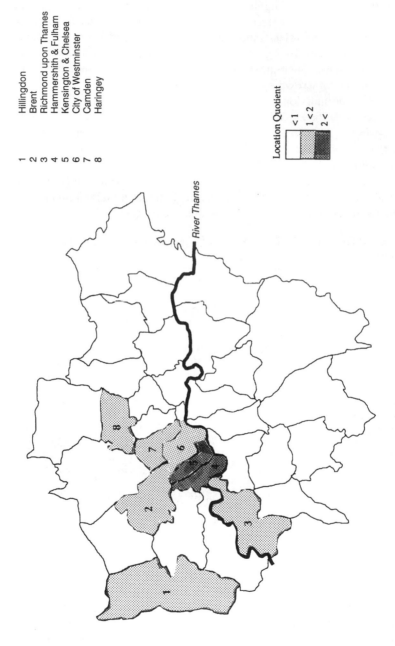

1 Hillingdon
2 Brent
3 Richmond upon Thames
4 Hammershith & Fulham
5 Kensington & Chelsea
6 City of Westminster
7 Camden
8 Haringey

Location Quotient
<1
1 < 2
2 <

River Thames

Figure 6.2 The concentration of tourism-related employment in London, 1991

accommodation industry during the 1980s. However, what is not clear is the degree to which labour costs have been kept low by the hotel trade moving towards a more casual labour force, employed on a daily or even a shift by shift basis (Wood 1991).

Tourism-related employment is far from evenly distributed among the boroughs of Greater London. As one may have expected from the location of tourist attractions and hotels, its employment is also heavily concentrated in the central west of the city, with most jobs to be found in Westminster (over 70,000), Camden (over 22,000), Kensington and Chelsea (almost 17,000), and Hammersmith and Fulham (16,000) (Figure 6.2). In these last two boroughs, employment in tourism accounted for over 20 per cent of the total, resulting in location quotients in excess of 2.0! Other boroughs where tourism-related employment was more than would be expected extend south and west from the centre of London following the line of the Thames. These are not only areas where important tourist attractions can be found (see Figure 6.1), but also ones where these very institutions helped to create high-status residential areas with above-average use of hospitality establishments. A further borough which must be noted is Hillingdon in the far west, the location of Heathrow airport. What is also clear from Figure 6.2 is that the east of London shows no important concentrations of tourist employment at all. A number of attempts have been made, and are still being made, to encourage the development of tourism in this area, but by 1991 they had made no significant impact at the borough scale of analysis. This, of course, does not mean that they were unimportant at the local scale (see pp. 174–5).

Unfortunately, if change in tourism-related employment between 1981 and 1991 is considered the east of London also performs relatively badly (Figure 6.3; Table 6.6). Most of the boroughs recording significant job losses, such as Barking and Dagenham, Hackney, Newham, and even Greenwich, the location of the National Maritime Museum, *Cutty Sark* and the Observatory, were all in the eastern half of the capital. The other boroughs to actually shed labour during this period were all centrally located, including Westminster, the City, and Lambeth. Excepting Haringey, the boroughs recording high rates of employment growth, such as Kingston upon Thames, Barnet, Brent and Hounslow, tended to be in the west of London.

In many parts of Great Britain tourism employment is often typified by part-time, seasonal, lowly paid jobs with a high proportion of female workers (Ball 1989). The official figures from the Census of Employment tend to underestimate the scale of casual and temporary employment in tourism (Bull and Church 1994). Nevertheless, there is quite strong evidence to suggest that in terms of the nature of tourism employment

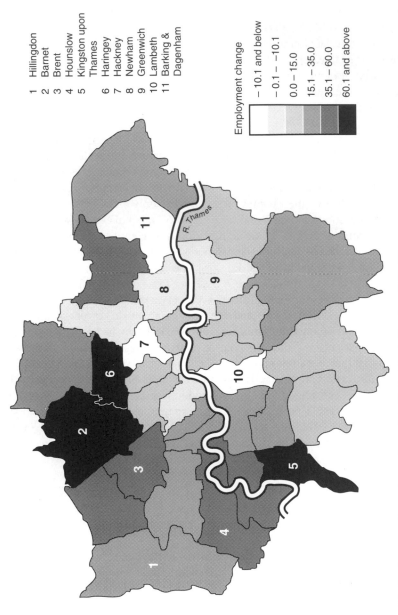

1 Hillingdon
2 Barnet
3 Brent
4 Hounslow
5 Kingston upon
   Thames
6 Haringey
7 Hackney
8 Newham
9 Greenwich
10 Lambeth
11 Barking &
   Dagenham

Employment change

- 10.1 and below
- 0.1 - -10.1
0.0 - 15.0
15.1 - 35.0
35.1 - 60.0
60.1 and above

R. Thames

Figure 6.3 Employment change in tourism-related industries in London, 1981–91

Table 6.6 Tourist employment in London, 1981 amd 1991: the importance of individual activity headings

	% importance	
	1981	*1991*
Eating places	15.12	17.62
Take-aways	1.31	2.93
Pubs	10.63	10.15
Night-clubs	3.98	4.17
Contract catering	12.91	9.96
Hotels	15.40	12.92
Other tourist accommodation	0.03	0.02
Tourist offices/community services	2.66	5.08
Radio/TV, theatres	13.73	13.90
Libraries, museums, galleries	5.35	4.90
Sport, other recreation services	18.59	18.18
Total	100.00	100.00

Source: NOMIS

London is slightly different to many other parts of Britain. For example, in London's hotel and catering sector in 1991, only a third of employees in employment were part-time workers compared to just over 60 per cent nationally. In addition, only 49 per cent of workers in this sector were female compared to two-thirds nationally (Census of Employment 1991). Office jobs in the headquarters of large tourism companies and the existence of some very large hotels and attractions may partly account for these differences. Nevertheless, a significant proportion of employment in London's tourism sector has traditionally been poorly paid with poor conditions (GLC 1985).

TOURISM POLICY FOR LONDON: THE EARLY YEARS

Policies for urban tourism usually require a network of co-operation between local government, tourist agencies and urban regeneration organizations. In London the policy environment is even more complex due in part to the larger number of government organizations involved and the geographically uneven economic role that tourism plays in the capital. Urban tourism policy in London, however, has a long history compared to cities elsewhere in the UK. Specific events like the British Empire Exhibition of 1924 and the Festival of Britain in 1951, which attracted large numbers of visitors to London, required a co-ordinated effort amongst local authorities to deal with the pressures that arose on London's infrastructure. By the early 1960s planning documents for the central London boroughs recognized the implications for planning policy of the land-use demands for new hotel construction. But it was the emergence of mass tourism in London in the 1960s that provided the key stimulus for the development of tourism policy. In 1963 the London Tourist Board (LTB) was established jointly by the London County Council and the private-sector-funded London Publicity Committee chaired by Lord Forte. The LTB started to implement tourism promotion policies for London, but the development of a more wide-ranging tourism policy linked to land-use planning was slower to emerge.

Eversley (1977) traces the development of a specific tourism planning policy for London back to the mid-1960s when the Greater London Council (GLC) and the boroughs of Westminster and Kensington and Chelsea, as part of the preparations for the Greater London Development Plan (GLC 1969), started to voice their concerns over the effect of tourism on housing land availability and transport. In a similar vein, the Green paper published by the GLC on tourism and hotels (GLC 1971) highlighted the negative effects of tourism on the land market, the transport system and working conditions. Not unexpectedly, the LTB tended to take a different view arguing that tourism growth should be vigorously encouraged and not be unnecessarily constrained by a restrictive planning policy for London (LTB 1970). The establishment in 1969 of the English Tourist Board and the British Tourist Authority provided further political support for the LTB's perspective.

Despite these differences attempts were made to devise a coherent tourism policy for London. In 1974 a tourism plan for London was produced by the GLC, four central London boroughs and the LTB and English Tourist Board (GLC 1974). This contained many good intentions, but Eversley (1977) argues that the organizations involved could not agree on what was needed for the encouragement and control of tourist growth in London. A GLC (1978) discussion paper and a later statement of policies for tourism (GLC 1980) both argued for more co-ordination and tended to be less restrictive towards tourism development. The lack of agreement identified by Eversley (1977) perhaps reflects the concern held by the GLC and local councils over the planning problems tourism created. Eversley (1977) lists the major planning issues associated with tourism as the conflict between hotels and local housing needs, the substitution of tourism employment for traditional jobs, seasonality, traffic congestion and the vulnerability of London's economy to tourist fluctuations. Clearly in the 1970s there were those who felt the problems of tourism growth might outweigh the positive opportunities it created.

TOURISM POLICY IN LONDON IN THE 1980s AND 1990s

Two recessions and the dramatic deindustrialization of London's economy have resulted in tourism plans for London that stress the economic benefits of tourism as opposed to its negative pressures. *The Greater London Industrial Strategy* produced in the early 1980s by the GLC (1985) recognized the growth potential of tourism-related employment but argued that government policy was essential to improve the working conditions of employees and to ensure the provision of high quality, low-priced accommodation. This approach reflected the interventionist tendencies of the socialist-controlled GLC in the early 1980s. After the abolition of the GLC in 1986, the LTB has taken the lead in developing London-wide tourism planning. In 1987 its Tourism Strategy for London (LTB 1987) was a key stimulus to the subsequent establishment of the Joint London Tourism Forum (JLTF). The JLTF brings together public and private tourism interests in order to provide guidance and co-ordination on the LTB's implementation of the Tourism Strategy for London. In particular, the JLTF seeks to ensure that support for the strategy is forthcoming from the tourist boards, central government and the thirty-three London boroughs (LTB 1993).

The objectives of the 1987 strategy were to develop tourism in order to promote economic growth, increase private and public incomes, generate employment, encourage urban renewal, contribute to environmental improvement and minimize the effect of visitor pressures. The Strategy is also based on the view that the development of tourism must benefit residents as well as visitors (LTB 1987). Such objectives will be similar to those adopted by tourism planning agencies in other cities (Law 1993). Overall, the London Strategy has a strong economic rationale, which is hardly surprising given the restructuring of London's economy and high levels of unemployment in contemporary inner London (LTB 1993).

The Tourism Strategy for London (1987) has been implemented by a series of Action Plans. The third Action Plan, published in 1993 (LTB 1993), identifies a number of the problematic issues currently facing tourism policy in London, many of which are similar to those listed by Eversley (1977). Transport infrastructure is seen as a key factor that could limit tourism's future development. An efficient and reliable public transport system will be needed to spread tourism away from the centre. In this context the JLTF has sought to exert a greater influence on transport policy by establishing a transport group and by sitting on the central government ministerial working group on Transport. The Action Plan (LTB 1993) also identifies certain particular transport problems for the tourist industry, such as the provision of space for coach parking, the lack of a high-speed rail link to the Channel Tunnel and the financial failure of the Riverbus on the Thames at a time when the LTB was trying to market the use of the river by tourists. Seasonality and the geographical concentration of tourism are still important problems (LTB 1993), despite increased visitors in off-peak periods and local borough policies (such as Discover

Islington) designed to attract tourists to less familiar locations. A further problem facing the tourist industry is the standard of all forms of tourist provision for which the Action Plans have developed a number of initiatives to raise its quality. Nevertheless, the problem is still a pressing one given research by a private sector grouping designed to promote London, called London First Visitor's Council, recently discovered from departing tourists at Heathrow a clear need to improve the value for money in London's restaurants, hotels and attractions (London Pride 1994).

It is also possible to identify certain policy issues that are perhaps particular to London. For example, a number of studies have identified London's competitiveness problems in the large conference/exhibition market due in part to the lack of a very large conference centre (Reid 1994). In 1985 the British Tourist Authority (1985) argued that the two major exhibition centres of Olympia and Earls Court needed to be significantly expanded and a new facility should be built in West London or London Docklands. Current redvelopment proposals for London Docklands include provision for a new exhibition centre but London still lacks the conference facilities many organizations feel the capital should have (Reid 1994).

A crucial current issue for tourism policy in London, however, is marketing and promotion. Despite the seeming luxury compared to other conurbations in the UK of having a regional tourist board just for London, many organizations still feel that the promotion of London is far from satisfactory. The abolition of the Greater London Council in 1986 removed the locally elected metropolitan government advocate for London. The JLTF's 1991 Action Plan (LTB 1990) argued that the lack of a 'voice' for London was the key factor that could limit the development of tourism in London in the 1990s. The need for a London 'voice' had been identified by many other private and public organizations and for a period in the early 1990s two organizations, London Forum and London First, had been established to promote the capital. These two merged in 1993 to form London First. This has now established the London First Visitors Council which aims to involve the private sector to a greater extent in the promotion of London as a tourist attraction.

In addition, to these organizations there are a number of other bodies that have a specified interest in tourism in London. The establishment of the Department of National Heritage created a single central government ministry responsible for many tourist-related issues. In March 1995 the Department of National Heritage published a thin policy document called *Tourism: Competing with the Best*. The main proposal on the supply side of the industry was for a co-ordinated voluntary grading system for accommodation establishments, while on the demand side special action was proposed to promote London, with up to £8 million in funding, of which 50 per cent was to be from government sources. To quote from the document 'If we do not exploit the potential of London the whole country will lose out' (p. 10), and 'The aim must be to restore London as a prime destination for first-time visitors to Europe . . . and to exploit to the full the growing intra-European visitor market' (p. 10). Evidence is given in the document which indicates, first, that many recent visitors to London have not been satisfied with the standard of their accommodation and, second, that tourism growth in other European cities is faster than in London. The latter could, of course, be in part a function of the former. Nevertheless, for whatever reasons, these findings have helped to move the government towards realizing the crucial importance of London to UK tourism and tourism to London. Whether London's tourism complex can adequately cope with a major increase in visitor numbers without additional co-ordinated infrastructural planning is quite another matter.

At the same time the newly established central government Millennium Commission clearly represents an opportunity for considerable new investment in certain leading cultural tourism attractions. The Commission will use approximately £75 million per annum from the National Lottery to support arts projects in London. A number of these will be designed to be major tourism attractions. Major regeneration projects such as at Greenwich Waterfront and Kings Cross are seeking support from the Millennium Commission for major new tourism and cultural attractions that will be key elements in these large redevelopment schemes. In addition, certain major cultural flagship projects are being promoted as possibilities for support from the Millennium Fund. These are all in central London and include the Albertopolis in the South Kensington Museum Quarter, a second Tate Gallery at Bankside, and the redevelopment of the Royal Opera House and the South Bank Theatre complex.

Recent changes elsewhere in the structures of central government also have implications for tourism in London. A central government Cabinet sub-committee for London has been established along with a government regional office for London and the appointment of a Minister for Transport for London. The consultation document on the future of London published by the Regional Office for London identified tourism as a key future growth sector and suggested central government agencies might be involved in its promotion. Despite this sudden proliferation of agencies with a regional remit the 1994–7 Tourism Action Plan (LTB 1993) is somewhat cautious about whether they yet constitute a London 'voice' and argues that the new bodies must obtain appropriate resources and set clear priorities.

Furthermore, co-ordination between the different organizations is by no means straightforward, with evidence of disagreements over priorities. For example, the London Planning Advisory Committee (LPAC), which since the abolition of the GLC advises central government on strategic planning issues for the capital, identified in its 1994 Advice (LPAC 1994) a shortfall in hotel accommodation, especially of the low-cost variety. It suggested that more hotels should be provided in accessible town centres outside central London, and that in central London more non-residential locations should be designated for hotel development. The 1994–7 Tourism Action Plan (LTB 1993) takes a slightly more cautious view, arguing that the emphasis should not be on encouraging hotel development but 'on looking for particular opportunities as and when they arise' and maintaining standards in the existing hotel stock.

There are also differences of opinion over the approach taken in promoting London. For example, the London Pride Partnership, which seeks to provide a forum for private sector concerns over planning in London, suggested that the LTB's overseas promotional strategy did not relate to the market many local boroughs were targeting. Furthermore, the LTB needed to do more to disperse tourists throughout London once they arrived and to stress the diversity of London's attractiveness (London Pride 1994). The LTB would counter this view by pointing to its Borough Liaison and Development Department, in which policy co-ordination is an important priority.

TOURISM POLICY FOR LONDON AT THE LOCAL LEVEL

The local boroughs provide another tier of government seeking to promote urban tourism in London. Of the thirty-three London boroughs fourteen have tourism officers and the English Tourist Board has made funding available to a number of local authorities to support tourism projects linked to local employment generation and urban renewal. For example, the Borough of Islington has formed a limited company in partnership with the English Tourist Board and local private sector companies, such as Thames Water, to develop its 'Discover Islington' strategy. This is aimed at attracting tourists to Islington who are seeking to escape from the mainstream London attractions and the dominance of international hotels and fast-food units.

Also at the local level certain urban regeneration bodies in London have developed tourism strategies. The London Docklands Development Corporation (LDDC) founded in 1981 instigated a specific visitor strategy in 1989 to attract more tourists to this major urban regeneration area in East London. Surprisingly, given that urban renewal agencies often place great emphasis on the role of tourism, it took eight years for the detailed strategy to come into being. Tourism had been identified in 1973 by an earlier regeneration organization as having a role to play in redeveloping London Docklands (London Docklands Study Team 1973). Indeed, the feasibility study undertaken by the GLC (1979) for the 1988 Olympics examined the potential of docklands as a base for the games and argued that the construction of new faciles in Docklands would have immense future tourism potential (GLC 1979). In the early 1980s a number of potential major tourism projects for Docklands were identified by the LDDC (Page and Sinclair 1989). In 1989 proposals existed for as many as eleven new hotels in Docklands with a combined capacity of over 4,000 beds (Page 1989). Many of these projects never came to fruition due to the national recession, but between 1981 and 1994 two new hotels and a youth hostel were built in Docklands. Other proposed schemes in the early 1980s included a people-draw area modelled on Quincey market in Boston USA, but this was overtaken by events as the major office development at Canary Wharf was on a neighbouring site. Plans for the Museum of London to find a home for Docklands-related artefacts has been a long running issue which may finally be resolved in 1995 with a Docklands Museum at West India Quay near Canary Wharf. The lack of an earlier formal LDDC tourism strategy was partly the result of the rapid pace of commercial and housing development in the mid-1980s, with tourists and visitors seen as something that would follow in the wake of large-scale office development (Church 1995).

Ironically, it was the downturn in the commercial office market that stimulated the emergence of a tourism strategy. In order to revive the commercial image of Docklands a new marketing team was established in 1989. As part of this initiative a visitor strategy was developed (Church 1995). The current visitor strategy seeks to develop and enhance visitor facilities, increase visitor numbers and encourage employment in the visitor industry in Docklands (LDDC 1994). Certain key elements in the regeneration process, such as the new Docklands Light Railway, are also marketed as tourism attractions (LDDC 1994) Recently the LDDC was part of a private/public partnership co-ordinated by the LTB that tried to adopt a more strategic approach to tourism in East London, and in particular in the Thames Gateway area identified by central government as a regeneration priority. This led to the development of an East London Tourism Initiative which took the form of an unsuccessful bid in 1994 to central government's Single Regeneration Budget.

The organizational complexity that now surrounds tourism policy in London might be seen as symptomatic of the competitiveness, fragmentation and diversity associated with post-modern urban politics. Such a theoretical explanation would in fact be rather inappropriate since in London, at least, tourism policy has been always thus. Eversley (1977) identified eleven major public sector organizations that in the late 1970s had a role in the promotion and regulation of tourism. This diversity, Eversley (1977) claimed, prejudiced the development of tourism policy. In the mid-1990s the implementation of the London Tourism Strategy (LTB 1987) suggests there is more unanimity of purpose, but there is still plenty of evidence that tourism policy for London is still a fractured jigsaw that the differing agencies are finding hard to assemble.

CONCLUSION

This discussion has demonstrated the importance of tourism in London, both nationally and within the capital itself. However, in the 1980s growth was relatively slow and probably more the result of fortuitous economic circumstances than a sustained co-ordinated policy. The economic boom of the South-East region during the last half of the 1980s raised local consumption demand which substituted for the slowing down of overseas numbers. This growth, however, appeared to have little effect on employment levels in many of the depressed areas of Inner London. During the early part of the 1990s interest in visiting the capital has been somewhat depressed by economic recessions in the UK and abroad. But by 1995 local and foreign demand had started to pick up, with a number of new hotels and significant refurbishments underway. But tourism in London still has certain major problems – especially its value for money, lack of a promotional 'voice', internal transportation difficulties and geographical concentration. The development of policies to overcome these fundamental problems requires co-ordinated action. Central government, despite the funds made available to tourist boards in the 1995 budget and potential grants for the London arts from the National Lottery funds, tends to view tourism as a mature industry that should deal with its own problems. Given the scale of tourism in London, the fragmented private sector and local agencies may find it hard to deal with the problems without greater involvement by central government. Again, however, economic circumstances and certain specific events will probably come to London's rescue and allow tourism to expand. The recovery of the European economy along with the Channel Tunnel will bring in more tourists from mainland Europe. The millennium celebrations are likely to increase both domestic and foreign visitor numbers. How long London's tourism sector can go on staggering from one lucky break to another without resolving some of the underlying problems remains to be seen.

ACKNOWLEDGEMENT

We are grateful to Tina Scally in the Geography Department at Birkbeck College for drawing the maps.

NOTES

1 In this chapter London refers to the thirty-three boroughs of Greater London, shown in Figures 6.1, 6.2 and 6.3.
2 Unless otherwise referenced, the empirical evidence used in this analysis comes from various editions of the London Research Group's *Annual Abstract of London Statistics*.

REFERENCES

Ambrose, P. and Colenutt, B. (1975) *The Property Machine*, Harmondsworth: Penguin.

Ball, R. (1989) 'Some aspects of tourism, seasonality and local labour markets', *Area* 21, 35–45.

British Tourist Authority (BTA) (1985) *Exhibition Facilities in London – Providing for the Future*, London: BTA.

British Tourist Authority (BTA) (1993) *Regional Tourism Facts: London*, London: BTA.

British Tourist Authority (BTA) (1994) Student information pack, London: BTA.

Buck, N., Gordon, I. and Young, K. (1986) *The London Employment Problem*, Oxford: Oxford University Press.

Bull, P.J. and Church, A.P. (1994) 'The geography of employment change in the hotel and catering industry of Great Britain in the 1980s: a sub-regional perspective', *Regional Studies* 28, 13–25.

Census of Employment (1991) *Census of Employment*, National On-line Manpower Information System, University of Durham, England.

Church, A. (1995) 'Diversification in the Cityport economy, the role of tourism', in B. Hoyle (ed.) *The Restructuring of Cityport Regions*, London: Wiley.

Department for National Heritage (1995) *Tourism: Competing with the Best*, London: DNH.

Essex, S. (1994) 'Tourism', in R. Gibb (ed.) *The Channel Tunnel: A Geographical Perspective*, London: Wiley.

Eversley, D. (1977) 'The ganglion of tourism', *The London Journal* 3(2), 186–211.

GLC (1969) *Greater London Development Plan*, London: Greater London Council.

GLC (1971) *Tourism and Hotels in London*, London: Greater London Council.

GLC (1974) *Tourism in London, A Plan*, London: Greater London Council.

GLC (1978) *Tourism – A Paper for Discussion*, London: Greater London Council.

GLC (1979) *1988 Olympic Games Feasibility Study*, London: Greater London Council.

GLC (1980) *Tourism, a Statement of Policies*, London: Greater London Council.

GLC (1985) *The Greater London Industrial Strategy*, London: Greater London Council.

Hall, P. (1989) *London 2001*, London: Unwin Hyman.

Hamilton, F.E.I. (1991) 'A new geography of London's manufacturing', in K. Hoggart and D.R. Green (eds) *London: A New Metropolitan Geography*, London: Edward Arnold.

HMSO (1991) *London: World City*, London: HMSO.

Hoggart, K. (1995) 'Regional Development in the UK: the South East', *Geography* 80, 80–4.

Hoggart, K. and Green, D.R. (eds) (1991) *London: A New Metropolitan Geography,* London: Edward Arnold.

Horwath and Horwath (1986) *London's Tourist Accommodation in the 1990s,* London: Horwath and Horwath (UK) Ltd.

Jeffrey, D. and Hubbard, N.J. (1988) 'Foreign tourism, the hotel industry and regional economic performance', *Regional Studies* 22, 319–29.

Law, C.M. (1993) *Urban tourism,* London: Mansell.

LDDC (1994) 'Visitor strategy update', Report to Corporation Board, 20 December, London Docklands Development Corporation, London.

London Arts Board (1994) *Capitalising on Creativity – Prospects for the Arts in London,* Mimeo.

London Docklands Study Team (1973) *Docklands Redevelopment Proposals for East London,* London: Department of the Environment.

London Pride (1994) *Tourism in London,* London: London Pride Partnership.

LPAC (1994) *Planning Advice for London,* London: London Planning Advisory Committee.

LTB (1970) *Seventh Annual Report,* London: London Tourist Board.

LTB (1987) *The Tourism Strategy for London,* London: London Tourist Board.

LTB (1990) *Tourism Strategy for London Action Plan 1990–93,* London: London Tourist Board.

LTB (1993) *Tourism Strategy for London Action Plan 1994–7,* London: London Tourist Board.

Martin, R. (1993) 'Remapping Britain's regional policy: the end of the north–south divide', *Regional Studies* 27(8), 787–805.

Page, S. (1989) 'London docklands: a tourism perspective', *Geography* 72, 59–63.

Page, S. and Sinclair, M.T. (1989) 'Tourism and accommodation in London: alternative policies and the docklands experience', *Built Environment* 15, 125–37.

Reid, L. (1994) *London Tourism,* London: London Pride Partnership (Mimeo).

Shaw, G. and Williams, A.M. (1994) *Critical Issues in Tourism: A Geographical Perspective,* Oxford: Blackwell.

Thornley, A. (ed.) (1992) *The Crisis of London,* London: Routledge.

Townsend, A. (1992a) 'The attractions of urban areas', *Tourism Recreation Research* 17(2), 24–32.

Townsend, A. (1992b) 'New directions in the growth of tourism employment?; propositions of the 1980s', *Environment and Planning* A, 24, 821–32.

Wood, R.C. (1991) *Working in Hotels and Catering,* London: Routledge.

7 Tourism in British provincial cities

A tale of four cities

Christopher M. Law

As a country Britain attracts visitors primarily for its cultural heritage and also for business reasons. This accounts for the fact that most foreign visitors go to London for all or part of their stay. When they venture out they tend to visit small historic towns like Bath or Stratford-upon-Avon, or rural areas like the Cotswolds with stately homes. For British tourists, the seaside, countryside and historic towns are again popular and the idea of visiting a major provincial and industrial centre would at first sight not hold much appeal. When in the early 1980s the Yorkshire woollen centre of Bradford attempted to sell itself as a tourist centre, the concept appeared incredible. Yet within a few years every major city in Britain was upgrading its tourism policies and seeking a role for the industry in economic development. The reason for this change, the policies they have evolved and the success they have had are the subjects of this chapter.

Many of the cities in provincial Britain are the products of industrial growth in the nineteenth century. We include here cities such as Birmingham, Bradford, Bristol, Cardiff, Glasgow, Hull, Leeds, Liverpool, Manchester, Newcastle upon Tyne, Nottingham, Sheffield and Stoke-on-Trent. Although this period has left behind some fine buildings, museums and art galleries, theatres, orchestras and sports teams, in the public mind it is the image of industry, poor housing and bleak environments which persists, and which makes it difficult for them to be taken seriously as tourist centres (Madsen 1992). During the twentieth century most of these cities have faced increasing economic problems as old industries declined, and as the economic life of the country became more focused in and around London. The recession of the early 1980s involving savage cuts to industrial employment was a turning point for most of these cities. In a post-industrial world it was no longer feasible to base economic development strategy on the premise of solely attracting manufacturing employment. Most of the jobs in the future would be in the service sector and consequently these industries must be promoted. It was from this perspective that tourism was selected for development, being perceived as a growth industry. It was never seen as a panacea for the economic problems of cities, as the sole industry which could save the city, but as one of several industries to be promoted. Its advantage also was that it could help raise the profile of cities, change their image, and through the improvement of facilities provide further reasons why people such as managers should come and live in the city. Again tourism was not perceived as an instant solution, but as a strategy for the long term requiring the improvement and development of new attractions, the creation of events, and the modernization of the environment.

In order to evaluate the progress of urban tourism in British provincial cities, this chapter will focus on the four main centres, Birmingham, Glasgow, Liverpool (Merseyside) and Manchester, but much of what applies to them is relevant to the other cities listed in the second paragraph of this chapter.

HISTORICAL BACKGROUND

By the First World War the population of three of the urban areas had reached 1 million, with Birmingham at 910,000 just below. Liverpool was primarily a port with port-related industries. Glasgow was also a port but its earlier interests in cotton and tobacco had given way to shipbuilding and heavy engineering. Birmingham had a diversified range of metal industries while Manchester had added on to its cotton and clothing industries various types of engineering. Service activities were relatively well developed, both those related to the main activities and those serving a wider region. The growing diversity of activities and the entrepreneurial strength suggested a promising future.

But this was not to be. The basic industries of Glasgow, Liverpool and Manchester went into long-term decline, although for a period this was hidden by a post-Second World War boom. Only Birmingham had a different trajectory as the car industry expanded from the 1920s to the early 1970s. With high unemployment in the Glasgow and Liverpool areas, governments awarded assisted area status so that new industries could be attracted. The decline of basic industries impacted on the service industries, and at the same time commercial activities were being incorporated into national concerns with their headquarters in London thus reducing the vitality of provincial cities. The physical expansion of these cities brought them into contact with neighbouring towns to create conurbations.

Deindustrialization accelerated from the late 1960s. With Britain's car industry going into decline in the 1970s, the economy of the Birmingham area began to suffer serious problems. In addition to these economic difficulties, the cities began to experience physical problems. As the middle class moved to the outer suburbs, not only did the population of the inner city decrease, but it became more dominated by the poor, with attendant social problems. Rather than helping these areas, redevelopment policies often made them worse. Falling inner-city population in some cases, such as Manchester, also affected the strength of retailing in the city centre. On the edge of·the city centre warehouses and transport facilities were closing leaving behind derelict and redundant premises. By the early 1980s it was obvious that city centres and inner-city areas were in need of economic, social and physical regeneration.

While certain trends are apparent in all four cities, there are also significant differences between them. Birmingham's central location and good accessibility is advantageous when seeking to attract activities. Its distance from London (120 miles) has enabled it to attract services moving out of the capital, but at the same time it can be overshadowed, as with the airport where growth has been limited. Birmingham City Council has the largest area and population of the four giving it municipal strength and enabling it to dominate other cities in the conurbation and give it unchallenged leadership.

Liverpool's decline has been the greatest of the four and its problems the most severe, a situation made worse by its poor image (Madsen 1992). In 1994 Merseyside was given Objective 1 status by the European Union so ranking it amongst the poorest regions in Europe. Since 1949 when it first received assisted area status many firms have moved to the area, but many have subsequently closed or reduced their labour requirements so that unemployment has remained high. Within North-West England, Liverpool is overshadowed by Manchester which is only 35 miles away, and as a consequence some of its activities are smaller than might be expected – for example, service activities and air transport. The population of Merseyside is declining, particularly in Liverpool, so reducing its importance amongst the five local authorities of the region.

Manchester's strength is in the role which it plays in the north of England. Many companies have their regional offices here. Its airport, centrally located, has been able to grow to serve this wider region, and is by far the largest of the four. However, the City of Manchester only has a small area and population, and thus resource-base, and this has hampered its leadership role in the urban area. With an urban area divided amongst several authorities, there is inevitably some competition.

Glasgow dominates west central Scotland which contains the largest concentration of people and industry in that country. While Edinburgh is the capital of Scotland, many Scottish companies are based in Glasgow. Scotland has more devolved government than the English regions, and appears to be more responsive to local problems. This has helped Glasgow to respond to its serious economic problems.

THE ORIGIN AND DEVELOPMENT OF TOURISM STRATEGIES

While the basic reasons why British cities are promoting tourism are similar, the balance of arguments and the evolution of policy may be different, as our four case studies illustrate. In any city the development of policy will be influenced by the inheritance of facilities, structure of economy, agencies and authorities and traditions of working.

Birmingham's involvement with tourism dates back to the 1960s. At that time manufacturing firms in what was a thriving city expressed a need for an exhibition centre to display their wares, as was found on the Continent. At the same time a national committee proposed that there should be a national exhibition centre. The Labour government invited bids and to many people's surprise Birmingham won (Law 1985). The bid was a partnership between the City Council and the Chamber of Commerce, who had to provide most of the funding, this being supplemented by a small grant. The National Exhibition Centre was opened in 1976 on the eastern edge of Birmingham adjacent to motorways, the main London railway and airport. It has been an outstanding success, so much so that in the late 1980s an expansion process was begun with the aim of doubling its size.

The success of the NEC encouraged city leaders to believe that there was a future for Birmingham in business tourism. In the early 1980s a convention and visitor bureau was established and plans prepared for a convention centre on North American lines in the city centre (Franks 1983). This became possible when Birmingham was given European funding and such a centre was opened in 1991. However, by then it was becoming obvious that business and pleasure tourism could not be neatly separated. Business and convention visitors would be deterred from coming to the city if there were few facilities, particularly the arts and entertainment. Consequently the city has pursued arts policies attracting the Royal Sadlers Wells Ballet and the D'Oyle Carte Opera Company.

These policies have been led by the City Council where the leadership in this area of a moderate Labour group was able to attract bipartisan support. It also had the support of the private sector. Recently, however, the cost of these projects has caused some concern, it being suggested that funds have been diverted from educational and social policies at the expense of poor residents (Loftman 1990; Loftman and Nevin 1992, 1994). In spite of this, tourism projects still figure prominently in the 1994 Civic Pride document and include a national stadium, a major visitor attraction, more events, and the enhancement of existing attractions (Birmingham City Council *et al.* 1994). A strategic review of tourism by consultants Greene Belfield Smith was completed in early 1995.

Glasgow's tourism drive got a kick-start in 1983 (van den Berg *et al.* 1994). In that year a long-held ambition came to fruition with the opening of a new gallery to house the Burrell Collection, built with a large grant from the Scottish Office, and was much acclaimed. The city provost also initiated a confidence-boosting campaign, 'Glasgow's miles better', which raised awareness, while the McKinsey report proposed a regeneration campaign led by a public private organization (later Glasgow Action) to promote amongst other things, the city centre and tourism. Behind this initiative was the Scottish Development Agency which also promoted the Scottish Exhibition and Conference Centre opened in 1985 and the Garden Festival in 1988. Later in 1990 Glasgow became the European City of Culture. Most of these developments were the result of a partnership between the City Council, the Strathclyde Regional Council, the Scottish Development Agency and Glasgow Action. In 1991 the last two gave way to a new organization called the Glasgow Development Agency which was funded by Scottish Enterprise. Within Glasgow a tourism strategy has received widespread support, and has been sold to the public as a way of creating jobs.

In contrast to Birmingham and Glasgow, Liverpool's development of a tourism strategy has had a more bumpy ride. With the decline of the port, many of the old enclosed docks became redundant and were closed. This included the Albert Dock surrounded by listed historic buildings and close to the pier-head and city centre. It was suggested that the release of docklands opened up possibilities for tourism, but without funding for reclamation and rehabilitation this was impossible. In 1981 the Merseyside Development Corporation (MDC) was established and amongst its first projects were the 1984 International Garden Festival and the restoration of the Albert Dock. Throughout its existence the MDC has given a high priority to the development of tourism in the area, saying that 'tourism is essential (a precursor) to change the image which is necessary to bring other types of development to Merseyside' (*Financial Times*, 19 October 1989). A tourism strategy was produced and a Merseyside Tourism Board established, largely paid for by the development corporation (Merseyside Tourism Board 1987). Merseyside County Council became involved through the establishment of a maritime museum in the Albert Dock where retailing was also located. When the County Council was abolished in 1986 Merseyside museums were handed over to a nationally funded body. Notably absent from these policies was Liverpool City Council which was either bogged down in internal conflict or led by a militant left group who had no sympathy for tourism policies. At the end of the 1980s, when the Council was led by a moderate Labour group, greater support was given to tourism policies; though, in practice, little finance was made available (Liverpool City Council 1987). The private sector has also given little support or at best erratic support. With the life of the Merseyside Development Corporation coming to an end in 1996 it is difficult to see who will take on the leadership and funding of tourism development.

The origin of Manchester's tourism strategy goes back to 1978 when the Greater Manchester Council purchased two railway properties on the southern side of the city centre (Law 1993). One of these properties contained the original 1830 station for the Manchester to Liverpool railway and was located in the Castlefield district where there were also Roman remains, early canal developments and other historic buildings, albeit amidst environmental degradation. The Greater Manchester Council gradually evolved a policy of creating this area into an Urban Heritage Park and relocating a science and industry museum to the railway property, which was opened in 1983. The second railway property contained the former Central Station, with a large train shed which it was felt was worth preserving. An alliance with an insurance company, plus government and European funding, resulted in G-MEX, a £30 million exhibition centre opened in 1986, shortly before the Greater Manchester Council was abolished. By now the private sector was becoming involved. Granada TV opened their studios to the public in 1988, creating a major tourist attraction, while hoteliers pushed for a promotional organization. About this time two development corporations were established, Trafford Park in 1987 and Central Manchester in 1988, and with the English Tourist Board they promoted a strategic development initiative (English Tourist Board 1989). Using this plan the Central Manchester Development Corporation have encouraged tourism in the Castlefield area.

Independent of these initiatives, a group of local people led by a theatre manager were advancing the claims of Manchester to host the Olympic Games (Law 1994). At their first attempt to be the British nomination in 1986 they were beaten by Birmingham. In 1990 and 1992 they succeeded in representing Britain but failed to win either the 1996 or 2000 Games. However, by 1993 (bidding for the year 2000 Games) their profile both locally and nationally had become high. They were able to persuade the government to fund a velodrome and a large indoor arena. The City

Council had also become involved and after many years of weak support in the 1980s was beginning to take tourism seriously. This is indicated by the 1994 City Pride document which lists several projects with a tourism dimension such as a national stadium, an extension to the City Art Gallery, a Communication Centre and a new Lowry Centre in Salford as a performing arts centre and art gallery (Manchester City Council 1994).

These brief sketches illustrate the way in which tourism policies have become adopted by cities and incorporated into economic development strategies. In each city there is a different group of actors, and the leaders have varied. However, in all cases it has been the public sector which has led. From this background we can now move on to look at the various components of tourism.

BUSINESS TOURISM

The term 'business tourism' is used both to describe persons travelling on business and also those attending conferences and exhibitions. Business tourism is important because generally these visitors are high spenders and therefore have greater economic impacts than other types of tourists, and in particular because they use and maintain hotels. A city which is important for business activities will be able to support a good stock of hotels which can become the basis for other types of tourism. Within Britain, London is the outstanding business centre, but Birmingham, Glasgow and Manchester are important centres, while Liverpool is less important.

We have already seen that Birmingham has promoted itself for business tourism for over twenty-five years. Recently it has adopted the slogan 'Europe's Meeting Place', emphasizing this role. The National Exhibition Centre opened in 1976, with an area of approximately 100,000 square metres, enabled it to host large shows, both trade and public, and quickly became the most important exhibition centre in Britain. In the year 1993–4 it hosted 183 events attracting 3.4 million visitors and supported 12,200 jobs in the region (KPMG Peat Marwick 1993). It also generates a significant profit for the city.

Currently it is the process of being doubled in size. Whilst primarily an exhibition centre it can also be used for concerts and, with its two hotels, for conferences. Birmingham's central location and many hotels, both in the city centre and on the periphery, have enabled it to be important for conferences – in particular for the small business meeting. The opening of the £180 million International Convention Centre (ICC) in 1991 enabled the city to host large conferences (Smyth 1994). In the year 1992–3 the ICC hosted 263 events attracting 114,000 visitors and, it is calculated, supported 2,700 jobs in the region (KPMG Peat Marwick 1993). However, because of the competition in the conference market it cannot charge high rates for usage and for 1993–4 was projected to lose £7 million. It has found it difficult to attract political and trade union conferences away from the coastal resorts but recently achieved some success when members of the Confederation of British Industry voted to prefer Birmingham over Bournemouth.

Glasgow has many facilities for conferences and exhibitions but its location in northern Britain limits its ability to attract delegates. The Scottish Exhibition and Conference Centre was opened in 1985, funded 40 per cent by the Scottish Development Agency, 40 per cent by the local authorities and 20 per cent from the private sector. Whilst well used it has run consistently at a loss. Conferences are also attracted to other halls in the city, to the hotels and to the university. The experience of Glasgow has been that having high profile events like the 1990 European City of Culture has helped it to attract conferences, thus emphasizing the interdependence of the different elements of the tourism sector.

Liverpool aspires to be important for conferences and exhibitions but, without either purpose-built facilities or a large hotel stock, it is in a weak position to compete with the likes of Birmingham. Currently there are proposals for a conference centre adjacent to the Albert Dock and it is hoped that Objective 1 funding can be used to finance the project.

Manchester has long been important for conferences and exhibitions. Old exhibition facilities at City Hall and Belle Vue closed down when G-MEX was opened in 1986 (see p. 184). This centrally located facility has only 10,000 square metres of space and so cannot host the large shows that the NEC is able to do. It is well used, but there is a high proportion of public shows drawing mainly local people so that its economic impact is reduced. A small conference facility has recently been added. Manchester has no purpose-built convention centre, but it is listed as a future project in the 1994 City Pride document. Elsewhere the hotels and universities attract many conferences.

Birmingham's important role in this sector is due to early initiatives and its central location. Other cities aspire to have a role but it is going to be difficult to achieve. The severe competition in the industry often ensures that economic rents cannot be charged and facilities are run at a loss. Such losses must be set against the positive economic impacts of the sector in the local economy and the publicity that sometimes conferences and exhibitions bring. The example of Birmingham also confirms experience elsewhere that the conference and exhibition industry cannot be undertaken as a self-contained activity. The city will be more successful if there is a wide range of attractions, a topic to which we now turn.

ATTRACTIONS

Nearly all large cities have an inheritance of museums and art galleries usually dating back to the nineteenth century. The scale of the facilities varies depending on how many gifts they have received and how far municipalities themselves were prepared to invest in buildings and stock. Both today, as well as in the past, a fine art collection located in a building of architectural distinction is perceived to add prestige to a city. Museums and art galleries are usually run by a city authority but also sometimes by a university or a private non-profit-making trust. These facilities were of course established to serve local people, but today they can also be used to attract visitors. Large collections of art by internationally renowned artists can attract visitors from across the world, but smaller collections of lesser-known artists are unable to do so. Most of the great collections are national ones located in capital cities with which provincial cities will find it difficult to compete. Nevertheless, in their attempts to provide reasons why people should visit cities they must upgrade collections and facilities and perhaps divide collections to create new museums. Other attractions in cities include cathedrals, royal palaces and other historic buildings, but these again are unlikely to be present in cities of the Industrial Revolution.

Birmingham has a fine museum and art gallery in the city centre and also a science and industry museum. Other attractions, generally on a smaller scale, are scattered in the suburbs. Until recently it appeared to be doing little to extend these facilities. However, in 1993 it opened the Gas Hall for special exhibitions and kicked off with the Canaletto collection which attracted 60,000 visitors. In 1991, on the edge of the city centre, it opened a Discovery Centre in the Jewellery Quarter and in 1995 opened Matthew Boulton House to illustrate Birmingham in the Industrial Revolution. The main private sector attraction is Cadbury World opened in 1990.

Glasgow is well endowed with museums and art galleries. Its Kelvingrove Art Gallery is one of the largest and most popular in the country. The Burrell Collection, donated by a rich merchant, was relocated from here to a new and striking museum in 1983. When Kelvin Hall was closed as an exhibition centre in 1985, part of the building was converted for a relocated and enlarged Transport Museum, opened in 1988. More recently Glasgow relocated its religious art to a new gallery, St Mungo's, near the cathedral. There are also plans for two new museums in the city including a Gallery of Modern Art which will open in 1996 and be housed in the former Stirling's Library. Glasgow has attempted to attract collections from elsewhere such as Thyssen-Bornemisza, and recently bid for a new national Scottish art gallery. A science museum is planned on the Garden Festival site.

Liverpool also has a good inheritance of museums, which until 1986 were run by the County Council and subsequently by National Museums and Galleries on Merseyside. The long-term goal of a Maritime Museum was achieved in 1983 when it was opened in the Albert Dock. In 1988 a branch of the Tate Gallery was established in the Albert Dock, while in 1993 the Museum of Labour History was also relocated to this area and renamed the Liverpool Life Museum. Liverpool is fortunate that all these facilities are funded by the state with no cost falling on local council tax payers. In addition to these attractions, two smaller ones – Beatles Story and Animation World, are also located in the Albert Dock. The Albert Dock is itself a major tourist attraction receiving over 5 million visitors a year. Unlike the other cities, Liverpool has two major (modern) cathedrals, one Anglican and one Roman Catholic, which add considerably to the appeal of the city. Its waterfront location is also a major attraction of the city.

Until 1983 Manchester only had one facility – the City Art Gallery – in the city centre, the rest being scattered, including two associated with the University of Manchester. In 1983 two museums, an Air and Space Museum and a Science and Industry Museum, were located and relocated in Castlefield in redundant buildings. The latter was made possible by the generosity of the Greater Manchester Council which bequeathed funding for the enlargement of the museum. In 1988, besides this museum, Granada TV opened their studios to the public, containing the *Coronation Street* set as well as others. This facility cost £8.5 million and received a £750,000 grant from the English Tourist Board. This private initiative has proved a great success, attracting 700,000 visitors a year. Interestingly, in its Civic Pride document, Birmingham suggested an attraction 'Birmingham Studios' which appears modelled on Granada.

Visitor numbers to existing attractions have varied over the years and not shown a significant increase, but total visitor numbers have grown because of the opening of new attractions (Table 7.1). The latter have certainly increased the appeal of the cities. Between 25 per cent and 33 per cent of visitors to these museums come from outside the metropolitan area. Most were either residents or day-trippers coming from the nearby regions. This suggests that these facilities are mainly regional serving. All the four cities are seeking to develop new attractions and particularly ones with at least a national reputation so that visitors will be attracted from a distance. With only a few exceptions, such as Granada Studios Tours and Cadbury World, most of the investment in attractions has come from the public sector.

Table 7.1 Visits to the principal attractions in the four cities

	1983	1988	1993
Birmingham			
Museum & Art Gallery	483,063	598,856	632,505
Science & Technology Museum	236,154	243,000	317,139
(Jewellery Q) Discovery Centre	–	–	20,000
Cadbury World	–	–	473,000
Glasgow			
Art Gallery ˉ	839,912	926,804	796,380
Burrell Collection	189,096	580,357	361,980
Transport Museum	265,675	671,821	493,577
People's Palace	121,010	415,764	312,606
Pollok House	132,600	149,223	113,722
McLellan Galleries	–	–	283,009
St Mungo Museum	–	–	159,227
Provand's Lordship	6,400	127,282	89,274
Liverpool			
Liverpool Museum	526,680	585,222	494,025
Maritime Museum	103,086	409,012	367,519
Walker Art Gallery	174,313	242,960	237,779
Tate Gallery North	–	490,952	624,111
Liverpool Life	–	107,307	200,173
Beatles Story	–	–	119,000
Anglican Cathedral	100,000	209,000	500,000
Catholic Cathedral	150,000	150,000	175,000
Manchester			
City Art Gallery	70,747	181,000	193,191
Museum of Science	70,241	250,000	255,850
Manchester Museum	232,000	223,000	200,000
Whitworth Art Gallery	72,843	112,790	107,337
Granada Studios Tour	–	233,000	750,000
Salford Art Gallery	104,037	57,712	65,000

Sources: British Tourist Authority/English Tourist Board, 'Visits to tourist attractions' (various)

Given their history, the role of industrial heritage is either surprisingly weakly developed or only developed relatively recently. Birmingham and Manchester have science and industry museums, Glasgow a transport museum and Liverpool a maritime museum. Birmingham has recently opened a Discovery Centre in the Jewellery Quarter and has plans for another museum. There are also museums in Glasgow, Liverpool and Manchester dealing with social history. Of course many *in situ* industrial heritage sites are found at some distance from the city centre and are being exploited but cannot be easily linked in with the city centre attractions. While these cities have belatedly come to value their industrial heritage and now wish to preserve it and use it for tourism, one problem they face is that these types of museums are still relatively lowly placed in the hierarchy of attractions. People will travel the world to visit an art gallery, but not as yet to see an early example of a cotton mill.

CULTURE, SPORT AND SPECIAL EVENTS

Cultural and sporting activities are mainly provided for local residents, but once again they can be reasons why tourists should visit a city, or if they are already in the city, help make their stay enjoyable. After a period of decline, cities are attempting to improve their basic facilities, theatres, concert halls, arenas, sporting stadia, and at the same time improve the standard of performances in these venues. To raise the profile of the city and to bring visitors to the city, special events are held. The higher the quality of these events, the more likely it is that visitors will come from a distance. Such events will also have a high profile and wide publicity and so be able to draw visitors from a distance. For cities that have a poor image and lack world-class attractions, special events are a way of bringing in the visitors.

Birmingham has been upgrading its cultural resources in recent years. The International Convention Centre, opened in 1991, contains the Symphony Hall, and the city has been prepared to provide extra funding to the Birmingham Symphony Orchestra, with its charismatic conductor Simon Rattle, in order to improve a world-class orchestra still further. The city has also upgraded two theatres and attracted the Royal Sadlers Wells Ballet, now the Royal Birmingham Ballet, and the D'Oyle Carte Opera Company. For many years Birmingham has had a Jazz Festival and a Readers and Writers Festival. In 1992 it was City of Music, and Simon Rattle has organized a series of special musical events every year up to the Millennium. The Gas Hall already mentioned is designed to hold special art exhibitions which will draw people to the city. On the sports side Birmingham opened the £51 million, 8,000 to 12,000-seat National Indoor Arena in 1991 on the edge of the city centre (Smyth 1994). In the year 1992–3 it hosted forty events and attracted nearly 600,000 visitors, two-thirds of these coming from outside the West Midlands. It lost £3 million in the year but is estimated to have generated 1,900 jobs in the region (KPMG Peat Marwick 1993). In its Civic Pride document the city is bidding for a national stadium. It has been unsuccessful in other areas however. A failed bid for the Olympic Games was not repeated. A car race around the inner city was abandoned. None the less, the private sector, supported by the City Council, is investigating a large event, 'Expo 2003'.

Glasgow is likewise an important centre for the arts and sport. It is the home of all the national performing arts organizations in Scotland, the Scottish Opera, the Scottish Ballet and the Scottish National Orchestra. The International Sports Arena was created in 1987 when part of the former exhibition centre, Kelvin Hall, was converted to form a faculty capable of seating 5,000. It has recently, in 1990, improved its facilities with the opening of the £29 million Royal International Concert Hall. However, it is for special events that it is best known (Booth and Boyle 1993). An annual Mayfest has been held since 1983. In 1988 a Garden Festival was held attracting over 3 million visitors, while in 1990 the city received very wide publicity when it was European City of Culture. Visitor numbers increased, only to fall back in 1991 and 1992 (Myerscough 1988a, 1991). To rekindle interest Glasgow is now planning a Visual Arts Festival in 1996 and has successfully bid for the City of Architecture in 1999.

Liverpool has a cultural and sporting tradition which it is fighting hard to maintain (Parkinson and Bianchini 1993; see also Myerscough 1988b). Its theatres and concert halls are underfunded thus threatening artistic standards, survival, and the maintenance of the fabric of buildings. In the last ten years it has had two major events, the International Garden Festival in 1984 and the Tall Ships Race in 1992, both sponsored by the Merseyside Development Corporation. On a lesser scale it has an annual Beatles convention and has held events to mark fiftieth anniversaries of the Second World War victories. Liverpool bid for the City of Architecture in 1999 (along with Edinburgh and Glasgow), but was unsuccessful.

Manchester's cultural and sporting activities appear to be thriving. In the 1980s its commercial theatres were modernized and, exploiting the good accessibility of the city in the motorway network, it began to pull in patrons from a wide area. A new concert hall, the Bridgewater Hall costing £42 million, is being built for 1996, while the spin-offs from the Olympic Bid have been the £9 million Velodrome (National Cycling Centre) and the £56 million Victoria Arena. The events held here should attract visitors from a distance. Manchester has a strong sporting tradition. Manchester United is one of the few football teams which attract supporters from all over the country. While unsuccessful in its Olympic bids, the city has been won over to the idea of bidding for events. It began with the City of Drama in 1994 and also attracted a Global Environmental Conference. It is now bidding for the Commonwealth Games of 2002, which it appears likely to win, there being no other candidates.

The evidence from the four cities shows how culture, sport and special events are being used to promote the city, improve the quality of life and attract visitors. Special events, as Glasgow shows, can raise the profile and win visitors, but if they are not followed by more events, visitor numbers fall away. New facilities have or are being built, but it is too early to assess their impact. In any case, while they may be individually successful, they should also be considered as part of a more comprehensive strategy of creating a large number of reasons why visitors should come to the city.

SECONDARY ELEMENTS

The term 'secondary elements' is used to describe activities which generally do not attract visitors to an area but which are important in providing for visitors' needs during the stay. In the case of hotels, they are essential if visitors are to stay overnight in serviced accommodation, while shops, restaurants and nightclubs can make a visit more enjoyable. The scale, range and location of these facilities is very important for the tourist industry of a city. In nearly all cases they are provided and operated by the private sector. It is important that they are constantly updated to remain competitive with facilities elsewhere.

Hotels have been developed in the past for the business traveller and therefore to an extent reflect the standing of the city as a business centre. With business overnights mainly occurring during the week, hotels have sought to encourage the weekend leisure break market to fill their rooms, offering significant discounts to achieve this. A large hotel stock is also important for the developing conference market, whether the conferences are held in the hotel or a purpose-built centre. Since urban tourism has mainly been focused in the city centre, the scale of the hospitality industry in this area is an important indicator of the state of the industry.

Three of the four cities have experienced a significant expansion of the hotel industries in their city centres. All four cities had about 1,300 hotel bedrooms in their centres in the early 1980s, but in the cases of Birmingham and Manchester this number has increased by over a thousand, in the case of Glasgow by over 600, but for Liverpool the increase has been much less, and significantly these have been mainly budget-price hotels. The development of conference and exhibition facilities has been a major factor encouraging this growth, and its absence in Liverpool may explain why there has been less expansion. In the three cities with a growing hotel industry, the opening of such facilities coincided with the opening of new hotels. In the case of the Hyatt Regency in Birmingham and the Forum in Glasgow, new hotels were directly linked to conference and exhibition facilities (Smyth 1994). In Birmingham several new hotels were built near to these facilities, but elsewhere the spatial association was absent.

Shopping is an activity which tourists spend much time on, whilst often declaring that this is not the purpose of their trip. They are looking for shops which sell goods that they are unlikely to find in their home area, either luxury or craft goods. While major cities in Britain have maintained good and sizeable shopping districts, they do not always provide this type of good, or in a setting which would appeal to visitors.

Glasgow maintains a good shopping centre which in recent years has expanded with the addition of St Enoch's. Another addition which appeals to tourists is the Princes Square shopping centre built around a large atrium. Liverpool has benefited from the development of the Albert Dock where a festival marketplace type of facility is found. Manchester has few new developments of this type, but the St Ann's Square/King Street area would have some appeal to tourists. Finally Birmingham has acknowledged that it is deficient in this area. It had hoped for a festival marketplace type of development at Brindley Place, but so far this has not materialized.

The evening activities of tourists need to be met by an exciting range of restaurants and possibly nightclubs. There has been a growth of these activities in recent years to meet the requirements of the local population, thus reflecting greater affluence. In most city centres many new restaurants have been opened and are of an increasing variety in terms of cuisine. Manchester is a good example of this. There are now over sixty restaurants in the city centre, of which just over a quarter are Chinese (Law *et al.* 1994). A Chinatown emerged in the 1980s complete with a Chinese Arch. The city centre also has a vibrant youth culture experienced in over twenty nightclubs. There is also a gay village within the area. Indian and Asian restaurants are not generally found in the city centre but in the inner-city district of Rusholme about a mile away. Under City Council policy this is to become a themed area with the name 'Little Asia'. Another recent feature of policy in Manchester is the concept of the '24-hour city'. An attempt is being made to allow clubs and pubs to stay open all night, or at least well into the night. It is hoped that public transport and taxis will also run well into the night. Underlying the concept of the 24-hour city is the idea of becoming like other European cities which are perceived to have this kind of life, including pavement cafés and bars. Whether this latter aspect can be translated into Britain with its wetter climate is debatable. While these changes may appear to have little direct link with tourism, they are very relevant to it. They make cities more exciting places to visit. They may even become the cause of a visit. At a local and regional level they can draw people in on a Friday and Saturday night from up to 50 miles away.

The other three cities are experiencing similar trends to Manchester. Birmingham is following an almost identical trend, with a Chinese Quarter and a themed area where visitors can have the 'Balti Experience' (Asian cuisine). Liverpool also has a Chinatown, much longer established than those in the other two cities.

THE ENVIRONMENT

Creating a good and hopefully memorable environment is a necessary path to follow to become a tourist city. Because at least some parts of industrial cities are bleak it is necessary for them to reinvent or recreate themselves and in doing so create a new product to sell (Ashworth and Voogd 1990). They need striking urban landscapes, landmark buildings and distinctive features with which to create a new image. Unfortunately much of the architecture of the 1960s and 1970s on redeveloped sites was poor and definitely unmemorable, and in some cases is already being pulled down. All the four case-study cities have given much thought to this topic, although it has often been difficult to put ideas into effect. General ideas involve pedestrianization, removing traffic from the city centre, creating open spaces, planting trees, having street sculpture, developing waterfronts, constructing striking new buildings, floodlighting buildings (particularly for attractions), and creating themed quarters where tourist activities are clustered.

In Birmingham the city fathers decided to create a tourism/convention quarter on the west side of the city centre along Broad Street (Figure 7.1). Here the International Convention Centre has been constructed, in front of which is the newly laid-out Centenary Square complete with a sculpture representing the people of the city costing £3 million in all. The canal environment behind the centre is being enhanced and on the other side of the water the Brindley Place project is proposed as well as the already complete National Indoor Arena. Originally Brindley Place was to be primarily tourism oriented with a festival marketplace, but the failure to find a private sector investor has caused the scheme to become more oriented towards office development (Smyth 1994). A revised plan announced in March 1995 proposed 50,000 square metres of offices, 150 housing units, plus leisure activities which include the relocated IKON Gallery, a Sealife Centre, a new theatre, and shops and restaurants. Within the city centre Victoria Square in front of the Town Hall has been significantly upgraded at a cost of £3.5 million, a cultural quarter has been created to the south, and other areas have been designated for theming and improvement including the Jewellery Quarter and Chinatown. The 1995 strategy review reinforced the case for developing tourism quarters. However, one of Birmingham's main problems is that the inner ring road, planned as far back as 1919, is too close in, and with numerous tunnels and overpasses creates a poor environment. A recent Birmingham Urban Design Study has attempted to find solutions to this problem so that a high quality city-centre environment can extend further outwards.

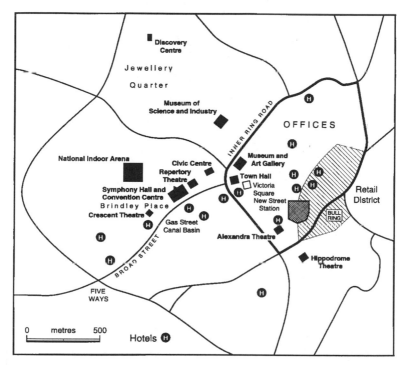

Figure 7.1 Tourism resources in central Birmingham

One of Glasgow's main problems is that its tourist loci are scattered and generally on the edge of, or just outside, the city centre (Figure 7.2). Therefore, an important policy has been to reinforce and develop the existing sites of attractions rather than create new locations. The Transport Museum was relocated to Kelvin Hall opposite the Kelvingrove Museum and Art Gallery. The Scottish Exhibition Centre is near to the old Garden Festival site where a tourist attraction is proposed. The Cathedral precinct has been enhanced and developed to include the new St Mungo Museum of Religious Life and Art. Within the city centre there

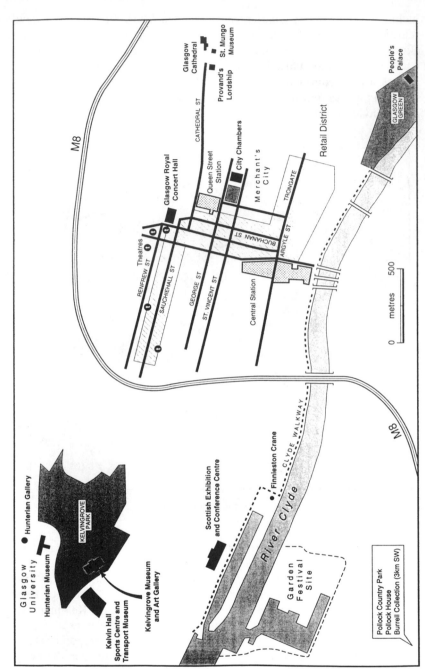

Figure 7.2 Tourism resources in central Glasgow

have been plans to rehabilitate the Merchant City and include some tourist attractions, but investment has been difficult to obtain. A report in March 1995 by Urban Cultures Ltd proposes that the quarter's renewal should be based on cultural industries and measures to develop the night-time economy. Finally Glasgow has a waterfront along the River Clyde which could be exploited in some as yet undefined way.

In most respects Liverpool has the best site of the four cities. There is the possibility of a classic waterfront urban landscape being created. Already the view across the Mersey to the pier-head – with the Liver, Cunard and Docks and Harbour buildings – provides a dramatic image of the city. The pier-head itself is in the process of being redesigned once again. With the closure of the docks on either side it has become possible to incorporate the magnificent Albert Dock into the public arena and to plan to use the other redundant spaces as sites for new uses and buildings (Figure 7.3). In the space of a few years in the 1980s the rehabilitated Albert Dock became the focus of tourism in Liverpool with five museums, shops and eating places. Overall it is estimated that over 5 million visits are made to it each year. Since its establishment in 1981 the Merseyside Development Corporation has been seeking to expand the tourism area, but a key site, the King's Dock adjacent to the Albert Dock remains undeveloped in spite of numerous proposals. This illustrates Merseyside's great weakness, its inability to attract private investment. The other task for tourism in Liverpool is to link the waterfront with the other attractions, the cathedrals and the St Georges Hall – museums area. This latter area, which includes the main theatre, is being developed as a cultural quarter.

Manchester's tourism environmental strategy has been to create a tourist quarter on the south side of the city centre (Figure 7.4). A tourism strategic initiative in 1989 (English Tourist Board 1989) reinforced this idea, with the addition of a linear zone along the River Irwell. The concept of a Castlefield Urban Heritage Park emerged in the late 1970s as some of Manchester's historic transport facilities became disused and derelict (see p. 184). The area was to be greatly improved in terms of its physical infrastructure and environment and it was hoped that private investment would be forthcoming to create tourist facilities. Three facilities, the Science and Industry Museum, Granada Studios Tours and G-MEX, have been very successful, but it has been difficult to develop other leisure uses. In order to get the land developed, the Central Manchester Development Corporation has been prepared to let sites go for housing and offices. It has been a similar story with the river corridor, although a museum and arena have been constructed north of Castlefield and there is still hope of leisure facilities coming to fruition in Salford Quays, particularly the Lowry Centre.

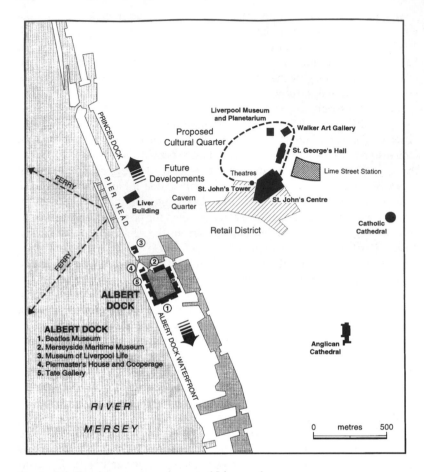

Figure 7.3 Tourism resources in central Liverpool

All four cities illustrate the fact that it is relatively easy to draw-up a physical planning strategy for tourism, but it is much more difficult to find the investment to realize the vision. It is likely that such strategies must be long term, requiring patience from the originators and main actors. Each city produced its plans in the boom period of the late 1980s only to find no takers for its proposals in the recession of the early 1990s.

PROMOTION

The selling of a city and the provision of visitor services is as important as the creation of tourism resources, and the scale of promotion is an indication of the importance attached to this role of the city. British cities have, of course, been promoting themselves for decades, but the effort devoted to this task was often erratic and generally small scale. Tourism leaflets were often produced by a public relations officer in the town clerk's department, who from time to time may have also provided copy to newspapers about the advantages of the city for industry. The growth of tourism generally, and the establishment of national and regional tourist organizations from the late 1960s, has stimulated the promotion of tourism and provision of visitor services at the local level. Best practice has been quickly passed downwards. The idea of Tourist Information Centres was borrowed from The Netherlands, while the idea of a quasi-private promotional organization came from the United States where every city has its Convention and Visitor Bureau. It has, however, been with some difficulty that the idea has become a reality (Bramwell and Rawding 1994).

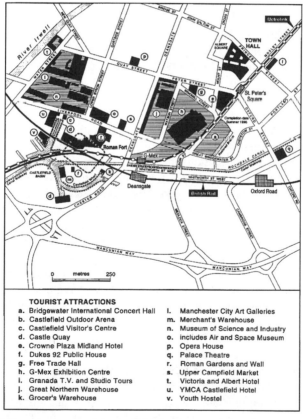

TOURIST ATTRACTIONS

a. Bridgewater International Concert Hall
b. Castlefield Outdoor Arena
c. Castlefield Visitor's Centre
d. Castle Quay
e. Crowne Plaza Midland Hotel
f. Dukes 92 Public House
g. Free Trade Hall
h. G-Mex Exhibition Centre
i. Granada T.V. and Studio Tours
j. Great Northern Warehouse
k. Grocer's Warehouse

l. Manchester City Art Galleries
m. Merchant's Warehouse
n. Museum of Science and Industry
o. includes Air and Space Museum
p. Opera House
q. Palace Theatre
r. Roman Gardens and Wall
s. Upper Campfield Market
t. Victoria and Albert Hotel
u. YMCA Castlefield Hotel
v. Youth Hostel

Figure 7.4 Tourism resources in central Manchester

With Birmingham modelling itself on the American experience, not surprisingly it was the first city to establish a semi-autonomous promotional company. The Birmingham Convention and Visitors Bureau (BCVB) was formed in 1982 and predominantly funded by the city. In 1990 it provided about £1 million of the £1.15 million income. In 1993 it was replaced by the Birmingham Marketing Partnership (BMP) combining the BCVB and the city's other promotional activities. The BMP was intended to market all aspects of the city, not just tourism, and to have greater involvement of the private sector. In its first year of operation it had an income of £2.2 million of which £1.6 million came from the city.

The Greater Glasgow Tourist Board was established in 1983 at the same time as a new structure for local tourism promotion came into being in Scotland. It covers Glasgow and some of the smaller towns round about. It is an autonomous organization with private sector membership. In the year 1992–3 it had a turnover of £2.3 million, of which £1.5 million came from the local authorities (including £1.2 million from the City of Glasgow).

The Merseyside Tourism Board was established in 1986 by the Merseyside Development Corporation and funded by them. In the year 1992–3 it had a budget of £700,000. It covers the County of Merseyside and thus is more than just Liverpool. In 1993 the Merseyside Tourism Board was wound up and replaced by the Merseyside Tourism and Conference Bureau, an autonomous body drawing funds from several sources. The Merseyside Development Corporation has greatly reduced its contribution, but the local authorities contribute, albeit only £68,000 (1993–4). With a contribution of £157,000 from the European Regional Development Fund, plus sales, it has maintained its budget at about £700,000 (Merseyside Tourism and Conference Bureau 1993).

Until 1986 tourism promotion in Greater Manchester was undertaken by the individual local authorities plus a separate conference office mainly funded by the County Council. In that year a Greater Manchester Tourism and Leisure Association was founded to co-ordinate the marketing of both the public and private sectors. Its main task was to develop the partnership which would lead to a more high-powered organization being created. This happened in 1991 when the Greater Manchester Visitor and Convention Bureau was formed. In the year 1993–4 it had an income of £677,000 of which £239,000 came from the local authorities, including £84,000 from Manchester and £53,000 from membership fees. It managed to earn £315,000 from fees and charges (GMVCB 1992–4).

It is clear that the scale of tourism promotion varies greatly between the cities. The Birmingham and Glasgow tourist organizations have relatively large incomes and are strongly backed by large local authorities. In contrast Liverpool and Manchester are poorly funded and have weak local authority support. They have to generate income from other sources as much as possible.

TOURISM IMPACT

This section will mainly examine the economic impact of tourism in terms of visitor numbers, overnights, expenditure and jobs created. There are of course many other impacts in terms of political attitudes and values, types of jobs, environment and so forth which are beyond the scope of this chapter. Most available data is obtained from national surveys of international and domestic tourism.

In terms of overseas visitor trips our four cities are in the third division behind the dominant London and the strong Edinburgh (Table 7.2). Glasgow received 430,000 visitors in 1992, Birmingham 360,000, Manchester 330,000 and Liverpool 170,000. The figures for the last three cities can be increased if conurbation statistics are quoted. All cities experienced growth over the previous ten years, in each case nearly doubling. In terms of the number of nights in 1992 the figures were Glasgow 2.8 million, Birmingham 2.4 million, Manchester 2.5 million and Liverpool 1.3 million.

Table 7.2 Overseas visitors to UK cities

		1983	1988	1992
1	London	7,560	9,080	9,980
2	Edinburgh	580	740	850
3	**Glasgow**	**210**	**290**	**430**
4	**Birmingham**	**220**	**290**	**360**
5	Oxford	210	300	340
6	**Manchester**	**200**	**260**	**330**
7	York	200	280	320
8	Cambridge	190	260	300
9	Bath	160	240	280
10	Brighton	210	250	260
11	Inverness	130	200	250
12	Bristol	130	180	210
13	Stratford-upon-Avon	120	170	170
14	Canterbury	110	140	170
15	**Liverpool**	**100**	**130**	**170**
16	Cardiff	80	130	160

Source: International Passenger Survey

For domestic staying visitors the 1992 figures suggest 1–2 million trips for each Glasgow, Merseyside and Greater Manchester and just over

2 million for the West Midlands. For nights the figures for the first three cities were 4–6 million and for the West Midlands 6–7 million. All cities experienced a fall in the early 1990s, probably reflecting the recession. In the case of Glasgow the decline may also reflect a fall away after the 1990 European City of Culture events.

In terms of expenditure in 1992 £300 million was spent in the West Midlands (perhaps £210 million in Birmingham), £240 million in Greater Manchester, £189 million in Glasgow and £156 million in Merseyside.

There are very few figures for jobs created. Two surveys for Merseyside undertaken in 1985 and 1990 suggest that the industry employed 14,000 (DRV Research 1986; Merseyside Information Services 1991). For Glasgow, a survey of 1989 suggested that 25,000 jobs were provided in the tourism and leisure sections, although not all of these are the result of visitor expenditure (Segal Quince and Wickstead 1989).

CONCLUSION

The account of these four cities illustrates how in the 1980s Britain's older industrial cities turned to tourism as a way of finding new jobs and raising their profile. There are no comprehensive and reliable statistics about local tourism trends, but data which is available, such as that for visits to attractions, overseas visitors and domestic visitors, suggest that they have had some success. Of the four cities Birmingham has probably been the most successful, followed by Glasgow and Manchester, and at the bottom Liverpool. However this success must be put in the context that many visitors are day-trippers and that they have difficulty in attracting large numbers from a distance to stay overnight, particularly the leisure tourist. They are mainly regional and national centres of tourism rather than international (see Chapter 1). They have difficulty in claiming attractions of world status and their image discourages visitors.

To attract visitors they must find good reasons to induce them to come. They can host conferences and exhibitions, stage events, and provide a large and ever-widening array of attractions in the hope that everyone will find something. Glasgow's experiences show the strength and weakness of this strategy. For several years it had an increasing number of visitors, but when it stopped having events in the early 1990s British visitor numbers fell away. Was this because all potential visitors have seen Glasgow and did not want to come back, or was it that without events they did not want to come? The fact that Glasgow is organizing events again suggests that the city leaders believe that it is the latter. In their quest for visitors these cities must constantly develop new products which are distinctive and unique and so demand a visit. It is debatable for how long they can go on doing this, and whether the cost is justified.

The development of tourism in these cities has mainly been led by the public sector, whether this be a city council, development corporation or agency, or arm of government. Public funding has provided improved environments, new attractions (mainly museums) and other resources, and funding for promotion. It has also been used to lever private funding as, for instance, when the city grant is used for a hotel. It has proved difficult to get private sector investment because of the risks involved. It has frequently been suggested, citing the evidence of urban revitalization programmes in American cities such as Baltimore, that the public sector has to lead, but when a certain threshold is reached – in this case visitor numbers – private funding will flow in. So far this has only happened to a very limited extent, as with hotels following the completion of conference and exhibition centres. The development of tourism to a successful conclusion appears to be a long haul in these cities, and one that may not be sustainable given the resource limitations of the public sector. Cities need to have access to varied sources of public funds from the local authority, regional government, national government to the European level, and from all their various agencies. The new British National Lottery has provided another source of funds. The successful city is one that can manipulate these sources to obtain finance. But if public funding reduces overall there will be decreasing opportunities to improve the tourism resource base. Not withstanding the disappointing levels of private investment, all cities are committed to involving the private sector in the organization, planning and promotion of the industry. This can take different forms as the example of the four cities shows.

The comparison of the cities has shown not only that there can be different trajectories, but also how difficult it can be for some cities. Problems include the local political culture, poverty in the area, political fragmentation of the area, the overshadowing by a neighbouring city, lack of a strong business sector, absence of a major airport, and distance from the major markets. Plus points are a large local authority base, a good airport, central location, initial advantages from developing a facility, a culture of partnership in the area, good leadership, and access to public sources of funds.

Despite setbacks and difficulties and possibly less funding in the future, it is highly likely that British cities will continue with their tourism strategies. With their economic problems they must promote any sector which is likely to be a source of new jobs. Existing programmes have now obtained inertia. Civic leaders are now aware more than ever before of inter-city competition and that tourism is both part of this and also a weapon in the wider economic strategies.

ACKNOWLEDGEMENTS

The author is grateful to Pam Wilsher of the Merseyside Tourism and Conference Bureau, George Sneddon of Glasgow City Council, Jane Cook of the Glasgow Development Agency and John Concannon of the Birmingham Marketing Partnership for help with this chapter.

REFERENCES

Ashworth, G.J. and Voogd, H. (1990) *Selling the City,* London: Belhaven Press.

Birmingham City Council *et al.* (1994) *Birmingham City Pride: First Prospectus 94*, Birmingham City Council.

Booth, P. and Boyle, R. (1993) 'See Glasgow, see culture', in F. Bianchini and M. Parkinson (eds) *Cultural Policy and Urban Regeneration*, Manchester: Manchester University Press.

Bramwell, B. and Rawding, L. (1994) 'Tourism marketing organisations in industrial cities', *Tourism Management* 15, 425–34.

DRV Research (1986) *An Economic Impact Study of Tourist and Associated Arts Developments*, Bournemouth (for Merseyside County Council).

English Tourist Board/Land Design Research (1989) *Manchester, Salford, Trafford Strategic Development Initiative: A Framework for Tourism Development*, London.

Franks, D. (1983) *International Convention Centre Birmingham: Feasibility Study*, Birmingham: Birmingham City Council.

GMVCB (Greater Manchester Visitor and Convention Bureau) (1992–4) *Annual Report(s)*, Manchester.

KPMG Peat Marwick (1993) *The Economic Impact of the International Convention Centre, the National Indoor Arena, Symphony Hall and the National Exhibition Centre on Birmingham and the West Midlands*, London: KPMG Peat Marwick.

Law, C.M. (1985) 'The British conference and exhibition business', *Urban Tourism Working Paper No. 2*, University of Salford, Department of Geography.

Law, C.M. (1993) 'Tourism in Greater Manchester', *Manchester Geographer* NS 14, 38–51.

Law, C.M. (1994) 'Manchester's Olympic Bid for the Millennium Games', *Geography* 79(3), 222–31.

Law, C.M., Fairweather, E.A. and Dundon-Smith, D. (1994) Metrolink and leisure activities in Greater Manchester', *Metrolink Impact Study Working Paper No. 15*, University of Salford.

Liverpool City Council (1987) *A Tourism Strategy for Liverpool: A Framework*, Liverpool.

Loftman, P. (1990) 'A tale of two cities: Birmingham the convention and unequal city', *Research Paper No. 6*, Birmingham Polytechnic, Faculty of the Built Environment.

Loftman, P. and Nevin, B. (1992) 'Urban regeneration and social equity: a case study of Birmingham 1986–1992', *Research Paper No. 8*, University of Central England in Birmingham, Faculty of the Built Environment.

Loftman, P. and Nevin, B. (1994) 'Prestige project developments: economic renaissance or economic myth: a case study of Birmingham', *Local Economy* 4, 307–25.

Madsen, H. (1992) 'Place-marketing in Liverpool: a review', *International Journal of Urban and Regional Research* 16, 633–40.

Manchester City Council (1994) *City Pride*, Manchester.

Merseyside Information Services (1991) *Visitors to Merseyside*, Liverpool.

Merseyside Tourism Board (1987) *Tourism: A Flagship for Merseyside*, Liverpool.

Merseyside Tourism and Conference Bureau (1993) *Action Plan 1994/5*, Liverpool.

Myerscough, J. (1988a) *Economic Importance of the Arts in Glasgow*, London: Policy Studies Institute.

Myerscough, J. (1988b) *Economic Importance of the Arts in Merseyside*, London: Policy Studies Institute.

Myerscough, J. (1991) *Monitoring Glasgow 1990*, Report for Glasgow City Council, Strathclyde Regional Council and Scottish Enterprise.

Parkinson, M. and Bianchini, F. (1993) 'Liverpool: a tale of missed opportunities', in F. Bianchini and M. Parkinson (eds) *Culture and Urban Regeneration*, Manchester: Manchester University Press.

Segal Quince and Wickstead Ltd (1989) *Glasgow Tourism Review*, Cambridge.

Smyth, H. (1994) *Marketing the City: The Role of Flagship Developments in Urban Regeneration*, London: E. & F.N. Spon.

Van den Berg, L., van der Borg, J. and van der Meer, J. (1994) *Urban Tourism*, Rotterdam: Erasmus University.

8 Tourism in United States cities

Uel Blank

Sing a song of cities, cities great and small,
Rhyming little ditties, tell about them all.
New York has her lobsters, Boston has her beans;
Baltimores the place for Oysters – but for lassies
New Orleans.
(Street Urchins' Medley, from *Grey Book of Favorite Songs*)

Cities are *the major* United States tourist destination.

Cities have occupied the role of major attractor for travel throughout United States history; their pattern is startlingly dynamic, complex, and varies strikingly from city to city. Despite variations, two factors operate in all cases to ensure the dominance of cities in tourism: the great majority (77.5 per cent) of the US population live in metropolitan areas (urban places with populations of over 100,000), and in addition to having the majority of the population, they attract travel at an even higher per capita rate than other parts of the state.

This chapter deals with tourism in United States cities, but in a special way. It primarily covers hinterland cities – those often considered as primarily industrial centres and lacking in amenities. We will see that while this may have been the conventional view in some past instances, it has never been true and is increasingly less true at the present (Blank and Petkovich 1980). Because of the focus on hinterland and so-called 'non-attractions' cities, this discussion will not treat extensively with cities perceived as high-amenity, high-profile tourist attractors such as New York, Miami, Washington, DC, San Francisco and Las Vegas.

Before proceeding further, it will be helpful to note the definition employed for 'tourist'. A tourist is any person away from the usual place of living, work or school. This definition does not initially make distinctions because of travel purpose, origin, length of stay, etc. Such distinctions are important to marketing procedures, but it is essential to begin with the total tourist system. For the destination city the most important consideration is this: the city has attracted its visitors by its complex of resident citizens, businesses, governmental and other headquarters, recreational and cultural opportunities, amenities, shopping and human and personal services. It then has opportunity to serve these travellers, thus generating jobs, profits, rents and taxes from the tourism industry.

CITIES AS TRAVEL ATTRACTORS

Now to look further into our central thesis; why are cities the major tourist destination in the United States? Travel occurs because cities are the focus of many and varied human activities and interactions. Many of these activities, as illustrated in Figure 8.1, involve both residents and tourists.

Figure 8.1 Community travel attractors

The following factors explain important elements of the complex, richly varied tapestry of human life that generates travel to cities in the United States.

Cities are, by definition, areas of high population density. Thus, travel to 'visit friends and relatives' constitutes a major tourism sector in nearly all cities. It has been found to be the largest single reason for travel to many hinterland cities.

Most cities are major travel nodes. Nearly all owe their establishment and early growth to an initial access advantage. Once established, subsequent travel developments focus upon the city, including railways, roads, and air routes. Thus, anyone travelling for any distance must go to a city whether they wish to or not.

Manufacturing, trade and finance concentrate in cities. For example, the Seattle Primary Metropolitan Statistical Area has 41 per cent of the state of Washington's population, but it accounts for 52 per cent of the value added in manufacture, 48 per cent of the value of retail trade and 75 per cent of the value of wholesale trade. All of these activities require a flow of travel and people interaction. An adequate set of hospitality businesses is needed to service this travel. Thus the tourism plant is essential to many components of the city's economy.

Just as commerce and industry concentrate in cities, so do all types of people services. These make up part of the agglomeration that constitutes a city. They include health care, education, government, and headquarters for industry, religious and other special interest groups and associations. In some cities, such as Rochester, Minnesota, health care is the primary tourist attraction; in many state capitals, governmental business generates the most travel.

Cities offer a wide and growing variety of cultural, artistic, and recreational experiences. This offering varies from opera performances to major sports; from art exhibits to nightclubs; and from historical interpretation to zoos. The first purpose of many such facilities is to improve residents' living quality. In addition, these facilities affect travel; many travellers make travel decisions based upon amenities offered (Brown 1990; Kavanaugh 1991). In many cases both residents and tourists gain from the interaction. Tourists enjoy a cultural/recreational experience offered by the city that would not otherwise be available; in turn, purchases by tourists in the use of these facilities may support facilities and programmes of a quality that the resident population alone could not afford.

The data in Table 8.1 specify the way in which certain hospitality services and economic activities concentrate in cities. Compared are per capita sales of four industry classes in five hinterland cities with sales in the state in which each city is located. Most lodging sales are to tourists; in one state 30 per cent of eating and drinking sales were tourist sales (Blank 1982a). A value of over 100 means more sales take place in the city on a per capita basis than in the respective state.

Only two values below 100 will be noted. Michigan's hospitality business in outstate areas is relatively large, thus Detroit's lodging sales per capita are not quite average for all of Michigan. In most of these cities wholesaling activities far outrank that in each respective state – Witchita,

Kansas is an exception. This is explained by the presence of other larger distribution points surrounding it: Kansas City to the East, Denver to the west, and Oklahoma City to the south.

Table 8.1 Relative shares of state hospitality, wholesale and retail sales for selected United States cities

City	Industry class (per capita share)			
	Eating & drinking	Lodging	Wholesale	Retail
Birmingham, Alabama	120	103	194	117
Dallas-Fort Worth, Texas	127	159	162	121
Detroit, Michigan	109	89	140	105
Indianapolis, Indiana	129	181	181	121
Wichita, Kansas	129	103	75	112

Source: US Census of Business (1987)
Note: The figures in Table 8.1 show the relative importance of sales in a given industry class, on a per capita basis, for each city in comparison with sales in the respective state. A figure of 100 would indicate that sales are of equal importance in both the city and the rest of its state. The figures are computed by dividing the percentage of the state's dollar sales in each class for each given city, by the percent of the state's population in that city. Example: Birmingham has 22.5 per cent of Alabama's population, but 26.9 per cent of the dollar value of Alabama's sales in Eating and Drinking Establishments were made in Birmingham; 26.9 is 120% of 22.5, as displayed.

Two cities rank high in all categories. Texas activities concentrate particularly in Dallas-Fort Worth. There is an even greater per capita concentration of Indiana's activities in Indianapolis. These indicators reflect the way in which hinterland cities act as the focus of economic and related travel activities.

EVERY CITY'S TOURISM IS UNIQUE

Not only does every city in the United States have a significant tourism industry, but the pattern varies strikingly from city to city. Some of this variety is illustrated in Table 8.2. There four hinterland cities are compared with each other and with a 'Speciality Tourist City' (discussed on p. 211).

In Kansas City 'visits to friends and relatives' make up almost half (46 per cent) of the total person-trips. Eight out of eleven cities investigated in making up Table 8.2 had 'visits to friends and relatives' as the largest single reason for tourists to travel there. 'Business and Conventions' dominate as the travel attraction for Chicago. While not the dominating factor, travel to Atlanta for 'entertainment and sightseeing' is at a rate almost twice that to Kansas City, and three times the rate to Detroit.

Table 8.2 Percentage distribution of tourist's person-trips to selected US cities

Purpose for travel	Atlanta, Georgia (%)	Chicago, Illinois (%)	Detroit, Michigan (%)	Kansas City, Missouri (%)	Orlando, Florida (%)
Visit friends and relatives	30	34	39	46	18
Business and conventions	34	37	26	30	12
Outdoor recreation	4	2	2	2	6
Entertainment and sightseeing	18	13	6	10	53
Personal business	11	10	24	9	5
Shopping	1	1	0	0	0
Other	2	3	3	3	5
Total	100	100	100	100	100

Source: US Census of Travel (1977)

Orlando, Florida is a different kind of city. There, over half of its tourist person-trips are for 'entertainment and sightseeing'. Orlando has one of the nation's premier attractions, Disney World, and supplements this with a major convention sales effort. These distinctions indicate the special make-up of travel to each individual city.

A CLASSIFICATION OF UNITED STATES CITIES BY TOURISM

United States cities may be classified according to their perceived endowment for offering tourism/recreational experiences. The three-part classification suggested there is probably more historical than applicable to tourism in the present day. It is valid, however, in the sense that this historical pattern persists as a destination image view of United States cities in the perception of many travellers, both residents of the United States and of other nations (Blank 1989).

The first two classifications: 'Cities With High Amenities' and 'Speciality Tourism Cities', will be seen as having a huge destination image advantage. In other words, travellers see them as attractive travel destinations. The third, 'Hinterland Metropolitan Areas', has not enjoyed such a favourable image. These cities are, in fact, situated in what many international travellers, as well as residents of the United States' east and west coasts, think of as 'flyover territory' having no appeal and only helping to hold that part of the world together. We will see that near-revolutionary changes within recent decades operate to alter the travel appeal of hinterland cities dramatically.

Cities with high-amenity sites

Some cities are endowed with high-amenity natural resources that serve as attractors to travel. These include mountains and other unique geology, water recreation, and winter sun. Phoenix and Tucson, Arizona appeal to those seeking relief from winter cold. Seattle, Washington and San Francisco, California offer beautiful ocean-based sites. San Diego, California and Miami, Florida combine both the appeal of winter sun and ocean beaches. The prevailing view of these cities is as places for sight-seeing, and fun in the sun and water. Their tourism industry, in actuality, consists not only of these elements, but much more.

Speciality tourism cities

Speciality tourism cities often lack the advantage of a high-amenity site, but have other characteristics causing them to rank high as tourist destina-tions in the conventional view. This characteristic is most usually man-made and/or historical. Examples abound, the most likely to come to mind is Orlando, Florida with its nearby Walt Disney World attraction. Equally prominent is Las Vegas, Nevada and its casinos. There are many others: Washington, DC – the seat of the United States government, and New York, which has a high destination image profile because of its huge scale, variety and history. The identification of Philadelphia and Boston with the United States' national origins ranks them high. And the great complex of Los Angeles/California combines sites near the ocean and in the winter sun with Hollywood, plus nearby recreational attractions such as Disneyland.

The city leaders of cities situated in high-amenity sites and those with speciality tourism features have historically had a better recognition of tourism's role in their city, compared with the next class. Nevertheless their support of this concept has sometimes been uneven.

Hinterland metropolitan areas

In the conventional view, inland metropolitan areas such as Wichita, Kansas; Sioux Falls, South Dakota; and Louisville, Kentucky lack the travel appeal of cities with high profile natural or man-made attractions enjoyed by the two classes of cities illustrated immediately above. In some views this class of United States cities is even thought of as the non-attractions hinterland area or, as noted earlier, flyover country. These dif-ferences are more in the public perception than actual.

All hinterland cities have locational advantages. The site may not be on an ocean, but nearly all are situated on waters, either inland lakes or rivers, and many of these sites are outstanding in their own right. Duluth, Minnesota, for example, is one of the most spectacularly sited cities in the world.

Every hinterland city has a surprisingly large tourism industry. This fact may be one of the best-kept secrets in the United States. Tourism has not been well-recognized by hinterland cities because their city fathers thought that their economic future depended upon factories. They considered tourism as limited to those travelling for recreation to the high-amenity sites and activities offered by the two classes of cities noted above, or to resorts in outlying areas (Law 1993).

An important part of the tourism of hinterland cities is based upon their 'trade centre' function of wholesale and retail trade, finance, and human services. Another major part bases upon their resident population that generates human interactions classed as 'visiting friends and relatives'. A high proportion of their tourist income thus comes through sales made by operations that also serve the resident population. Hospitality services are necessary, but often are not the major source of tourist dollars. Even though relatively large in the aggregates, tourism income of this nature is dispersed throughout many firms. It thus has a low profile, and is often misunderstood and seriously underestimated (Blank and Petkovich 1979).

Many hinterland cities are moving aggressively to upgrade their offering of amenities for residents' living and for use by tourists, to enhance their tourist image and to market their tourism resources (Millman 1991; Anderson 1994). The history, patterns and results of these activities are treated in detail in the sections immediately following.

An important consequence of the upgrading underway is that hinterland cities often have tourism offerings and appeals that rival or even surpass those of the 'high-amenity' and 'speciality' cities. Illustrated here is the principle that ingenuity in upgrading, development and new investment can overcome the initial disadvantage of limited resource endowment (Blank 1989).

THE DYNAMICS OF CHANGE IN UNITED STATES CITIES

Since cities are the focus of human interaction, the evolving change in human society also concentrates in cities. Throughout the past century there have been massive alterations in the way in which the United States lives, works and plays. This change has accelerated in recent decades.

The Industrial Revolution produced its first major impact upon United States life early in the nineteenth century. It brought factories and 'mill towns' in which workers often lived crowded closely together in cheap living quarters. Factories also brought the smells and smoke from processing operations and power production. These reduced the livability of many city sectors and their effects persisted into and beyond the decade of the 1940s.

Industrial production, despite its many negatives, produced wealth. Corporate structures were devised, along with better-adapted, impersonal means of financing. This, in part, enabled the construction of large downtown buildings for trade, services and finance, bringing about the forerunners of the large city centres of today.

Transportation and communications technology produced a profound effect upon many cities. So long as travel was mainly by foot or beasts of burden there was a limit to the size of cities, as well as a barrier to expansion of population away from the East Coast and into the vast undeveloped continent. Water transportation was an early primary means of access into the interior. The location of many United States cities on major rivers and lakes attests to the early role of water travel. Canals were dug in some applicable locations to supplement natural water systems but the cost and adaptability of canals imposed strict limits on the extent of their use.

The steam locomotive was a major, Industrial Revolution, technology breakthrough. Its impact upon access to new territories, city locations, and the subsequent development of cities was tremendous. At the time of the Louisiana Purchase from France in 1803, the then president, Thomas Jefferson, is said to have commented 'It will take a thousand years for us to populate the area' (the Louisiana Purchase included a vast area from what is now the Central United States, the Mississippi River to the Pacific Ocean). Jefferson did not foresee the mass in-migration of land-hungry peoples from Europe or the California Gold Rush. Especially he did not foresee the development of railways.

Most hinterland cities were founded and/or experienced their time of major development during the period when steam locomotives dominated transportation in the United States. With improved transportation urban sprawl could take place. Earlier, the wealthy business leaders built their homes near the urban centres where there was commercial interaction. With the development of light rail, especially the electric-propelled trolleys of the late nineteenth century, the city could spread, and the wealthy could retreat from the factory din and smoke and from city-centre living congestion. Suburbs and commuting to work evolved on to the urban scene.

Suburbs were among the first vestiges of urban development arising from the quest for 'quality of living' (Blank 1989: 94). Suburbs allowed a choice in style and quality of living. They are made possible by the rising affluence of the middle and upper classes, and especially by the easy mobility of light rail and, in the past sixty years, the mobility and flexibility of the motor car.

In the United States the car-induced urban sprawl surrounding hinterland cities is, at best, a mixed blessing. Suburbs expand choices. But at the same time the city is imposed, often recklessly, upon the country. The sprawl allowed by the car often makes for inefficient development in the provision of roads, sewers and water. Further, most suburbs are difficult to adapt to public transportation, should this be required by energy efficiencies.

Most United States suburban development is poorly planned and managed. This occurs because the 'frontier spirit' is still alive and well within most citizens. The 'frontier' is long gone, but it typifies a spirit in which one felt compelled to move when neighbours got 'too close', or when resources were exhausted. The view says that resources are in inexhaustible supply and one needs only to move on to new space and to commandeer new resources. It also defies authority, each person is a law unto himself and may do as he or she pleases with the space and resources commanded. With many in the population thus psychologically attuned there is unwillingness to curtail one's individual actions, and 'rights', to achieve a better-organized living community.

Every action has a reaction. As the more affluent left the city centre, property values fell. This made it possible for poorer people, most of whose jobs were downtown, to move into the vacated properties. These properties had been well maintained and often upscale, but this condition did not continue for long. Living capacities became overcrowded, maintenance was reduced, and there was widespread decay in the city centres. The extent of this blight is sometimes difficult to imagine. In a large city such as Chicago the squalid living conditions, with maintained islands interspersed, extend for over eighty city blocks south from the Loop (Chicago's downtown business area). In some cities even the downtown business area became overwhelmed with the blight. The serious tragedy of this development is that squallor and poverty breed more poverty and crime, and blight the life opportunities for those people who are captured within it.

There is still further reaction; each metropolitan area is subdivided into a number of jurisdictions. Usually there is the major city from which the area gets its name. This major city is hemmed in by multiple suburbs, none of which, including the major city, has jurisdiction over the other. As the affluent leave the city, and the poor move in, the tax base of the major city changes – it falls! It has a growing, desperate need for infrastructure and human needs; but it has a declining income. This is the plight in which municipal governments in the United States find themselves (Lodd and Linger 1989).

The nature of manufacturing, processing and trade changed continuously throughout the past century. This change was in response not only to advances in physical technology such as those in transportation and power, but also to institutional inventions. These paralleled, added to, and were part of a city's difficulties. Among the more serious were those changes affecting numbers employed at given jobs, and requirements for human skills. These often acted to impose further hardships upon the most disadvantaged human classes, and continue to do so.

The above is background to understanding United States cities. Great and small, rich and poor, richly endowed by nature or poorly endowed; all, to one extent or another, have grown, blossomed, suffered blight, and struggled to overcome the difficulties besetting them. It is small wonder that tourism industry development has taken a back seat in many of them. The amazing thing is that many have achieved major progress. Many have mounted a considerable effort towards the development of their tourism industry. Human problems are also being treated. In some cases, instead of solutions, these problems are encapsulated – isolated from many residents and visitors. Still, while much remains to be done, there has been genuine progress towards restoring the city centre (Holstrom 1994).

Since 1950 most major cities have largely rebuilt or refurbished their downtown areas (Byrum 1992). In most cases this has been both a private and public effort. In many cities, the rebuilding has accomplished in twenty-five years what originally required 50–100 years to do. Cities, often with federal government assistance, have cleared away dilapidated buildings, built highway access and streets, established pedestrian malls and built public offices. Corporations have built hotels, shopping space and office buildings.

Much else has been accomplished:

- In many northerly cities skyways have been built connecting most of the downtown with above-the-traffic enclosed passages.
- Downtown parks have been established or enhanced, and human-scale areas have been added where downtown visitors can relax and where human interaction can occur.
- Many cities have added sports stadia, or enclosed sports domes. Here sports events can be enjoyed while protected from weather.
- Convention/conference centres have been added to many larger cities, or an existing centre has been upgraded and enlarged.
- Many cities now have one or more major theme/recreational parks, with an estimated 600 nation-wide (Millman 1991).
- Opera houses, other cultural facilities and museums have been added to most cities (Brown 1990; Kavanaugh 1991).

- Previously blighted areas adjacent to the downtown have been revitalized as upscale living areas in many cities.

Two developments deserve special note as adding to the livability and tourist appeal of 'nonattractions' hinterland cities:

- Up until the 1930s and 1940s many of these cities could be thought of as smoky, industrial cities. Most have now achieved victory over the air pollution, and have substantially restructured their industries so that their negative impact is less.
- Many cities are situated on rivers. Up until recent decades rivers were thought of as secular and profane; to be used, in many cases as open sewers. There has now been a dramatic upgrading of river frontage, where in many cases a severe eyesore and liability has been converted into a key tourist asset. In the case studies that follow immediately, Pittsburgh, Pennsylvania and St Louis, Missouri are examples of outstanding river-front redevelopment.

The net result of the above positive developments are greatly to reduce the initial advantage in tourism appeal enjoyed by cities having major natural sites, or man-made advantages. Many hinterland cities formerly thought of as stodgy by travellers have the ability to deliver a superior travel/vacation experience.

VIGNETTES OF SELECTED HINTERLAND CITIES

In this section hinterland cities are reviewed. These are cities that have undergone a metamorphosis as dramatic as the transformation of a caterpillar into a butterfly. Their histories and conventional travellers' images are reviewed. We will then see that they have progressed from industrial centres and nonattractions for tourists in the popular view, to offering an eclectic selection of things to see and do that is geared to the modern domestic and international traveller.

Detroit, Michigan

Detroit is a near-classical manufacturing/rustbelt United States city. In its 1950s heyday it was known as the 'Car Capital of the World'. Since that time it has undergone vicissitudes of fortune, and while it retains a strong orientation to car manufacture, many changes have occurred.

French explorers visited the Detroit River area, which connects lake St Clair with Lake Erie, as early as 1648. The French built Fort Detroit there in 1701, which passed into British control in the mid-eighteenth century. It was incorporated as a village in 1802, became the seat of government of the Michigan territory and for ten years (1837–47) was Michigan's capital. It served mostly as an agricultural centre until 1870. Then, in common with many northern United States cities after the Civil War, it developed manufacturing, including railway equipment.

Detroit owes its development as a car manufacturing centre to its manufacturing background, its location in the United States heartland, and especially to the vision, ingenuity and determination of a group of Detroit men including Henry Ford, Walter Chrysler and Ransom Olds. Detroit produced thousands of trucks and armoured vehicles during the First World War. During the Second World War, its entire automotive productive capacity was converted into the manufacture of war machines. The quarter-century 1940 to 1965 represented the zenith of Detroit's car manufacturing activity.

Three factors conspired to alter the manufacturing pattern in the United States. Manufacturing/assembly of cars was disseminated throughout the nation. Military machines depended less upon the wheels, more upon air power and high technology – centres for these activities included many locations in addition to Detroit. Added to these, serious competition from car producers in other nations developed.

While the above was going on there were also social developments. Jobs in car manufacturing attracted in-migration. Immigrants came both from within the United States and other countries. Particularly appealing was Henry Ford's then revolutionary $5 per day to his factory workers. It attracted disadvantaged United States citizens, especially from southern states. The demand for manufacturing workers during the Second World War further reinforced this people movement. The immigration continued for a decade after the strong demand was no longer there. This in-flow of relatively poor people, along with a lack of employment opportunities, impoverished some sections of Detroit as it did other similar northern United States cities that had been manufacturing centres. The social unrest resulting must be understood as a part of the overall history of these cities.

Detroit reached a zenith as a manufacturing city. It suffered a period of depression but is now recovering. In common with many hinterland cities its tourism offering and its downtown skyline have been transformed in the past two decades.

Detroit continues as the hub of United States car manufacture. Closely linked to the history of the manufacturing era is the Henry Ford Museum and Greenfield Village. Mainly the museum and village are a tribute to the genius of extraordinary individuals: Thomas Edison, Henry Ford, Noah Webster and Orville and Wilbur Wright. It is a 'must see' for any visitor.

The downtown now has a 4.7-kilometre (2.9 mile) long, overhead people mover. The Renaissance Center includes the city's largest office and hotel complex. Adjacent is the 28-hectare (300,000 square feet) Civic Center development. It includes Cobo Hall, a conference/exhibit centre that has recently been expanded to offer 7 hectares (700,000 square feet) of exhibit space. Also there is the 20,000-seat Joe Louis Arena which is primarily used for sports events and commemorates the famous athlete/boxer from Detroit. In close proximity there are other arenas, hotels and shopping facilities. Nearby in the Detroit River is the 400-hectare (1,000 acres) Belle Isle Park. Among other things it has an aquarium, and offers nature walks.

Art exhibits, theatre and cultural opportunities are in many forms. These include Orchestra Hall, home of the Detroit Symphony Orchestra; the Fox, Gem and State Theatres; the Detroit Institute of Arts and the Detroit Historical Museum. There are many others.

Detroit's ethnic variety is reflected in many ways. Near the downtown centres noted above is a two-block 'Greek Town', offering authentic Greek food and entertainment. Its African-American heritage is partly displayed in the North American Black Historical and Culture Center, the African-American Heritage Cultural Center, and the American Black Artists Museum. Polish culture can be found in the city of Hamtramck. Detroit thus reflects the American experience and culture in a wide-ranging way, and makes it available to the visitor.

Pittsburgh, Pennsylvania

In the 1950s Pittsburgh produced more steel than any other city in the world. It is from this activity that Pittsburgh acquired its reputation for steel manufacturing just as Detroit developed its reputation as a car manufacturing centre. At one time steel mills lined the rivers on which Pittsburgh is sited for 32 kilometres (20 miles), and it was reported that the great steel furnaces cast a red glow across the night sky that could be seen for miles away. It justifiably acquired the nickname 'Smoky City'.

Whatever its reputation, Pittsburgh is now a drastically transformed city. In addition, it is spectacularly sited in the 'western Appalachian Mountains of Pennsylvania and at the confluence of three rivers – the Allegheny, Monongahela and Ohio.

After contesting control of the area with the French, the British established Fort Pitt on what is now the present site of Pittsburgh in 1754. Interestingly, tourism was a factor in the early nineteenth century; Pittsburgh was the departure point for travellers on their way west. In the mid-1800s coal, gas and oil were found in the vicinity. These resources, together with its access to river transportation, gave Pittsburgh a major advantage, propelling it into the lead as a steel- and glass-making city. This occurred during and immediately following the Civil War – a period in which many cities were transformed into manufacturing centres.

In the early twentieth century Pittsburgh's living quality was less than ideal. There was great activity on the rivers and railways moving coal, coke and iron ore. The bustling mills, coke ovens and foundries spewed out a thick, gritty cloud of soot requiring that the street lights remained on all day. There was labour unrest and a high rate of industrial accidents.

Efforts at smoke abatement began in 1941. In the late 1940s city leaders funded a $500 million renewal programme. This included smoke control, development of a 15-hectare (36 acres) Point State Park on what is now the Golden Triangle, and an airport.

Steel production in Pittsburgh declined in the 1960s; today no steel is produced within the city limits. In the 1980s another downtown renewal, funded at $3 billion, produced a Convention Center, a major hotel, seven office/shopping complexes and a light rail system. Today the Golden Triangle where Pittsburgh's three rivers join has these and many other amenities, including historic Fort Pitt, and, just across the river, the Carnegie Science Center and a major sports stadium.

Today over 800 firms employing 85,000 people are involved in advanced technology in the Pittsburgh area. There are also thirty-one colleges and universities, over 200 performing arts groups, a symphony orchestra, and more golf courses per capita than any other United States city. In 1991, Pittsburgh received the National Building Museum's Honour Award for 'Its collective efforts over the last 45 years to successfully overcome urban decay and economic diversity and bring renewed vitality to Pittsburgh's metropolitan area.'

The dynamic pattern of international production and commerce now presents another interesting possibility for Pittsburgh. Steel-making technology is shifting to mini-mills. These may partly revive Pittsburgh's steel industry (Belsie 1994; Baker and Alexander 1994).

Birmingham, Alabama

A 17-metre (56 feet) high, cast-iron statue of Vulcan, the mythical god of fire and metalworkers, overlooks Birmingham. Vulcan appropriately symbolizes Birmingham, which was named after the steel-producing city in England, and has been referred to as 'The Pittsburgh of the South'.

Birmingham's setting is a scenic, southern extension of the Appalachian Mountains. Its origin is relatively recent, having been founded in 1871 at the junction of two railways. Abundant iron ore, coal and limestone in the area enabled it to become the leading producer of iron and steel in the Southern United States.

An industry diversification/transformation effort began shortly after the Second World War. Today only 15 per cent of its workforce have jobs in manufacturing. It still has iron foundries but its iron- and steel-workers have been largely replaced with medical and engineering professionals.

Today one can experience a bit of Birmingham's past iron-producing days – with a visit to Vulcan, standing high on Red Mountain; by touring the Sloss furnaces, near the downtown, and maintained as a National Historic Landmark; and with a visit to nearby Tannehill Historical State Park where primitive iron-making began in the 1800s.

Birmingham was a focal point for the Civil Rights Movement of the 1960s. Events that shaped the Movement and the course of the nation regarding civil rights occurred there. These are interpreted in the Birmingham Civil Rights Institute.

Complementary to the experience of Birmingham's industrial and human history are many entertainment, cultural, and artistic events and facilities. To note a few:

- The Birmingham Race Course, with a schedule of both thoroughbred and greyhound racing.
- It is home to more than a dozen performing arts groups, including ballet, theatre and music.
- Birmingham has the largest municipally owned art museum in the south-east United States. The museum recently underwent a $20 million renovation and expansion.
- The Alabama Sports hall of fame is in an outstanding botanical garden.
- The Birmingham-Jefferson Civic Center; with recent expansion it now includes a 19,000-seat coliseum indoor arena, and a 3,000-seat concert hall, along with an exhibition hall (20,400 square feet) for hosting trade shows.

Birmingham typifies the transition from an industrial to a service-oriented community.

Saint Louis, Missouri

Located at almost the mid-point of the United States, St Louis played a pivotal role in the westward expansion of the nineteenth century. The pattern of its economic history differs somewhat from that of the three cities detailed above, but like them its downtown area blossomed, atrophied, and has undergone a remarkable renaissance.

St Louis' site, near the confluence of the continent's two greatest rivers – the Missouri and the Mississippi, has long been inhabited. The Cahokia Indians developed a major culture here from AD 700–1400. Their settlement is now preserved in the 880-hectare (2,200 acres) Illinois State Park. There their way of life is interpreted, and includes a 30-metre (100 feet) high mound, along with many other smaller mounds.

European settlement began in 1764, when two French fur traders established a fur trading post on the site. It grew rapidly as French settlers moved into the area around the post.

In 1804, the claim to ownership was transferred to the United States as a part of the Louisiana Purchase from France. Almost immediately, the town became a key in westward expansion. The exploratory expeditions of Zebulon Pike and of Meriwether Lewis and William Clark started from St Louis. In that period the rivers were the primary arteries of transportation.

Eads Bridge, the first to span the Mississippi River, was completed in 1874. This bridge greatly improved railway access and overland commerce with Eastern cities. In this immediate post-Civil War period St Louis grew rapidly as a manufacturing and trading centre.

Unlike the three cities detailed above, St Louis' economy was never tied primarily to a single industry. It did not thus experience a fully comparable economic metamorphosis. But its economic activities changed dynamically over the years. It began as a fur trading post. Later came grain marketing, livestock exchange and meat packing activities. These continue, but are relatively less important as country buying points and other market shifts occurred. A few decades ago St Louis was the largest shoe manufacturer in the United States. This too has diminished in importance. In the process of dispersing car production out of Detroit, St Louis has now become one of the nation's largest car manufacturing centres. Other important economic activities now also include brewing, chemicals and high performance aircraft.

In common with nearly all of the larger cities in the United States, St Louis' social/demographic history includes considerable drama. Its middle-class, white population deserted the downtown area for the suburbs as soon as transportation developments permitted. Underprivileged minorities, mostly black in-migrants from the South, then occupied the downtown living quarters, parts of which deteriorated into wretched squalor. Not surprisingly, parts of the downtown business and shopping area also atrophied. An early attempt at redevelopment of the blighted housing area resulted in one of the nation's greatest public housing fiascos. Sub-standard housing was cleared, and the high-rise community Pruett-Igo built. This proved a serious mistake as it became impossible to control crime adequately, and to provide proper maintenance under these crowded living conditions. In a fanfare of publicity, Pruett-Igo was demolished. Despite these events black citizens are increasingly integrated into the social and economic life of the community.

Ethnic influences are strong in St Louis, in addition to that of the black population, just noted. The influence of the French shows in place-names throughout the city, and many elements of French culture are apparent. The nineteenth century saw a large influx of Germans to the central United States. Large numbers settled in St Louis and then up the rivers, especially westward along the Missouri River. One result is that St Louis shares beer-brewing fame with Milwaukee, where Germans also settled. The Germans also developed large wine-producing areas along the Missouri River. The wineries were abolished during the period of Prohibition of the 1920s. Many have now been re-established and lend a German/European aura to many small nearby communities.

More than almost any other city St Louis acquired a distinctive trademark image in the process of rejuvenating its downtown. It did this by erecting a 192-metre (630 feet) high, stainless steel arch on prime river frontage. A thumbnail sketch of the process is instructive. Farsighted individuals began intensive work in the 1930s to authorize a National Riverfront Park that would commemorate St Louis' role in the westward expansion of the nation. National legislation for this authorization was passed in the 1930s and signed by President Roosevelt. The Second World War intervened, and little action was taken throughout the war's duration. Then came a major job of clearing the waterfront of warehouses, and developing the park. A competition was held to determine the structure to be erected and Eero Saarinen's entry proposing a stainless steel arch was selected. Construction of the arch was not completed until the 1960s. Thus fully thirty years were required for this phase, with development efforts continuing into the 1990s.

Visitors may now view St Louis from the top of the Arch. Under it is the large Museum of Westward Expansion interpreting, among other things, the Lewis and Clark expedition in graphic detail. The Arch stands in front of the old Federal Courthouse, which is now a museum of St Louis city. Westward, for twelve blocks from the Courthouse, Market street is lined with Federal Courts and other office buildings, terminating in the former Union Railroad Station, and a massive fountain. The converted station now houses a hotel and many shops. The fountain 'The Meeting of the Waters' symbolizes the confluence of the Missouri and Mississippi Rivers. On the park grounds with the Arch is the 160-year-old Cathedral, St Louis' oldest church. Immediately adjacent to the waterfront park are thirteen hotels. Nearby is Busch Memorial Stadium, Cervantes

Convention/Conference Center, and the City Center (a shopping centre of 130 shops).

Forest Park is another unusual feature of St Louis. At 552 hectares (1,380 acres) it is one of the largest of central city parks. It was initially developed for the World's Fair of 1904, commemorating the Louisiana Purchase. Now it incorporates the St Louis Art Museum, an open-air Municipal Opera, the Jewell Box (an impressive greenhouse), the Zoo, and the St Louis Science Center.

UNITED STATES CITIES IN THE POSITIVE GENERATION OF THE TOURISM INDUSTRY

We have seen some examples. What, in general, are hinterland United States cities doing to generate the tourism industry? The first question might well be, why?

Traditionally hinterland city leaders pursued means other than tourism for generating economic activity; specifically industrial plants and operations handling tangible products. Tourism, since it dealt with intangibles, produced 'nothing'. Increasingly this view has been altered and there is growing understanding of tourism as a possible supplement to other economic activities. How much return? In one comprehensive study of a hinterland city, Minneapolis-St Paul, Minnesota (population 2 million), tourism sales amounted to 17 per cent of all retail and selected services sales (US Census of Business Classifications that include nearly all goods and services sold at retail) (Blank and Petkovich 1979). A percentage this large makes a substantial difference in the city's economy.

Many of the developments noted in the four cities sketched were not done solely or even intentionally for tourism industry purposes. Most were undertaken because of pride in one's home community, and to achieve a better lifestyle for residents. Air-quality improvements, parks, major sports centres, restaurants, evening entertainment, streets, airports, historical interpretation, art museums and cultural and artistic performances all add to living quality. But in the complex fabric of the interaction between residents, businesses, services and visitors they also add to tourist appeal and potential for tourism income.

Noted below are specific organizations and activities in pursuit of the tourism industry, by hinterland cities.

Chambers of Commerce

All cities have a Chamber of Commerce, whose function, broadly, is to promote economic health. Typically they see their role as that of attracting investment in industrial production, trade and competition; such a function is needed. While not directly intended, industrial development expands tourism in the form of business travellers (Snepenger and Miller 1990; Weaver *et al.* 1993). Until recently few Chambers of Commerce in large cities had actively worked at tourism development except for the provision of literature about the city and efforts to attract conventions.

Convention/conference

Nearly all larger United States cities have Convention and Visitor Bureaux. Most of these are directly a part of the Chamber of Commerce, or affiliated in some manner. While often overlooking other components of tourism there has been a long-standing rivalry for the convention trade. Emphasis upon conventions fits logically into the urban pattern. Large meetings and conventions are big business in the United States, with a total 1992 spending estimated at $61.4 billion (*Successful Meetings* 1993). These large gatherings primarily are made up of corporate employees and members of associations. Cities seek conventions not only for the direct income but because in this way they can focus the attention of key groups of decision-makers upon the city's potential for professional and business location and development. These are prominent among the reasons why nearly all large cities have located convention centres downtown in close juxtaposition to a high-amenity offering of activities to help make a good impression upon these visitors.

Powerful motivating forces in convention competition are the larger hotel/motel facilities. Convention travel represents an important part of their business and they thus are among the strongest supporters of Convention and Visitor Bureaux, along with support from major downtown food, entertainment and shopping services that also stand to gain directly from convention travel. Not only do conventionaires patronize these latter, but some research has found that in as many as 70 per cent of the cases other family members travel to the convention city and may also make purchases in the vicinity (Braun 1992).

A growing number of Convention and Visitor Bureaux now have appointed a tourism director. This person's function is to deal broadly with development of the tourism industry. Tourism directors may carry out or assist with many of the activities noted below.

Group planners and travel guides

More than three out of four of major hinterland cities surveyed were able to supply a good quality group planner. A 'group planner' is a document providing detailed information about meeting facilities and their capacities, attractions (things to see and do), lodging, food, cultural and artistic events and facilities, nightlife, transportation, and other services that a visiting group might need.

Group planners are made available primarily to professional travel organizations and leaders of professional groups that show interest in the city. These may include:

- The person(s) responsible for organization of a conference/convention for a business, professional, or special interest group. The decision for a given conference site is often made a number of years in advance. Among other things, facilities that fit both the group's needs and the amenities offered by the city are important ingredients in the sitting decision.
- Motor tours, organized bus trips, are growing at a rapid rate. Those who plan motor tour itineraries need information about the facilities and things to see and do in a city and its vicinity in order to include it upon the travel schedule.
- Travel wholesalers, businesses that organize package tours, also need information about each city. Tour packages are developed for a wide variety of travel groups from motor tours noted above, to cyclists, to international travellers having both general and specialized travel interests.

Every city contacted was able to provide a general travel guide (sometimes called a 'lure book'), of good to excellent quality. A travel guide, in general, is the literature sent in response to a request from an individual for travel information about the city. This literature has been sharply upgraded by United States cities in recent decades. A short while ago it was common to receive poorly organized information, mainly consisting of ads for individual lodging and other travel-oriented businesses.

Many travel guides still contain considerable advertising. Ads are included as a means of paying for the production of the literature. But excessive advertising sometimes makes it difficult for a user to find the information wanted.

Promptness in providing travel information appears to be a difficulty in some cases. About half of the travel guides were received within one month. But some cities required as much as three months to respond! Three months is beyond the travel-planning horizon of many individual travellers.

Other marketing activities

Contact with convention organizers and planners and the provision of literature as discussed above are major travel marketing activities of United States cities. Through their various agencies cities also engage in a variety of other marketing activities, which may include:

1 FAM Tours, or Familiarization Tours as they are known by a more descriptive term, are conducted by nearly all larger cities. These are events in which people involved are hosted overnight and given a descriptive tour of travel facilities and attractions. Usually most of the cost is borne by the hosting city by a combination of inputs. The hotel association may provide lodging and, along with restaurants and nightclubs, food and evening entertainment. Airlines may provide all or part of the travel cost. Kinds of people invited may include travel writers, convention planners, motor coach tour operators, travel agents, travel wholesalers and package tour operators. FAM Tours offer a means of giving a personalized travel experience in the host city for travel decision-makers.

2 Information centres are often operated at key points of travel entrance and where visitors congregate. Where air travel is important, most cities participate with the airport authority in providing traveller information. Some cities provide information at key highway entrance locations, although this is less commonly done than the provision of information at airports. In some downtown locations, and in malls, information may be available. Some experimenting has been done with electronic information systems in central locations and in hotel rooms. In a number of cases the city teams up with private attractions to make general information available to the visitor of the given attraction. A difficulty with manned information stations, in addition to cost, is posed by their hours of operation. Information services that operate only on a regular 8-hours-per-day, 40-hours-per-week schedule miss large numbers of travellers, who often need information after 5 p.m. and at weekends.

3 Signs can be combined with and used as complements to information centres. These can include directional and facility information on streets and entrance roads; interpretation of attractions; and silent guides at information centres when personnel aren't on duty. Unfortunately much intrusive and ugly signing now exists and detracts from the travellers' experience. Thus, much remains to be explored in the design and use of signs by United States cities.

4 Educational programmes can tap the large potential of the city's resident population to promote travel. Nearly all cities surveyed indicated that their educational programmes were inadequate. Two important kinds of tourism educational programmes may be noted. The first is hospitality

training for those business persons who come into direct contact with travellers. Clients for this training include retail clerks, hotel and car-rental clerks, waitresses, employees of vehicle services, and taxi drivers. These people need to be aware of visitors, and be able to provide information that will give the travellers a good experience in the city (Zemke and Schaaf 1979). A second type of educational programme can be directed towards the resident population. Every citizen needs to understand the role of tourism in the local economy. They need also to understand the city's attractions and amenities so that these can be 'displayed' to their family visitors. Of one city's residents, 75 per cent have been found to eat out on the occasion of entertaining out-of-town guests, and they also frequently take them to entertainment facilities and cultural attractions (Blank 1982b).

5 Advertising is one aspect of promotion that includes spreading the word about the city by means of radio, television and various forms of print media. Table 8.3 indicates the estimated breakdown of advertising effort by larger hinterland cities. Note that on the average advertising is directed almost equally in three ways: instate, out-of-state but within 500 miles, and nationally. These averages cover large differences; one Midwestern city expended almost its entire effort instate while another directed all advertising nationally. Annual advertising budgets range from $30,000 to multiple millions of dollars. In many cases it is expected that commercial facilities, such as a complex of large hotels, may spend more for advertising than the city.

Table 8.3 Geographic distribution of advertising report by hinterland US cities

Geographic area	Percentage
Instate	25
Out-of-state, but within 500 miles	35
Nationally	35
Internationally	5
Total	100

Source: 1994 survey by HTR Group

6 The international advertising effort is noted in Table 8.3 as relatively small, at only 5 per cent of the total. While some hinterland cities indicated in their reports that they were mounting a substantial international sales effort, this 5 per cent indicates a generally low level of awareness or expectation for the potential of the international travel markets. With one exception, the cities showing interests in international tourism promotion were on or near the coast. In just the past six years the international travel

pattern has transformed itself. Between 1988 and 1994 the United States' dollar income from international travel more than doubled, increasing by 111 per cent. In the same period it went from a net deficit of $1.4 billion (the difference between what outbound United States travellers spent and dollars spent by inbound foreigners) to a net surplus of $24.8 billion (Erdmann 1993). The low level of interest in international travel indicates that hinterland cities are aware of their past 'flyover' status, and that they may not be aware of recent changes and/or are waiting for the United States Travel and Tourism Administration to demonstrate the potential to them before taking a substantial initiative on their own part.

Understanding tourism: research

Understanding of tourism and its potential contribution to hinterland cities has been limited. The lack of reliable tourism data has been a major factor in this limited understanding, and for good reason. Comprehensive tourism research is difficult to conduct (Blank 1994).

Important progress has been made. Two-thirds of the hinterland cities surveyed in 1994 reported the availability of some tourism data. Unfortunately, few studies of tourism are fully comprehensive, leaving city decision-makers with incomplete tourism information. Among the most common forms of tourism data generation are intercept interviews at selected points such as lodging places, airports and recreational attractions. The data thus generated are difficult to adjust reliably to the total traveller population. Further progress in research procedures is needed.

Nearly all tourism segments overlap in a complex pattern, but among the understated groups are those travelling by personal car. This is a huge segment; United States citizens now travel 3.2 billion kilometres (2 billion miles) annually. Of this travel, 86 per cent is by car. Among other often understated tourism components are those travelling to conduct non-convention business, both personal and economic; and those visiting friends and relatives. Many in these segments patronize commercial hospitality and recreational businesses and are thus counted, but in addition they deal with a wide variety of other rank and file businesses, as indicated earlier.

The impact of some of these partly overlooked segments may be large. One comprehensive research study fund that those present in the city to 'visit friends and relatives' spent more in retail stores for shopping than convention-goers spent for all purposes combined (Blank and Petkovich 1979).

Research that is fully comprehensive regarding all tourists is more difficult than that primarily treating the tourism components that deal mostly with commercial tourism-related firms. Further, marketing and services to stimulate the less visible tourists are less direct and more complex. But United States city agencies treating the tourism industry should be fully aware of the entire spectrum of its tourism components. Fortunately many of the actions that are undertaken do address the needs of all tourists. These include the upgrading of living quality, improvements in shopping opportunities, and developments in the recreational, cultural and artistic offerings.

THE FUTURE OF THE TOURISM INDUSTRY IN INDUSTRIAL/HINTERLAND UNITED STATES CITIES

What are the prospects for the tourism industry's future in hinterland United States cities?

There is a place for optimism. This optimism is based partly upon growth in travel by United States and world citizens, upon the upgrading of facilities, noted immediately above and at other points in this chapter, and in the observed upgrading in tourism marketing procedures (Kotler *et al.* 1993). Finally, tourism depends upon a complex of domestic and international trends and events.

Much hinterland city tourism depends upon population shifts. The largest tourism segment, 'visiting friends and relatives', is particularly affected. For example, people who have moved from the Midwest to California and Florida come 'back home' to visit. Further, their Midwestern relatives travel to visit them. Of course, those who do not move so far away also come back home to visit.

Population shifts within the United States are complex. There has been a pattern of net movement away from the hinterland to the Southeast and the Southwest. But renewed growth of industrial development in the Midwest may alter this pattern. Retirees are a relatively growing group in the United States. Their net movements, historically, have been into the sunbelt. Even this pattern is not guaranteed, and large Midwestern retirement cities such as at Bella Vista, Arkansas have been developed and now attract people to return from the sunbelt area. Even areas of northern Minnesota attract substantial numbers of retirees.

Business and conference travel will be influenced by economic competition, the general economy, and may be strongly impacted by communications technology. Many United States firms have down-sized and drastically cut expenses. These efforts reduce both the number of business and conference trips and the length of stay.

Overall, conferencing has increased and can be expected to continue to do so since many kinds of groups and interests find conferences useful, and numbers of these groups are proliferating.

Telecommunications will be a factor; how much and how rapidly it will produce change is difficult to predict. In a five-year period (1988–93) the number of teleconference centres in the United States increased from 800 to 2,800. Telecommunications also affects business operation and locations. For some operations it is no longer important to be located in large downtown office buildings near other businesses. Instead these locate where living amenities are to the liking of their executive officer and conduct business by means of telephone, fax, e-mail and other newly available means. As yet this latter is not a major, overall factor.

Along with communications technology, transportation technology and trends will influence domestic travel. What, for example, will change if rapid rail service is developed between cities, or if there are large changes in the means of car propulsion?

Dollar spending of international travellers to the United States has been noted to more than double in a recent six-year period. The current improvement in the economic health of European economies will contribute positively to this growth.

Transportation technology has had a major long-run impact upon international travel. Developments within the age of air travel alone are remarkable. Air travel moved forward rapidly in the twenty years from the 1930s to the 1950s: from the China clipper of the 1930s with its manually synchronized engines that caused the entire craft to vibrate, to the Boeing Stratocruiser of the late 1940s whose exhaust ports glowed cherry red as it struggled to claw its way up to its 20,000-foot cruising altitude, to jet craft that seem to leap effortlessly to 35,000-foot altitudes and that cruise at speeds in excess of 800 kilometres (500 miles) per hour. Is supersonic or some other transportation technology to be a major future factor?

The ease and speed of jet travel has now put every travel destination in the world into direct competition with all other travel destinations. United States hinterland cities have not been important on the agenda of overseas travellers. At the same time, these cities appear to have put little effort into attracting overseas travellers. This factor is undergoing change because of the growing importance of travel to the United States from abroad, the increasing ownership of United States businesses by other nations, and the varied ethnic background of United States residents. This potential in international tourism provides another, and an important, opportunity for hinterland cities to share the unique experience that each can offer with citizens of other nations, along with reaping increased jobs, profits, rents and tax returns from the tourism industry.

REFERENCES

Anderson, K. (1994) 'Modern Atlanta museums play up city's "Gone with the Wind" roots', *Christian Science Monitor*, 18 August, p. 14.

Baker, S. and Alexander, K.L. (1994) 'Nice work – if you can get it', *Business Week,* 29 August, p. 38.

Belsie, L. (1994) 'U.S. steelmakers hammer out lean profitable future', *Christian Science Monitor,* 10 August, p. 9.

Blank, U. (1982a) 'Interrelationship of the food service industry with the community', in A. Pizam, R.C. Lewis and P. Manning (eds) *The Practice of Hospitality Management,* Westport, Conn.: AVI Publishing Co., Inc.

Blank, U. (1982b) 'Life-style tourism interrelationships of Minneapolis-St Paul residents', pp. 82–9 in Staff Paper, Department of Agriculture and Applied Economies, University of Minnesota, St Paul, Minn.

Blank, U. (1989) *The Community Tourism Industry Imperative,* State College, Pa.. Venture Publishing Co.

Blank, U. (1994) 'Research on urban tourism destinations', in J.R. Brent Ritchie and Charles R. Goeldner (eds) *Travel, Tourism and Hospitality Research, A Handbook for Managers and Researchers,* New York: John Wiley & Sons, Inc.

Blank, U. and Petkovich, M. (1979) *Minneapolis-St Paul's Travel-Tourism,* St Paul: University of Minnesota.

Blank, U. and Petkovich, M. (1980) 'The metropolitan area: a multi-faceted travel destination complex', in D. Hawkins, E. Shafer and J. Rovelstad (eds) *Tourism Planning and Development Issues,* Washington, DC: George Washington University Press.

Braun, B. (1992) 'The economic contribution of conventions: the case of Orlando Florida', *Journal of Travel Research* 30(3).

Brown, M. (1990) *The Mayor's Task Force on Public Support for Cultural Organizations in Metropolitan Milwaukee,* City of Milwaukee, Wisconsin.

Byrum, O.E. (1992) *Old Problems in New Times, Urban Strategies for the 1990s,* Chicago, Ill.: American Planning Association.

Edgell, D. Sr (1990) *International Tourism Policy for the Future,* New York: Van Nostrand Reinhold.

Erdmann, R. (1993) 'The outlook for international travel', *1994 Outlook for Travel and Tourism,* Washington, DC: US Travel Data Center.

Holstrom, D. (1994) 'Inner cities being re-done American way – self help', *Christian Science Monitor,* 22 April, p. 4.

Kavanaugh, M.B. (1991) 'Tourism and the arts in San Francisco: a case study', *Tourism: Building Credibility for a Credible Industry, Proceedings,* Travel and Tourism Research Association, USA.

Kotler, P., Haider, D.H. and Rein, I. (1993) *Marketing Places: Attracting Investment, Industry and Tourism to Cities, States and Nations,* New York: The Freepress.

Law, C.M. (1993) *Urban Tourism: Attracting Visitors to Large Cities,* New York: Mansell.

Lodd, H. and Linger, J. (1989) *America's Ailing Cities: Fiscal Health and the Design of Urban Policy,* Baltimore, Md.: Johns Hopkins University Press.

Millman, A. (1991) 'The role of theme parks as a leisure activity for local communities', *Journal of Travel Research,* 29(4).

Snepenger, D. and Miller, L. (1990) 'Semographic and situational correlates of business travel', *Journal of Travel Research* 28(4).

Successful Meetings (July 1993), New York.

Weaver, P.A., McCleary, K.W. and Zhao Jinlin (1993) 'Segmenting the business traveller market', *Journal of Travel and Tourism Marketing* VI(4).

Zemke, R. and Schaaf, D. (1979) *The Service Edge,* New York: New American Library.

9 Tourism

A new role for Japanese cities

Kazutoshi Abe

The aim of this chapter is to analyse the role of tourism in major cities in Japan. Very little has been written on this topic and therefore this chapter is something of a pioneering work. Tourism has been studied by many academics in Japan, including geographers, and tourism geography is an established and important part of the discipline. However, most attention has been given to areas which have either environmental attractions (Type 1) or areas with historic buildings (Type 2). One purpose of this chapter is to suggest that there should be a Type 3 – namely, urban areas.

Type 1 areas include places where people can enjoy hot springs, go climbing or skiing, or partake in marine sports. In these sports, people make an active approach to the natural environment, but others may simply come to enjoy the view. The pleasure people get from the countryside can be seen in the recent boom in camping. Type 2 areas include places with religious facilities such as shrines and temples, as well as other historic buildings. The former are very popular, and attract many people who have no particular religious viewpoint. Table 9.1 shows that national features and religious buildings are very popular visitor attractions in urban areas in Japan. It is probably for this reason that geographers concerned with tourism have given most of their attention to these topics and to rural areas. Much effort has been spent on evaluating these attractions and the economic impact that they have on localities.

While some religious and historic buildings with associated gardens are found in cities, this has almost been regarded as incidental. The attractions have been studied but not the urban context. Japanese cities are largely the products of a period of rapid urbanization which has lasted just over one hundred years. The urban landscape is overwhelmingly modern, and unfortunately much of it does not have great appeal. For tourism geographers the significance of cities concerns their function as the origin of tourists. With a population of 123 million, of whom over 75 per cent live in cities, it is inevitable that the bulk of tourists to rural areas should come from cities. As the Japanese have increased their income, gained more leisure time and acquired cars, the number of visitors to rural areas has grown rapidly as more people have sought to escape from the cities (Graburn 1995). However, this view is far too narrow and it is the intention of this chapter to show that Japanese cities do attract visitors in large numbers. As elsewhere in the world cultural tourism is not dependent on historic features. The modern city is creating a new culture or cultures which will attract people. In addition business activities which lie at the heart of the urban economy generate an increasing flow of visitors. This business tourism has so far not been included within the conventional use of the term 'tourism' in Japan. When all these aspects are considered it is clear that in spite of the popularity and attention given to tourism in rural areas, tourism in cities is very important. Expenditure is high and most modern hotel accommodation is found there (Witherick and Carr 1993).

Table 9.1 Number of visitors by type of tourist destination in Japan (thousands)

	1975	1983	1988	1991
Type 1 Aso[a] (volcano in Kyushu)	4,973	5,192	7,685	
Type 1 Beppu[a] (hot spring in Kyushu)	12,035	12,006	11,991	
Type 2 Dazaifu[a] (shrine near Fukuoka)	5,068	6,408	7,121	
Type 2 Atsuta[b] (shrine in Nagoya)			8,280	8,285
Type 3 Zoo and botanical garden[b] (in Nagoya)			2,683	2,856
Type 3 Three museums[c] (in Tokyo)				1,586
Type 3 Two museums[c] (in Kyoto)				738

Sources: [a] Kyushu Economic Research Institute, *Resort and Regional Development* (in Japanese); [b] Nagoya City Office, *Nagoya of Industry 1992* (in Japanese); [c] *A Tourism White Paper of Japan* (in Japanese)

The growth of tourism in Japan needs to be set in the context of the dramatic economic and social changes which have occurred in the country since the Second World War. After recovery and sustained economic success, Japan forged ahead in the 1980s to become a major economic power in the world, second only to the United States. The country has become rich and its huge balance of payments has caused the yen to rise in value since the mid-1980s. This in turn has made the Japanese people amongst the most wealthy in the world. The question arises how Japan has used this new position to develop its country.

Japan has always looked to the West for inspiration. It has modelled its industrial system and products on the best it saw elsewhere. In the 1980s it sought to adopt the most modern that it saw elsewhere and also to be an international country, playing its role in the world and having the status that its economic power should have given it. It is not surprising that many of the innovations that appeared in the urban economy from the 1980s onwards should have been imported from elsewhere. These include convention centres, convention hotels, modern hotels, museums, aquariums, and theme parks. The introduction of these functions has extended the urban economy and inevitably enlarged the role of tourism. These changes have gone hand in hand with individual rising affluence and increased leisure time which again have inputted into the tourist system.

REGIONS AND MAJOR CITIES IN JAPAN

Before proceeding to the analysis of tourism in major cities in Japan, it is necessary to differentiate the regions and major cities in Japan. Although there are various ways of doing this, the classification adopted is that shown in Figure 9.1. The names of each region, plus the population in each region in 1990, are shown in this figure. Population in Japan is unevenly distributed, with the largest population of just over 38.5 million in the Kanto region (around Tokyo); the least, of almost 4.2 million, is in the Shikoku region; which is only 10.9 per cent of that in the Kanto region.

Major cities to which this chapter refers are those with populations of over 1 million people. There are eleven major cities in this category (Figure 9.1). Needless to say, the city with the most population is Tokyo with almost 8.2 million people, which is eight times of that of the eleventh city, Kitakyushu city. There are approximately 30 million people in the Tokyo metropolitan area living within a radius of 50 kilometres of the city.

Similarly, there are approximately 16 million people living within a radius of 50 kilometres of Osaka and about 8.2 million in the Nagoya metropolitan area. These three metropolitan areas are generally regarded as the largest in Japan, and are the centres of politics, economy and culture. Seven of the eleven major cities with populations of over 1 million are included in these three metropolitan areas. Of the other four major cities, Sapporo is the central city of Hokkaido, Hiroshima for the Chugoku region, and Fukuoka and Kitakyushu for the Kyushu region. These eleven major cities are analysed in the following sections.

As in other parts of the world, the economic structure of Japanese cities has been subject to change. Old heavy industries have been closing down and the early port zones have become redundant, often leaving waterfront zones ready for redevelopment. Landowners and cities have been seeking new functions. While unemployment has generally been low, there has been concern as to whether there will be enough jobs for young people. It is these types of problems that have encouraged cities to be more proactive in finding new economic functions and often to compete with one another for prestige projects. Additional powers have enabled prefectures and cities to invest in theme parks, convention centres and other attractions as well as developing suitable infrastructure. As will be seen later many of these new projects have a tourist dimension.

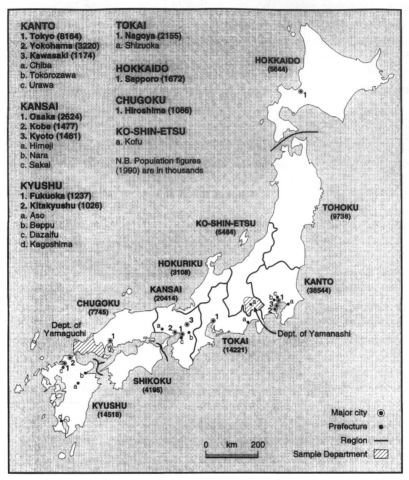

Figure 9.1 Japanese cities and regions

THE DEMAND FOR LEISURE AND TOURIST FACILITIES

Japan has traditionally been a work-oriented society, which tended to mean that Japanese people worked long hours each week and took few holidays. By the mid-1980s the average Japanese worked twenty more days a year than US citizens and forty-five more days a year than West

Germans. The average Japanese was entitled to 14.6 days holiday a year, but only took 8.2 days (56 per cent). Frequently the only long holiday a Japanese took was when on honeymoon. By the mid-1980s, with over thirty years of rising incomes, Japanese people were ready to take increased leisure time and enjoy the fruits of economic prosperity. Table 9.2 shows trends in leisure time for the last twenty years; it can be seen that this has increased, especially on Sundays. Inevitably most of this leisure time will be spent near home rather than in making long trips to other areas. By the late 1980s the government was encouraging the Japanese to have more leisure time and take longer holidays. To this end it set up a Leisure Development Centre and encouraged investment in leisure facilities. The 1987 Law for the Development of Comprehensive Resort Areas enabled prefectures to designate recreational districts, which would qualify for tax refunds and low interest loans.

Table 9.2 Average leisure time per day of people in Japan (minutes)

	1970	*1975*	*1980*	*1985*	*1990*
Weekdays	25	27	27	36	38
Saturday	37	37	42	48	59
Sunday	63	71	63	83	91

Source. Nihon Hoso Kyokai

By the mid-1980s the huge balance of payments surplus was a problem for the government. To offset this it was decided to encourage the Japanese to take their holidays abroad. A target was set to persuade 10 million Japanese to have an overseas holiday. Outbound tourists rose from 3.52 million in 1978, to 5.5 million in 1986, to 11.8 million in 1992 (Economist Intelligence Unit 1992; Witherick and Carr 1993). In this latter year expenditure abroad was $35.4 billion. These foreign trips have obviously reduced the demand for tourist facilities within Japan.

Compared to other countries Japan is noticeable for the relatively small number of foreign tourists visiting the country. This may be due to the fact that at present Japan's primary attractions – its culture, history, custom and traditions – appeal to only a small segment of the long-haul tourist market, but in the long term there is the opportunity to sell the country to the tourist looking for the exotic. Another deterrent may be the language and cultural barrier. For tourists from North America and Europe travel costs are likely to be high, while for all visitors the rising value of the yen has made a holiday in Japan expensive. These factors will obviously dampen the leisure tourism market. However, as Japan has become a major economic power its business links with the rest of the work have increased, resulting in a growing business travel market.

Tourist arrivals are well below the levels of outbound movements. They have increased from 1.04 million in 1978, to 2.06 million in 1986, and to 3.58 million in 1992. Over half of these tourists come from South and East Asia, from Taiwan, South Korea, Hong Kong and Singapore. These visitors not only benefit from lower travel costs, but are attracted by the modernity of Japan. In 1992 visiting tourists spent $3.5 billion. Until 1991, reflecting balance of payments considerations, the Japanese government gave low priority to attracting foreign visitors. Since then a new policy has set a target of 5 million visitors and a Two-Way Tourism 21 programme. Since the late 1980s the government have also attempted to gain international prestige by hosting conferences and special events (see pp. 244–6), which will inevitably attract more foreign visitors.

Most foreign tourists arrive by the two main gateways of Tokyo and Osaka airports, and tend to stay in the Tokyo-Osaka corridor visiting temples and historic sites along the 'Golden Route'.

TOURISM IN MAJOR CITIES IN JAPAN

There are three types in tourism generally preferred by Japanese people. First, as has been pointed out on p. 233, there is tourism with the theme of nature (Type 1). The second type centres on visiting historic ruins, including religious buildings (Type 2). The third type consists of urban areas which have attractions. Table 9.1 shows the salient examples of those three types, with the number of visiting tourists.

It can be noted from Table 9.1 that the number of tourists who enjoy natural areas such as hot springs and volcanoes is considerable; similarly, large numbers visit religious buildings. The number of tourists in these two areas has been gradually increasing for the last couple of years because of the traditional custom for Japanese to visit shrines and temples on every new year. For instance, over 2 million people visit Atsuta and Dazaifu Shrines for the first three days of every new year. Excluding people visiting religious places due to this unique Japanese custom, a large number of people visit famous religious places and buildings every year.

In the case of attractions in major cities, the number of visitors is much fewer than those concerning nature (Type 1) or religious buildings (Type 2). For instance, as shown in Table 9.1, the numbers of visitors in 1991 to the zoo in Nagoya and the three museums in Tokyo were only 2,856,000 and 1,586,000 respectively. Although it seems from these figures that tourism in major cities with such attractions is inferior to that in those with Type 1 and 2 attractions, it is not necessarily the case.

There are three main reasons why it can be said that tourism in major cities is as important as Types 1 and 2 tourism. First, there are many facilities in urban cities which are attracting more people than those with Type 1 and 2 features, though the number of visitors to each facility is less than the number visiting Types 1 and 2. Second, major cities can attract a huge number of people when big events, such as the Olympics, are held in urban areas. Third, major cities are attracting many tourists, using the term in a broad sense, whose visits include concerts, sports, and art exhibitions which can be only held in major cities. These three reasons are analysed in the sections which follow.

Table 9.3 shows the number of tourists in recent years in major cities in Japan excluding Tokyo and Osaka. It can be noted that Kyoto is a well-known tourist spot for both Japanese and foreign tourists from all over the world. There are a number of precious historically famous buildings in Kyoto. For that reason, Kyoto has a different character from that of other major cities.

Table 9.3 Number of visitors in major Japanese cities

	Period	*Number of visitors*
Sapporo	1990.4–1991.3	12,630,000
	1991.4–1992.3	13,180,000
Kawasaki	1990.4–1991.3	12,120,000
	1991.4–1992.3	12,120,000
Yokohama	1990.4–1991.3	23,910,000
	1991.4–1992.3	23,320,000
Nagoya	1990.4–1991.3	16,580,000
	1991.4–1992.3	18,680,000
Kyoto	1990.4–1991.3	40,850,000
	1991.4–1992.3	39,300,000
Kobe	1990.4–1991.3	23,320,000
	1991.4–1992.3	23,960,000
Hiroshima	1990.4–1991.3	8,340,000
	1991.4–1992.3	8,630,000

Source: Sapporo City Office (tourism section)

Historic buildings in other major cities are less important, hence there is less attraction compared to that of Kyoto. Two other major cities attracting many tourists are Yokohama and Kobe. They both developed as port cities with unique features of exoticism and many young people prefer to visit these two towns for a walk. Their proximity to Tokyo and Osaka is also one of the reasons why many people visit them.

ART GALLERIES AND MUSEUMS

There are numerous art and other exhibitions held every day in Japan, especially in metropolitan cities. They are among the major attractions of the cities and are important resources for tourism in urban areas. Although it is not possible to know the exact number of exhibitions held in Japan, the number held in museums in major cities during November 1990 is shown in Table 9.4. Art and other museums in the major cities listed are holding expositions all year round. While the full number of exhibitions is not known the figures shown in Table 9.4 are probably a good indication of the number of opportunities available to people in the major cities. There are many small art galleries in Japan, but they are not included in the table. Although no detailed data exist to show how many people visit the wealth of art and other museums in Tokyo, for example, available data on some facilities are shown in Table 9.5. These facilities are very important resources for tourism in major cities.

PUBLIC PERFORMANCES BY VISITING FOREIGN ARTISTS

Between April 1990 and March 1991, a total of 1,063 foreign artists and groups gave performances in major cities in Japan. Table 9.6 shows the types and numbers of performances given in each region. It also shows how the various regions compare with each other. Using a base figure of 100 for the Tokyo metropolitan area, percentages are given for the other regions. When compared, it can be seen that performances by foreign artists are more frequent in the Tokyo metropolitan area than in any other region, and that the Hokkaido region suffers from a comparative dearth of such performances.

Table 9.4 Number of exhibitions held by museums, November 1990

Kanto		Kansai		Tokai	
Tokyo	48	Osaka	13	Nagoya	11
Yokohama	3	Kyoto	4	Others	31
Kawasaki	1	Kobe	4		
Others	20	Nara	5		
		Others	14		

Source: Local information books

Table 9.5 Number of visitors to national museums

Museum	Number ('000s)
Tokyo National Museum	618
Kyoto National Museum	298
Nara National Museum	335
Tokyo National Museum of Modern Arts	283
Kyoto National Museum of Modern Arts	440
National Museum of Western Arts (Tokyo)	685
National Museum of International Arts (Osaka)	40
Total	2,699

Source: Agency for Cultural Affairs

Table 9.6 Number of performances by foreign artists, by region, from April 1990 to March 1991

		Tokyo metropolitan area	*Kansai*	*Tokai*	*Kyushu and Yamaguchi*	*Hokkaido*
Number of foreign artists (total)	1,063	933 (100)	665 (71.3)	318 (34.1)	152 (16.3)	55 (5.9)
Classical music	449	391 (100)	234 (59.8)	90 (23.0)	60 (15.3)	8 (2.0)
Other music	536	467 (100)	381 (81.6)	196 (42.0)	79 (16.9)	40 (8.6)
Plays etc.	78	75 (100)	50 (66.7)	32 (42.7)	13 (17.3)	7 (9.3)

Source: Abe (1992)
Note: Figures in parentheses are percentages, compared to a Tokyo base of 100

Only the types of performances given regionally are shown in Table 9.6, so it would be interesting to analyse data from each major city. The total number of performances in each major city are 846 in Tokyo, 573 in Osaka (about two-thirds that of Tokyo), and 308 in Nagoya (approximately one-third of Tokyo). Following these cities are Yokohama, Fukuoka, and Kyoto, but the numbers of performances in each of these cities are under 20% of the Tokyo figure. Performances in Kobe (63) and Sapporo (55) are still fewer, being only 7.4% and 6.5% of those given in Tokyo.

THEME PARKS

Following the success of Disneyland in the United States there has been an explosion of theme parks in North America, Western Europe and other parts of the world. Japan has not missed out on this trend. Unfortunately there is no precise definition of a theme park so that surveys using different definitions can give very different results. Whilst broadly defined as a themed family entertainment complex this can include both old fairgrounds and innovative museums.

A survey by Jones (1994) of twenty-seven theme parks found that six had been built between 1965 and 1986, including Disneyland near Tokyo, which was opened in 1983. The 1987 General Recreation Resort Development Act allowed cities to give grants or low-interest loans to theme parks where they would help regenerate areas and create jobs. This policy was encouraged by the Ministry of International Trade and Industry (MITI) which has guided Japanese development as a way of meeting the expected increased demand for organized leisure as well as utilizing redundant industrial land and creating jobs for the unemployed. Subsequently twenty-one theme parks were opened between 1988 and 1991 and at least eleven more were in the planning stage. These examples have diverse themes, but many are historical whilst even more could be described as educational. The distribution of these themes shows a concentration in the core region, but several are in Kyushu, including Space World at Kitakyushu near Fukuoka, an old steel works site which received a 30 per cent grant. This example illustrates a distinctive Japanese approach to new leisure industries. The Yawata works at Kitakyushu City in northern Kyushu was built by the government in 1901 as the first integrated iron and steel works in the country (Shapira 1993). More recently, as part of Nippon Steel, it has felt the effects of rationalization and seen the number of jobs fall from 43,700 in 1963 to 12,300 in 1988. Since Japanese firms do not like making workers redundant they seek to create new businesses to which displaced workers can be transferred. As a consequence, Nippon Steel constructed the $214 million Space World, opened in April 1990, on a 20-hectare derelict site having borrowed the idea from a theme park at Huntsville, Alabama. It employs about 250 full-time and 500 part-time workers. Other companies such as Sumitomo, Mitsui Mining, Matsushita, Honda and Nissan have also built theme parks. Eight of these theme parks attract over 1 million visitors, with Disneyland topping the list at 15 million. Generally these successful theme parks are in the major cities. Another survey suggested that there were over 374 theme parks, with eleven attracting over 1 million visitors a year, seven of which were in the Tokyo region. The major theme parks, such as Disneyland, are also important for foreign tourists from Asia.

SPORTS

Watching sports and games is also one of the major attractions which people can generally only enjoy in major cities. Here, an attempt is made to analyse the impact of the most important popular sports in Japan, baseball and sumo, in the major cities.

There are twelve professional baseball teams in Japan. Each team is franchised by the city where the team is based. Cities where a professional baseball teams are franchised are Tokyo (3 teams), Chiba (1 team), Tokorozawa (1 team), Yokohama (1 team), Nagoya (1 team), Osaka (1 team), Kobe (2 teams), Hiroshima (1 team) and Fukuoka (1 team). Regional distributions following the classification described earlier are Kanto (6 teams), Tokai (1 team), Kansai (3 teams), Chugoku (1 team) and Kyushu (1 team). There is no city in northern Japan where a professional baseball team is franchised as the game is generally played in regions where the weather is warm. In addition, the population density in Japan is more concentrated in the southern part of Japan. Hence people in the northern part of Japan seldom have the opportunity to watch professional baseball games except on television. Enthusiastic fans do come to the Kanto region by train or air especially to watch a game, or attend when on business trips; it can thus be said that the northern half of Japan is the hinterland of the Kanto region.

During the summer season professional baseball teams often visit regions where the weather is too cold during winter to play games. On such occasions, the baseball stadium is usually fully packed with people.

Professional baseball teams in Japan play 130 games during one season. Of the 130 games, sixty-five are usually played in the city where the team is franchised. Although there are some games played in other cities close to the franchising city, at least sixty games are played in that city. In this context, 180 games are played in Tokyo. If the entire metropolitan region of Tokyo is included, a total of 360 games are played, including those in Chiba, Yokohama, and Tokorozawa.

The Kansai region, with 180 games, is next to Kanto in the total number of games played. The ratio between the figure in Kanto and that in Kansai is approximately 6:3, while between Kanto and the other regions it is 6:1.

The number of games played is, of course, only partly related to the number of people who actually go to watch. Although there are differences in the capacities of baseball stadiums, on average the small stadium has a capacity of 30,000 while the big stadium holds about 55,000. Since a popular team can always attract a full capacity crowd, it is estimated that over 3 million people come to certain stadia every year. Even an unpopular team can attract approximately 800,000 people throughout the season. It can be seen, then, that the professional baseball game is a very important component of tourism in urban cities in Japan.

In the case of another popular sport in Japan, sumo wrestling, there are six fifteen-day tournaments held in the major cities each year – three in Tokyo (a total of forty-five days), and one each in Osaka, Nagoya and Fukuoka. Besides these six regular tournaments held in major cities, sumo wrestlers tour various parts of Japan or sometimes overseas, providing opportunities for people in other areas to watch sumo; real tournaments, though, can be seen only in the above-mentioned four major cities. Crowd capacities in these cities are 11,098 (Tokyo), 8,300 (Osaka), 11,000 (Nagoya), and 9,774 (Fukuoka), respectively.

SPECIAL EVENTS

In Japan, various expositions are held every year in different parts of the country. These expositions are usually only held once and do not attract people continuously as do historic and religious buildings. However, there are some cities which are successfully creating situations to attract people continuously by holding small-scale events frequently. Table 9.7 shows the number of visitors to expositions held in major cities in Japan in 1989; names of expositions are not included.

The cities with the largest number of visitors to expositions are Nagoya and Yokohama with over 10 million people. As shown earlier, the number of visitors to Atsuta Shrine in Nagoya averages over 8 million people annually. In this context, it can be said that large-scale events held in metropolitan areas attract more people than a famous religious building.

The average number of daily visitors is also shown in Table 9.7, as the total number of visitors to the events varies from one event to another depending on the duration of the events. It can also be noted from the table that the numbers of daily visitors to the events held in metropolitan cities are far higher than those for events held in other cities; this is because of advantages in size that the metropolitan cities possess.

In addition to annual events Japan has sought hallmark or mega-events of world-wide significance. World Fairs or Expos have been held at Osaka in 1970 and Tsukuba in 1985. The Olympic Games were held in Tokyo in 1964, and the Asian Games took place in Japan in 1994.

Table 9.7 Number of visitors to expositions, 1989

City	Population ('000s)	Number of visitors ('000s)	Daily number of visitors
Kagoshima	537	880	14,667
Fukuoka	1,237	8,229	48,125
Shizuoka	472	1,071	16,476
Himeji	454	1,582	20,028
Sakai	808	939	14,677
Yokohama	3,220	13,337	69,828
Hiroshima	1,086	3,298	28,934
Nagoya	2,155	15,184	112,474
Kofu	201	556	9,259

Source: Hakurankai Kenbutsu (in Japanese), Gakugei Shuppan

THE CONVENTION BUSINESS

As part of its thrust to be a modern and international economy Japan has embraced the concept of conventions, a term which may be used to include both conferences and exhibitions. In 1988 the Ministry of Transport, which is responsible for tourism, announced the designation of 'International Convention City'. To be recognized a city had to have facilities above a minimum standard and also have a convention bureau. Cities and prefectures were given powers to provide funds to upgrade facilities, develop infrastructure and establish convention bureaux. For their part, local authorities perceived conventions as a way of attracting visitors, generating income, creating employment and helping to revitalize areas.

To promote international conferences the Japanese Convention Bureau was established within the National Tourist Organization of Japan. In 1994 a further piece of legislation made it possible for companies financing international meetings to gain a tax advantage. At the same time a target was set of increasing Japan's share of international meetings from 4 per cent to 8 per cent.

International Convention Cities

CHUGOKU	KO-SHIN-ETSU	SHIKOKU
1. Hiroshima	1. Fujiyoshida	1. Matsuyama
2. Matsue	2. Matsumoto	2. Takamatsu
3. Okayama	3. Nagano	3. Tokushima
HOKKAIDO	4. Niigata	**TOHUKU**
1. Asahikawa	5. Ueda	1. Akita
2. Kushiro	**KYUSHU**	2. Morioka
3. Sapporo	1. Beppu	3. Sendai
HOKURIKU	2. Fukuoka	4. Tsuroka
1. Fukui	3. Kagoshima	5. Yamagata
2. Kanazawa	4. Kitakyushu	**TOKAI**
3. Toyama	5. Kumamoto	1. Gifu
KANSAI	6. Miyazaki	2. Hamamatsu
1. Kobe	7. Nagasaki	3. Nagoya
2. Nara	**OKINAWA**	4. Shizuoka
3. Osaka	1. Ginowan	
KANTO	2. Naha	
1. Chiba	3. Okinawa	
2. Maebashi	4. Urazoe	
3. Narita		
4. Tokyo		
5. Yokohama		

Figure 9.2 International convention cities in Japan
Source: *Conference and Incentive Travel*, March 1995

Prior to 1988 there were only a few convention centres in Japan. The Kyoto International Conference Hall was built in 1966 and the Kobe Convention Centre in 1981. However, between 1987 and 1992 sixteen convention centres were opened and several are planned to be completed during the 1990s. These convention centres are often accompanied by large luxury hotels. The number of International Convention Cities has risen from twenty-five in 1988, to thirty-three in 1992, to forty-six in 1995 (Figure 9.2). Meanwhile the number of international conferences has risen from 371 in 1981 to 764 in 1988, and to 1,665 in 1993, the latter attracting 63,134 delegates (Figure 9.3). The main areas for international conferences are, not surprisingly, the Kanto region (including Tokyo, Yokohama and Makuhari), the Kansai region (including Kyoto, Kobe and Osaka), plus Nagoya.

The facilities that have been constructed in recent years are of the highest international standards, and much has been learnt from the United States and Germany. The Chiba prefecture, which lies between downtown Tokyo and Narita airport, is constructing a new town which has at its core a convention centre. Opened in 1989, the Makuhari Messe, also known as the Nippon Convention Centre, includes 54,500 square metres of exhibition space, an arena seating 7,500, a conference hall for 1,600, as well as other facilities. At Yokohama the Minato Mirai 21 Scheme is a waterfront redevelopment scheme which at its centre has the Pacifico-Yokohama Convention Centre. This has 67,000 square metres of exhibition space and a conference hall seating 5,000. Whilst most of these convention centres, including the largest, are being built in the core region of Japan, some are also being built in the more peripheral regions.

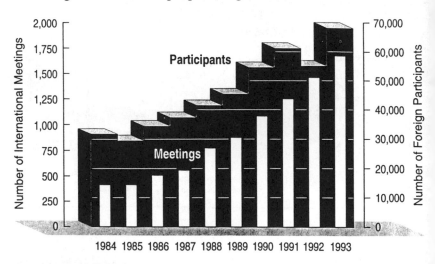

Figure 9.3 Growth of conventions and participants in Japan
Source: *Conference and Incentive Travel*, March 1995

NAGOYA: A CASE STUDY

With a population of 2,155,000 in 1990, Nagoya is the fourth largest city in Japan. It is sometimes described as the 'Birmingham of Japan'. Like the British city it lies in the centre of the country with good communications north and south. It is also an industrial city, the birthplace of the Toyoda Spinning and Weaving Company, the forerunner of the giant Toyota car firm situated in a nearby town. As a bustling industrial city it could not be described as beautiful.

Nagoya is not as big as Tokyo, nor like Kyoto with its many famous shrines and temples. However, it does contain two very famous historic and religious buildings in Nagoya Castle and Atsuta Shrine. Table 9.8 shows the number of visitors to attractions in the city. Atsuta Shrine attracted the largest number, with over 8 million in both 1987 and 1991, accounting for over 40 per cent of the visitor numbers. The figure of 8 million includes over 2 million who visited the shrine during the first three days of the new year. While over 50 per cent of the visitor numbers went to the two main attractions, over 40 per cent went to others. These include an art museum, the Toyota car museum, and the Zoo and Botanical Gardens (attracting 2.9 million visitors in 1991). There are also factory tours.

Table 9.8 Number of visitors to tourist attractions in Nagoya ('000s)

	1987		1991	
Nagoya Castle	1,088	6.2%	1,235	6.5%
Atsuta Shrine	8,780	49.9%	8,285	43.9%
Others[a]	7,744	43.9%	9,370	49.6%
Total	17,612	100.0%	18,890	100.0%

Source: Nagoya City Office, 'Nagoya of Industry 1992' (in Japanese)
Note: [a] Includes figures of 2,856 and 15.1 per cent for the Zoo and Botanical Gardens

The Nagoya Congress Centre was opened in 1990 and a new wing was added in 1994. It now has three halls with seating capacities of between 1,000 and 3,000, exhibition space of 3,000 square metres and thirty-nine syndicate rooms. As a consequence of these developments the number of conferences and delegates has increased markedly (Table 9.9). International meetings account for 8 per cent of its business. The city also opened a cultural centre in 1992 with a 2,500-seat theatre.

Through all these facilities Nagoya is able to attract over 18 million visitors a year. It also acts as a gateway for visitors to the mountains and coasts. There are now over 13,000 hotel bedrooms. Its plans for the future include a new art gallery in 1996, an outstation of Boston Museum housing its Far Eastern Collection, and hosting an International Expo in 2005.

Table 9.9 International conferences and attendance in Nagoya, 1986–93

	Number of international conferences	Attendance
1986	22	34,493
1987	15	4,411
1988	33	13,976
1989	51	16,974
1990	87	28,958
1991	146	35,421
1992	105	22,901
1993	141	39,451

Source: Kokusai Kanko Shinkokai

CONCLUSION

This chapter has reviewed tourism in major cities in Japan through analysis of major activities; a synthesis of the important points follows. In the past, the objectives of study in tourism geography were natural environments and regions with beautiful natural landscapes (Type 1) or regions with historic or religious facilities/buildings (Type 2). In other words, the objectives of study were not urban cities but rather mountainous or coastal regions/areas. However, the bigger a city grows the more concert halls, art galleries, museums and sports facilities are constructed to attract visitors. These facilities are often perceived by tourists to be the major attractions of cities, and are included in the Type 3 category. Past study in tourism in major cities had been mainly in Types 1 and 2, study in Type 3 having been neglected. This chapter has attempted to analyse tourism with the focus being on Type 3 facilities.

The purpose of this chapter has been to demonstrate that Type 3 tourism (that found in major cities) is as important as Types 1 and 2, although it should be noted that there is some overlap between these categories. Type 3 tourism in major cities has been evaluated by studies of the usage of facilities in cities for events, concerts by visiting foreign artistes, sports and other facilities such as art galleries, museums, convention centres and theme parks, all of which attract large numbers of people; they are also important in metropolitan areas. With Japan's growing wealth these facilities are being increasingly developed and are laying the resource base for tourism in cities in the future.

REFERENCES

Abe, Kazutoshi (1992) 'A comparative study of regions and cities based on the number of performances presented by foreign artists in Japan, *Chirigaku-Hyoron* (Geographical Review of Japan), Series A, 65(12), 911–19 (in Japanese).

Economist Intelligence Unit (1992) *International Tourism Reports: Japan*, no. 4, 5–35.

Graburn, N.H.H. (1995) 'The past in the present in Japan: nostalgia and neo-traditionalism in contemporary Japanese domestic tourism', in R. Butler and D. Pearce (eds) *Change in Tourism: People, Places, Processes*, London: Routledge.

Jones, T.S.M. (1994) 'Theme parks in Japan', in C.P. Cooper and A. Lockwood (eds) *Progress in Tourism, Recreation and Hospitality Management* 6, 111–25.

Shapira, P. (1993) 'Steel town to space world: restructuring and adjustment in Kitakyushu city', in K. Fujita and R.C. Child (eds) *Japanese Cities in the World Economy*, Philadelphia, Pa.: Temple University Press.

Witherick, M. and Carr, M. (1993) *The Changing Face of Japan: A Geographical Perspective*, London: Hodder & Stoughton.

10 Conclusion

Christopher M. Law

The case studies in this book have confirmed the growing importance of urban tourism. This partly reflects spontaneous trends as consumers are drawn to the amenities which large cities provide and which they continue to develop, and partly the deliberate effort by cities to develop facilities and events which will attract visitors. However, while the contributors have been able to assemble a commendable range of data it is also obvious that there is a lack of knowledge and understanding about the phenomenon of urban tourism. Accordingly this concluding chapter will be used to discuss a number of research issues for the future (see Haywood 1992 for a similar list).

The short-break leisure market is critical to the future of tourism in large cities yet there appears to be relatively little detailed research on how consumers make their decisions. There are surveys which show how tourists have chosen between seaside resorts, rural areas, historic cities and big cities, but the reasons for their choices are not known. What roles do cost, travel time and type of amenity play in their decisions? For those choosing the large city there is a secondary decision as to which city to visit. What considerations influence their choice? How much do they know of these cities? How does image influence the choice? Do events play any role in the decision?

A second general area concerns the behaviour of tourists in cities. It was noted in Chapter 1 how some visitors come for one purpose only, others for a main purpose but with secondary aims, and others because of the general appeal of the city. We need to know the proportions of these groups in the total visitor population (see chapter by Schnell in this book). For those in the second and third categories it would be useful to know how their time and expenditure was divided between different activities. Do visitors come with ideas of how to use their time or do they spontaneously respond to opportunities? How does the geography of the city influence these opportunities, and is the behaviour of tourists significantly different when tourism resources are strongly clustered? When they are not clustered, how do transport considerations influence their decisions?

Nearly all studies of urban tourism reveal how little is known about the impact of the activity on cities. There is a need for more impact studies, but as a preliminary there should be agreement as what is to be covered in the studies. As the case studies have shown, business tourism and day-trippers are often excluded yet these are important elements of tourism in cities. There is also a need to define how far a visitor has to travel before he can be counted as a tourist.

There is relatively little detailed research on the negative impacts of tourism in cities. A full audit would consider both the benefits and costs. Public expenditure, both capital and revenue, is high on tourism-related projects and there is a need to show local people that the benefits claimed for the activity do happen. There are costs of congestion, of wear and tear and clearing-up behind tourists. At the same time tourism may divert both attention and resources from other activities such as the welfare services. In order to attract tourists certain values are promoted through images and the development of facilities. What effects are there on the community of these actions?

The innovators or promoters of tourism in cities is another area for research. Who is pushing tourism? Who has the strategic vision for urban tourism? The public sector has an important role to play as was discussed in Chapter 1, but within this sector either councillors or officers may take the lead, and from different departments or sections. The rise of tourism policy has not been without contest. In certain councils, such as Bristol and Liverpool, policies have been overturned. What have been the arguments and interests for and against tourism? To what extent has the community been involved in discussing these issues? Within the private sector it has often appeared that there has been weak leadership; each entrepreneur has been content to do his own thing. Indeed competition often discourages co-operation. However, with the rise of public–private partnerships for promotion, members of the private sector have come to occupy positions of influence. What kind of background do they have and what kind of vision do they have?

The question of strategic vision raises a whole series of other issues. How detailed are tourism strategies? Cities like Birmingham very clearly decided they would go for business tourism while Indiana decided on sport. But other cities appear to have no clear policy on which area of tourism is to be favoured; in fact they are often very pragmatic. Related to this issue is how cities position themselves in the marketplace, both in terms of appeal and markets (see Chapter 2). How do cities come to make such decisions? This topic can also be linked to that of image. How does a city decide what image it wants to project?

Another question for research is the influence tourism is having on the geography of the city. In part there are spontaneous developments which are changing the character of quarters in the city. Successful activities may result in a natural clustering of firms, sometimes with negative effects for residents and other firms. At the same time there have been many policies to create tourism quarters and to regenerate decayed areas, often on the edge of the city centre. These have had varying degrees of success.

The planning of tourism in cities is effected by the division of the area into local authority districts. As the chapter on London showed, there can be a large number of jurisdictions. There is clearly a need for co-operation since tourists do not recognize these boundaries. What are the factors encouraging/discouraging co-operation? What kind of institutional arrangements for this co-operation have been made? Given that the importance of tourism is likely to be uneven across the urban area, how is this co-operation managed?

Most of the published research on urban tourism concerns Western Europe and North America, but tourism in cities is becoming important elsewhere, for example Hong Kong and Singapore. There is clearly a need to incorporate these studies into the syntheses that are being made about the topic.

REFERENCE

Haywood, K.M. (1992) 'Identifying and responding to challenges posed by urban tourism', *Tourism Recreation Research* 17(2), 9–23.

Index

Page numbers appearing in **bold** refer to figures. Page numbers appearing in *italic* refer to tables.